hay un

cierran

-do you ___ ___ ___
at night?

Spanish

lonely planet

phrasebooks
and
Marta López

Spanish phrasebook
4th edition – February 2011

Published by Lonely Planet Publications Pty Ltd
ABN 36 005 607 983

Lonely Planet Offices
Australia Locked Bag 1, Footscray, Victoria 3011
USA 150 Linden St, Oakland CA 94607
UK 2nd fl, 186 City Rd, London, EC1V 2NT

Contact
talk2us@lonelyplanet.com.au
lonelyplanet.com/contact

Cover illustration Mark Adams

ISBN 978 1 74179 339 0

This 4th edition of Lonely Planet's *Spanish* phrasebook is based on the previous three editions by the Lonely Planet Language Products team, Marta López for the Spanish translations and pronunciation guides, and Peter and Marta Gibney as proofers of the Spanish text. For this edition, new content was added by Spanish translator Cristina Hernández Montero. *¡Gracias Cristina, Marta, Peter y Marta!*

Thanks also to the others who contributed to the previous editions on which this one is based:

Jane Atkin, Karina Coates, Francesca Coles, Adrienne Costanzo, Ben Handicott, Jim Jenkin, Piers Kelly, Yukiyoshi Kamimura, Emma Koch, Paul Piaia, Fabrice Rocher, Karin Vidstrup Monk, Meg Worby, and last but not least, Patrick Marris who created the inside illustrations.

Lonely Planet Language Products

Associate Publisher: Tali Budlender
Managing Editor: Annelies Mertens
Editor: Branislava Vladisavljevic
Managing Layout Designer: Celia Wood
Layout Designer: Wibowo Rusli
Cartographer: Wayne Murphy
Production Support: Yvonne Kirk, Glenn van der Knijff

make the most of this phrasebook ...

Anyone can speak another language! It's all about confidence. Don't worry if you can't remember your school language lessons or if you've never learnt a language before. Even if you learn the very basics (on the inside covers of this book), your travel experience will be the better for it. You have nothing to lose and everything to gain when the locals hear you making an effort. Spanish is, of course, spoken in Spain, but also in many countries in Latin America. Spanish is also spoken in parts of the Pacific (ie the Philippines) and Africa (ie Equatorial Guinea).

finding things in this book

For easy navigation, this book is in sections. The Tools chapters are the ones you'll thumb through time and again. The Practical section covers basic travel situations such as catching transport and finding accommodation. The Social section gives you conversational phrases, pick-up lines, the ability to express opinions – so you can get to know people. Food has a section all of its own: gourmets and vegetarians are covered and local dishes feature. Safe Travel equips you with health and police phrases, just in case. Remember the colours of each section and you'll find everything easily; or use the comprehensive Index. Otherwise, check the two-way traveller's Dictionary for the word you need.

being understood

Throughout this book you'll see coloured phrases on the right hand side of each page. They're phonetic guides to help you pronounce the language. You don't even need to look at the language itself, but you'll get used to the way we've represented particular sounds. The pronunciation chapter in Tools will explain more, but you can feel confident that if you read the coloured phrase slowly, you'll be understood.

communication tips

Body language, ways of doing things, sense of humour – all have a role to play in every culture. 'Local talk' boxes show you common ways of saying things, or everyday language to drop into conversation. 'Listen for ...' boxes supply the phrases you may hear. They start with the phonetic guide (because you'll hear it before you know what's being said) and then lead in to the language and the English translation.

spanish

United States
of America

Mexico

Cuba

Dominican Republic
Puerto Rico

Guatemala
El Salvador
Honduras
Costa Rica
Panama
Ecuador

Nicaragua

Venezuela

Colombia

Peru

Bolivia

Paraguay

Uruguay

Argentina

Chile

national language

widely understood

For more details, see the **introduction**.

Spanish, or Castilian, as it's also called in Spain, is the most widely spoken of the Romance languages, the group of languages derived from Latin which includes French, Italian and Portuguese. Outside Spain, it's the language of most of Latin America and the West Indies and is also spoken in the Philippines and Guam, as well as in some areas of the African coast (Equatorial Guinea) and in the US. Worldwide, there are more than 30 countries or territories where Spanish is spoken.

Spanish is derived from Vulgar Latin, which Roman soldiers and merchants brought to the Iberian Peninsula during the period of the Roman conquest (3rd to 1st century BC). By 19 BC Spain had become totally Romanised and Latin became the language of the peninsula in the four centuries that followed. Today's Castilian is spoken in the north, centre and south of Spain.

People are intensely proud of their language and generally expect visitors to know at least a little. English is less widely spoken in Spain than in many other European countries, especially outside the major cities.

This book gives you the practical words and phrases you need to get by, and the fun, spontaneous phrases that lead to a better experience of Spain and its people. Need more encouragement?

at a glance ...

language name: Spanish

name in language:
Español es·pa·*nyol*

language family: Romance

key country: Spain

approximate number of speakers: more than 390 million worldwide

close relatives: Portuguese, Italian, French

donations to English: alligator, bonanza (lit: fair weather), canyon, guerilla, rodeo, ranch, stampede, tornado – and many more familiar words ...

introduction

Remember, the contact you make through using Spanish will make your travels unique. Local knowledge, new relationships and a sense of satisfaction are on the tip of your tongue, so don't just stand there, say something!

> basque, catalan & galician

We also give you the basics of these languages because they are each considered official in Spain, even though Spanish, or Castilian, covers by far the largest territory.

Basque, a non-Romance language, is spoken in parts of the north. Catalan is spoken in the east and Galician in the north-west. These last two are also Romance languages, so are closer in origin to Spanish.

If you're travelling widely in Spain, see the special section on these regional languages for some basic expressions (page 100).

> abbreviations used in this book

f	feminine	sg	singular
inf	informal	pl	plural
m	masculine	pol	polite

Spanish pronunciation isn't difficult, as most sounds are similar to the sounds found in English. The relationship between Spanish sounds and their spelling is straightforward and consistent. There are some easy rules to follow and once you learn them you shouldn't have problems being understood. Like in most languages, Spanish pronunciation can vary according to region – this book focuses on Castilian Spanish.

word stress

There is word stress in Spanish, which means you emphasise one syllable in a word over another. Rule of thumb: when a written word ends in *n*, *s* or a vowel, the stress falls on the second-last syllable, eg *lejos* le·khos (far), *casa* ka·sa (house). Otherwise, the final syllable is stressed, eg *hablar* a·blar (talk). If you see an accent mark over a syllable, it cancels out these rules and you just stress that syllable instead, eg *número* noo·me·ro (number).

vowel sounds

symbol	english equivalent	spanish example	transliteration
a	alms	*agua*	a·gwa
ai	aisle	*bailar*	bai·lar
e	red	*número*	noo·me·ro
ee	bee	*día*	dee·a
o	go	*ojo*	o·kho
oo	book	*gusto*	goo·sto
ow	cow	*autobús*	ow·to·boos
oy	boy	*hoy*	oy

consonant sounds

symbol	english equivalent	spanish example	transliteration
b	**b**ig	*barco*	*bar·ko*
ch	**ch**illi	*chica*	*chee·ka*
d	**d**in	*dinero*	*dee·ne·ro*
f	**f**un	*fiesta*	*fye·sta*
g	**g**o	*gato*	*ga·to*
k	**k**ick	*cabeza,* *queso*	*ka·be·tha,* *ke·so*
kh	as in the Scottish *loch*	*jardín,* *gente*	*khar·deen,* *khen·te*
l	**l**oud	*lago*	*la·go*
ly	mi**lli**on	*llamada*	*lya·ma·da*
m	**m**an	*mañana*	*ma·nya·na*
n	**n**o	*nuevo*	*nwe·vo*
ny	ca**ny**on	*señora*	*se·nyo·ra*
p	**p**ig	*padre*	*pa·dre*
r	**r**un (but stronger and rolled)	*ritmo,* *burro*	*reet·mo,* *boo·ro*
s	**s**o	*semana*	*se·ma·na*
t	**t**in	*tienda*	*tyen·da*
th	**th**in	*Barcelona,* *manzana*	*bar·the·lo·na,* *man·tha·na*
v	soft 'b', between 'v' and 'b'	*abrir*	*a·breer*
w	**w**in	*guardia*	*gwar·dya*
y	**y**es	*viaje*	*vya·khe*

reading & writing

There are some key things to remember about consonants in written Spanish:

- The letter *c* is pronounced with a lisp, eg *cerveza* ther·ve·tha, except when it comes before *a*, *o* and *u* or a consonant, when it's pronounced hard, like the *k* in 'king'.
- When ending a word, the letter *d* is also pronounced soft, like a th, or it's so slight that it hardly get pronounced at all.
- The letter *j* stands for a harsh and guttural sound, and we use the kh symbol in our pronunciation guides.
- Try to roll your double *r*'s.
- The letter *q* is pronounced hard, like a k.
- The letter *v* sounds more like a b, said with the lips pressed together.
- There are a few letters which don't appear in the English alphabet: *ch*, *ll* and *ñ*. You'll see that these letters have their own entries in the Spanish–English dictionary.

spanish alphabet

A a	a		*B b*	be		*C c*	the
CH ch	che		*D d*	de		*E e*	e
F f	e·fe		*G g*	khe		*H h*	a·che
I i	ee		*J j*	kho·ta		*K k*	ka
L l	e·le		*LL ll*	e·lye		*M m*	e·me
N n	e·ne		*Ñ ñ*	e·nye		*O o*	o
P p	pe		*Q q*	koo		*R r*	e·re
S s	e·se		*T t*	te		*U u*	oo
V v	oo·ve		*W w*	oo·ve do·vle		*X x*	e·kees
Y y	ee·grye·ga		*Z z*	the·ta			

pronunciation

false friends

Beware of false friends – those words that sound like familiar English, but could land you in a bit of trouble if you use them unwittingly in Spanish. Here are some mistakes it's a little too easy to make:

el suburbio   el soo·*boor*·byo   **slum district**
    not 'suburb' which is *el barrio*, el *ba*·ryo

Estoy   es·*toy*   **I have a cold.**
constipado/a. m/f   kons·tee·*pa*·do/a
    not 'I'm constipated' which is *estoy estreñido/a* m/f
    es·*toy* es·tre·*nyee*·do/a

Estoy   es·*toy*   **I'm pregnant.**
embarazada.   em·ba·ra·*tha*·da
    not 'I'm embarassed' which is *estoy avergonzado/a* m/f
    es·*toy* a·ver·gon·*tha*·do/a

la injuria   la een·*khoo*·ree·a   **insult**
    not 'injury' which is *la herida*, la e·*ree*·da

largo/a m/f   *lar*·go/a   **long**
    not 'large' which is *grande*, *gran*·de

los parientes   los pa·ree·*yen*·tes   **relatives**
    not 'parents' which is *los padres*, los *pa*·dres

sensible   sen·*thee*·ble   **sensitive**
    not 'sensible' which is *prudente*, proo·*den*·te

This chapter is designed to explain the main grammatical structures you need in order to make your own sentences. Look under each heading – listed in alphabetical order – for information on functions which these grammatical categories express in a sentence. For example, demonstratives are used for giving instructions, so you'll need them to tell the taxi driver where your hotel is, etc. A glossary of grammatical terms is included at the end of the chapter to help you.

adjectives & adverbs

describing people/things • doing things

When using an adjective to describe a noun, you need to use a different ending depending on whether the noun is masculine or feminine, and singular or plural (see **gender** and **plurals**). Most adjectives use the following four endings:

	singular		plural	
m	*fantástico*	fan·*tas*·tee·ko	*fantásticos*	fan·*tas*·tee·kos
f	*fantástica*	fan·*tas*·tee·ka	*fantásticas*	fan·*tas*·tee·kas

a fantastic hotel	*un hotel fantástico*	oon o·*tel* fan·*tas*·tee·ko
	(lit: a-m-sg hotel fantastic-m-sg)	
a fantastic meal	*una comida fantástica*	oo·na ko·*mee*·da fan·*tas*·tee·ka
	(lit: a-f-sg meal fantastic-f-sg)	
some fantastic books	*unos libros fantásticos*	oo·nos *lee*·bros fan·*tas*·tee·kos
	(lit: some-m-pl books fantastic-m-pl)	
some fantastic tapas	*unas tapas fantásticas*	oo·nas *ta*·pas fan·*tas*·tee·kas
	(lit: some-f-pl tapas fantastic-f-pl)	

Adjectives generally come after the noun in Spanish. However, adjectives expressing quantity (such as 'much', 'a lot', 'little/few', 'many') always precede the noun. See also **demonstratives** and **possessives**.

a comfortable hotel	*un hotel cómodo*	oon o·*tel* ko·mo·do
	(lit: a-m-sg hotel comfortable-m-sg)	
many tourists	*muchos turistas*	*moo*·chos too·*rees*·tas
	(lit: many-m-pl tourists)	

Most adverbs in Spanish are derived from adjectives by adding the ending *-mente* ·*men*·te to the singular feminine form of the adjective (ie the form ending in -a), just like you add the ending '-ly' to the adjective in English. In Spanish, adverbs are generally placed after the verb they refer to.

a slow train	*un tren lento*	oon tren *len*·to
	(lit: a-m-sg train slow-m-sg)	
to speak slowly	*hablar lentamente*	ab·*lar* len·ta·*men*·te
	(lit: to-speak slowly)	

articles

naming people/things

There are four words for the definite article (ie equivalents of 'the' in English) in Spanish, used depending on the gender and the number of the noun (see **gender** and **plurals**). The masculine singular form of the definite article is joined to some prepositions when it's placed after them, so eg *a el* (to the) becomes *al* al and *de el* (of the) becomes *del* del. See also **prepositions**.

definite articles			
m sg	the car	*el coche*	el *ko*·che
m pl	the cars	*los coches*	los *ko*·ches
f sg	the shop	*la tienda*	la *tyen*·da
f pl	the shops	*las tiendas*	las *tyen*·das

Similarly, Spanish has four words for the indefinite article (ie 'a/ an' in English), depending on the gender and number of the noun.

indefinite articles			
m sg	an egg	*un huevo*	oon *hwe·vo*
m pl	some eggs	*unos huevos*	oo·nos *hwe·vos*
f sg	a house	*una casa*	oo·na *ka·sa*
f pl	some houses	*unas casas*	oo·nas *ka·sas*

be

describing people/things • making statements

Spanish has two words for the English verb 'be': *ser* ser and *estar* es·*tar*, which are used depending on the context.

use of *SER* (to be)		
permanent characteristics of persons/things	*Liz es muy guapa.* leez es mooy *gwa·pa*	Liz is very beautiful.
occupations or nationality	*Ana es de España.* a·na es de e·*spa·*nya	Ana is from Spain.
time or location of events	*Son las tres.* son las tres	It's 3 o'clock.
possession	*De quién es este bolso?* de kyen es es·te *bol·*so	Whose bag is this?
use of *ESTAR* (to be)		
temporary characteristics of persons/things	*La sopa está fría.* la *so·*pa es·*ta free·*a	The soup is cold.
time or location of persons/things	*Estamos en Madrid.* es·*ta·*mos en ma·*dree*	We are in Madrid.
mood of a person	*Estoy contento.* es·toy kon·*ten·*to	I'm happy.

SER (to be) – present tense

I	am	*yo*	soy	yo	soy
you sg inf	are	*tú*	eres	too	e·res
you sg pol	are	*Usted*	es	oo·*ste*	es
he she	is	*él* *ella*	es	el e·lya	es
we	are	*nosotros* m *nosotras* f	somos	no·*so*·tros m no·*so*·tras f	*so*·mos
you pl inf	are	*vosotros* m *vosotras* f	sois	vo·*so*·tros m vo·*so*·tras f	*so*·ees
you pl pol	are	*Ustedes*	son	oo·*ste*·des	son
they	are	*ellos* m *ellas* f	son	e·lyos m e·lyas f	son

ESTAR (to be) – present tense

I	am	*yo*	estoy	yo	es·*toy*
you sg inf	are	*tú*	estás	too	es·*tas*
you sg pol	are	*Usted*	está	oo·*ste*	es·*ta*
he she	is	*él* *ella*	está	el e·lya	es·*ta*
we	are	*nosotros* m *nosotras* f	estamos	no·*so*·tros m no·*so*·tras f	es·*ta*·mos
you pl inf	are	*vosotros* m *vosotras* f	estáis	vo·*so*·tros m vo·*so*·tras f	es·*ta*·ees
you pl pol	are	*Ustedes*	están	oo·*ste*·des	es·*tan*
they	are	*ellos* m *ellas* f	están	e·lyos m e·lyas f	es·*tan*

demonstratives

giving instructions • indicating location • pointing things out

To point something out, the easiest phrases to use are *es* es (it is), *esto es* es·to es (this is) or *eso es* e·so es (that is).

It's a guide to Seville.

Es una guía de Sevilla.   es oo·na gee·a de se·vee·lya
(lit: is a-**f-sg** guide of Seville)

The Spanish words for 'this' and 'that' vary, depending on whether something is close (ie 'this'), away from you (ie 'that') or even further away in time or space (ie 'that over there'). Each of these words changes form depending on the gender and number of the noun it refers to. See also **gender** and **plurals**.

demonstratives				
	m sg		m pl	
this (close)	*éste*	e·ste	*éstos*	e·stos
that (away)	*ése*	e·se	*ésos*	e·sos
that (further away)	*aquél*	a·kel	*aquéllos*	a·ke·lyos
	f sg		f pl	
this (close)	*ésta*	e·sta	*éstas*	e·stas
that (away)	*ésa*	e·sa	*ésas*	e·sas
that (further away)	*aquélla*	a·ke·lya	*aquéllas*	a·ke·lyas

gender

naming people/things

In Spanish, all nouns (words which denote a thing, person or idea) have either masculine or feminine gender. You can recognise the noun's gender by the article, demonstrative, possessive or any other adjective accompanying the noun, as they change form to agree with the noun's gender (see **adjectives & adverbs**, **articles**, **demonstratives**, **possessives**). The gender of words is also indicated in the dictionary, but here are some general rules:

- a word is masculine/feminine if it refers to a man/woman
- words ending in *-o* or *-or* are generally masculine
- words ending in *-a*, *-d*, *-z* or *-ión* are usually feminine

The masculine and feminine forms of words are indicated with m and f throughout this phrasebook where relevant. See also the box **m (masculine) or f (feminine)?**, page 125.

have

possessing

Possession can be indicated in various ways in Spanish (see also **possessives**). One way is by using the verb *tener* te·*ner* (have). For negative forms with 'have', see **negatives**.

TENER (to have)					
I	have	*yo*	*tengo*	yo	*ten·go*
you sg inf	have	*tú*	*tienes*	too	*tye·nes*
you sg pol	have	*Usted*	*tiene*	oo·ste	*tye·ne*
he/she	has	*él/ella*	*tiene*	el/e·lya	*tye·ne*
we	have	*nosotros* m *nosotras* f	*tenemos*	no·so·tros m no·so·tras f	te·*ne*·mos
you pl inf	have	*vosotros* m *vosotras* f	*tenéis*	vo·so·tros m vo·so·tras f	te·*ne*·ees
you pl pol	have	*Ustedes*	*tienen*	oo·ste·des	*tye·nen*
they	have	*ellos* m *ellas* f	*tienen*	e·lyos m e·lyas f	*tye·nen*

The impersonal form of the verb *haber* ha·*ber* (have) is used to mean 'there is/are' and in questions for 'is/are there ...?':

Is there hot water? ¿*Hay agua caliente?* ai a·*gwa* ka·*lyen*·te
(lit: is-there water hot-f-sg)

negatives

negating

To make a negative statement in Spanish, just add the word *no*
no (not) before the main verb of the sentence:

I'm not going to try that.
   No voy a probarlo.   no voy a pro·*bar*·lo
   (lit: not I-go to try-it)

Contrary to English, Spanish uses double negatives:

I have nothing to declare.
   No tengo nada que declarar.   no *ten*·go *na*·da ke dek·la·*rar*
   (lit: not I-have nothing to declare)

personal pronouns

making statements • naming people/things

Personal pronouns ('I', 'you' etc) change form in Spanish depending on whether they're the subject or the object in a sentence. It's the same in English, which has 'I' and 'me' as the
subject and object pronouns (eg 'I see her' and 'She sees me').
The subject pronoun is usually omitted in Spanish as the subject
is understood from the corresponding verb form (see **verbs**).

I'm a student.   *Soy estudiante.*   soy es·too·*dyan*·te
                   (lit: I-am student)

subject pronouns

I	*yo*	yo	we	*nosotros* m *nosotras* f	no·*so*·tros m no·*so*·tras f
you sg inf	*tú*	too	**you** pl inf	*vosotros* m *vosotras* f	vo·*so*·tros m vo·*so*·tras f
you sg pol	*Usted*	oo·*ste*	**you** pl pol	*Ustedes*	oo·*ste*·des
he	*él*	el	**they**	*ellos* m	e·lyos m
she	*ella*	e·lya		*ellas* f	e·lyas f

grammar

19

As the tables show, Spanish has two 'you' forms. With people familiar to you or younger than you, it's usual to use the informal form of 'you', *tú* too, rather than the polite form, *Usted* oo·*ste*. Phrases in this book use the form of 'you' that is appropriate to the situation. Where both forms are used, they are indicated by pol and inf. See also the box **using your manners**, page 77.

object pronouns

me	*me*	me	us	*nos*	nos
you sg inf	*te*	te	you pl inf	*vos*	vos
you sg pol	*lo/le* m *la/le* f	lo/le m la/le f	you pl pol	*los/les* m *las/les* f	los/les m las/les f
him it	*lo/le*	lo/le	them	*los/les* m *las/les* f	los/les m las/les f
her it	*la/le*	la/le			

*the forms separated by a slash are direct/indirect object pronouns

The direct and indirect object pronouns differ only for the third person ('he', 'she', 'it', 'they') and the polite 'you' forms.

I don't know her.	*No la conosco.*	no la ko·*no*·sko
	(lit: not her I-know)	
I'm talking to her.	*Le hablo.*	le *a*·blo
	(lit: to-her I-talk)	

The object pronouns generally come before the verb. The indirect object pronoun comes before the direct object pronoun.

I'll show it to you.	*Te lo mostraré.*	te lo mos·tra·*re*
	(lit: to-you-sg-inf it I-will-show)	

plurals

naming people/things

To form plurals in Spanish, add -s if the noun ends in a vowel and -es if it ends in a consonant. In this book singular and plural forms are indicated with sg and pl respectively where needed.

singular			plural		
bed	*cama*	ka·ma	beds	*camas*	ka·mas
woman	*mujer*	moo·kher	women	*mujeres*	moo·khe·res

possessives

possessing

A common way of indicating possession is by using possessive adjectives before the noun they refer to. Like other adjectives, they agree with the noun in number, and in case of 'our' and 'your' they also agree in gender (see also **gender** and **plurals**).

our daughter *nuestra hija* nwes·tra ee·kha
(lit: our-f-pl daughter)

possessive adjectives					
my	*mi/* *mis*	mee/ mees	our	*nuestro/* *nuestros* m *nuestra/* *nuestras* f	nwes·tro/ nwes·tros m nwes·tra/ nwes·tras f
your sg inf	*tu/* *tus*	too/ toos	your pl inf	*vuestro/* *vuestros* m *vuestra/* *vuestras* f	wes·tro/ wes·tros m wes·tra/ wes·tras f
your sg pol	*su/* *sus*	soo/ soos	your pl pol	*su/sus*	soo/soos
his her its	*su/* *sus*	soo/ soos	their	*su/sus*	soo/soos

*the forms separated by a slash are used with a singular/plural noun

Another way to indicate possession is by using possessive pronouns, which also agree in gender and number with the noun.

The book is mine. *El libro es mío.* el lee·bro es mee·o
(lit: the-m-sg book is mine-m-sg)

possessive pronouns

mine	mío	mee·o	ours	nuestro	nwes·tro
	míos	mee·os		nuestros	nwes·tros
	mía	mee·a		nuestra	nwes·tra
	mías	mee·as		nuestras	nwes·tras
yours sg inf	tuyo	too·yo	yours pl inf	vuestro	wes·tro
	tuyos	too·yos		vuestros	wes·tros
	tuya	too·ya		vuestra	wes·tra
	tuyas	too·yas		vuestras	wes·tras
yours sg pol	suyo	soo·yo	yours pl pol	suyo	soo·yo
	suyos	soo·yos		suyos	soo·yos
his hers its	suya	soo·ya	theirs	suya	soo·ya
	suyas	soo·yas		suyas	soo·yas

*the four alternatives are used with m sg, m pl, f sg and f pl nouns

Ownership can also be expressed in Spanish using the construction '*de* de (of) + noun', just like in English. See also **have**.

my friend's bag
  el bolso de mi amigo   el *bol*·so de mee a·*mee*·go
  (lit: the-m-sg bag of my-m-sg friend)

prepositions

giving instructions • indicating location • pointing things out

Like English, Spanish uses prepositions to explain where things are in time or space. Common prepositions are listed in the table below. For more prepositions, see the **dictionary**.
  When certain prepositions are followed by a definite article, they are contracted into a single word (see **articles**).

prepositions					
after	*después de*	des·*pwes* de	from	*de*	de
at (time)	*a*	a	in (place)	*en*	en
before	*antes de*	an·tes de	to	*a*	a

questions

The easiest way of forming 'yes/no' questions in Spanish is to add the phrase *verdad* ver·*da* (literally 'truth') to the end of a statement, similar to 'isn't it?' in English. You can also turn a statement into a question by putting the verb before the subject of the sentence, just like in English.

This is the right stop, isn't it?
  ¿Esta es la parada, verdad?   es·ta es la pa·ra·da ver·da
  (lit: this-f-sg is the-f-sg stop truth)

Is this the right stop?
  ¿Es esta la parada?   es es·ta la pa·ra·da
  (lit: is this-f-sg the-f-sg stop)

As in English, there are also question words for more specific questions. These words go at the start of the sentence.

question words					
how	*cómo*	*ko·*mo	where	*dónde*	*don·*de
what	*qué*	ke	who	*quién* sg *quiénes* pl	*kyen* sg *kye·*nes pl
when	*cuándo*	*kwan·*do	why	*por qué*	por ke

verbs

There are three verb categories in Spanish – those whose infinitive ends in *-ar*, *-er* or *-ir*, eg *hablar* ab·*lar* (talk), *comer* ko·*mer* (eat), *vivir* vee·*veer* (live). Tenses are formed by adding various endings for each person to the verb stem (after removing *-ar*, *-er* or *-ir* from the infinitive) or infinitive, and for most verbs these endings follow regular patterns. The verb endings for the present, past and future tenses are presented in the tables on the following pages. For negative forms of verbs, see **negatives**.

> present tense

present tense		hablar	comer	vivir
I	yo	hablo	como	vivo
you sg inf	tú	hablas	comes	vives
you sg pol	Usted	habla	come	vive
he/she	él/ella	habla	come	vive
we	nosotros m nosotras f	hablamos	comemos	vivimos
you pl inf	vosotros m vosotras f	habláis	coméis	vivís
you pl pol	Ustedes	hablan	comen	viven
they	ellos m ellas f	hablan	comen	viven

See also **be** and **have**.

> past tense

past tense		hablar	comer	vivir
I	yo	hablé	comí	viví
you sg inf	tú	hablaste	comiste	viviste
you sg pol	Usted	habló	comió	vivió
he/she	él/ella	habló	comió	vivió
we	nosotros m nosotras f	hablamos	comimos	vivimos
you pl inf	vosotros m vosotras f	hablasteis	comisteis	vivisteis
you pl pol	Ustedes	hablaron	comieron	vivieron
they	ellos m ellas f	hablaron	comieron	vivieron

> future tense

In case of the future tense, the endings follow the same pattern for all three verb categories, and they are simply added to the infinitive (dictionary form of the verb), not the verb stem:

future tense				
		hablar	*comer*	*vivir*
I	*yo*	*hablaré*	*comeré*	*viviré*
you sg inf	*tú*	*hablarás*	*comerás*	*vivirás*
you sg pol	*Usted*	*hablará*	*comerá*	*vivirá*
he/she	*él/ella*	*hablará*	*comerá*	*vivirá*
we	*nosotros* m *nosotras* f	*hablaremos*	*comeremos*	*viviremos*
you pl inf	*vosotros* m *vosotras* f	*hablaréis*	*comeréis*	*viviréis*
you pl pol	*Ustedes*	*hablarán*	*comerán*	*vivirán*
they	*ellos* m *ellas* f	*hablarán*	*comerán*	*vivirán*

word order

making statements

Spanish has a basic word order of subject–verb–object, just like English. However, the subject pronoun is usually omitted in Spanish because the subject is understood from the corresponding verb form (see **verbs**) – so both of the following examples are correct but the second one is more common:

I study business.

Yo estudio comercio.   yo es·*too*·dyo ko·*mer*·thyo
(lit: I I-study business)

Estudio comercio.   es·*too*·dyo ko·*mer*·thyo
(lit: I-study business)

See also **negatives** and **questions**.

grammar glossary

adjective	a word that describes something – 'he was the **greatest** toreador of his time'
adverb	a word that explains how an action is done – 'he turned around **quickly**'
article	the words 'a', 'an' and 'the'
demonstrative	a word that means 'this' or 'that'
direct object	the thing or person in the sentence that has the action directed to it – 'and the bull missed **him**'
gender	classification of *nouns* into classes (like masculine and feminine), requiring other words (eg *adjectives*) to belong to the same class
indirect object	the person or thing in the sentence that is the recipient of the action – 'the public yelled to **him**'
infinitive	dictionary form of a *verb* – '**to be** careful'
noun	a thing, person or idea – 'the **fight** was exciting'
number	whether a word is singular or plural – 'and **they** sent in new **toreadors**'
personal pronoun	a word that means 'I', 'you' etc
possessive adjective	a word that means 'my', 'your' etc
possessive pronoun	a word that means 'mine', 'yours' etc
preposition	a word like 'for' or 'before' in English
subject	the thing or person in the sentence that does the action – 'his **cape** fell on the ground'
tense	form of a *verb* that tells you whether the action is in the present, past or future – eg 'run' (present), 'ran' (past), 'will run' (future)
verb	a word that tells you what action happened – 'when the bull **charged** again'
verb stem	part of a *verb* that doesn't change – eg '**mov**e' in '**mov**ing' and '**mov**ed'

There are two words for 'Spanish': *español* es·pa·*nyol* and *castellano* kas·te·*lya*·no. *Español* is used in Spain, whereas *castellano* is more likely to be used by Latin Americans.

I speak a little Spanish.
Hablo un poco de español.　　　ab·lo oon po·ko de es·pa·nyol

I'd like to practice Spanish.
Me gustaría practicar　　　me goos·ta·ree·a prak·tee·kar
español.　　　es·pa·nyol

Do you speak English?
¿Habla inglés?　　　ab·la een·gles

Does anyone speak English?
¿Hay alguien que hable　　　ai al·gyen ke ab·le
inglés?　　　een·gles

I need an interpreter who speaks English.
Necesito un intérprete　　　ne·the·see·to oon in·ter·pre·te
que hable inglés.　　　ke ab·le een·gles

Do you understand?
¿Me entiende?　　　me en·tyen·de

I (don't) understand.
(No) Entiendo.　　　(no) een·tyen·do

How do you pronounce this word?
¿Cómo se pronuncia　　　ko·mo se pro·noon·thya
esta palabra?　　　es·ta pa·lab·ra

How do you write 'ciudad'?
¿Cómo se escribe　　　ko·mo se es·kree·be
'ciudad'?　　　thee·oo·da

listen for ...		
ko·mo	¿Cómo?	**Pardon?**
no	No.	**No.**
see	Sí.	**Yes.**

What does ... mean?
¿Qué significa ...?   ke seeg·nee·*fee*·ka ...

Could you repeat that?
¿Puede repetir?   pwe·de re·pe·*teer*

Could you please ...?	*¿Puede ..., por favor?*	pwe·de ... por fa·*vor*
speak more slowly	*hablar más despacio*	ab·*lar* mas des·*pa*·thyo
write it down	*escribirlo*	es·kree·*beer*·lo

dirty latin

Over the last 500 years, the Spanish spoken in Latin America has developed differently to the Spanish spoken in Europe. Variations in pronunciation, vocabulary and even grammar can lead to confusion or embarrassment. Here are two examples that could get you into trouble.

Quiero coger el autobús.
kye·ro ko·*kher* el   **I want to catch the bus.**
ow·to·*boos*
(Latin America: I want to bonk the bus.)

Hay un gran bicho en el baño.
ai oon gran *bee*·cho   **There's a huge bug in**
en el *ba*·nyo   **the bathroom.**
(Latin America: There's a big prick in the bathroom.)

cardinal numbers

los números cardinales

0	*cero*	*the*·ro
1	*uno*	*oo*·no
2	*dos*	dos
3	*tres*	tres
4	*cuatro*	*kwa*·tro
5	*cinco*	*theen*·ko
6	*seis*	seys
7	*siete*	*sye*·te
8	*ocho*	*o*·cho
9	*nueve*	*nwe*·ve
10	*diez*	dyeth
11	*once*	*on*·the
12	*doce*	*do*·the
13	*trece*	*tre*·the
14	*catorce*	ka·*tor*·the
15	*quince*	*keen*·the
16	*dieciséis*	dye·thee·*seys*
17	*diecisiete*	dye·thee·*sye*·te
18	*dieciocho*	dye·thee·*o*·cho
19	*diecinueve*	dye·thee·*nwe*·ve
20	*veinte*	*veyn*·te
21	*veintiuno*	veyn·tee·*oo*·no
22	*veintidós*	veyn·tee·*dos*
30	*treinta*	*treyn*·ta
40	*cuarenta*	kwa·*ren*·ta
50	*cincuenta*	theen·*kwen*·ta
60	*sesenta*	se·*sen*·ta
70	*setenta*	se·*ten*·ta
80	*ochenta*	o·*chen*·ta
90	*noventa*	no·*ven*·ta
100	*cien*	thyen

101	*ciento uno*	*thyen·to oo·no*
102	*ciento dos*	*thyen·to dos*
500	*quinientos*	kee·*nyen* tos
1000	*mil*	mil
1,000,000	*un millón*	oon mee·*lyon*

ordinal numbers

los números ordinales

1st	*primero/a* m/f	pree·*me*·ro/a
2nd	*segundo/a* m/f	se·*goon*·do/a
3rd	*tercero/a* m/f	ter·*the*·ro/a
4th	*cuarto/a* m/f	*kwar*·to/a
5th	*quinto/a* m/f	*keen*·to/a

fractions

las fracciones

a quarter	*un cuarto*	oon *kwar*·to
a third	*un tercio*	oon *ter*·thyo
a half	*un medio*	oon *me*·dyo
three-quarters	*tres cuartos*	tres *kwar*·tos
all	*todo*	*to*·do
none	*nada*	*na*·da

amounts

las cantidades

a little	*un poquito*	oon po·*kee*·to
many	*muchos/as* m/f	*moo*·chos/as
some	*algunos/as* m/f	al·*goo*·nos/as
more	*más*	mas
less	*menos*	*me*·nos

For more amounts, see **self-catering**, page 158.

telling the time

dando la hora

What time is it?	¿Qué hora es?	ke o·ra es
It's one o'clock.	Es la una.	es la oo·na
It's (10) o'clock.	Son (las diez).	son (las dyeth)
Quarter past one.	Es la una y cuarto.	es la oo·na ee kwar·to
Twenty past one.	Es la una y veinte.	es la oo·na ee veyn·te
Half past one.	Es la una y media.	es la oo·na ee me·dya
Twenty to one.	Es la una menos veinte.	es la oo·na me·nos veyn·te
Quarter to one.	Es la una menos cuarto.	es la oo·na me·nos kwar·to
It's early.	Es temprano.	es tem·pra·no
It's late.	Es tarde.	es tar·de
At what time?	¿A qué hora?	a ke o·ra
At …	A las …	a las …
am	de la mañana	de la ma·nya·na
pm	de la tarde	de la tar·de

days of the week

los días de la semana

Monday	lunes m	loo·nes
Tuesday	martes m	mar·tes
Wednesday	miércoles m	myer·ko·les
Thursday	jueves m	khwe·ves
Friday	viernes m	vyer·nes
Saturday	sábado m	sa·ba·do
Sunday	domingo m	do·meen·go

the calendar

el calendario

> months

January	*enero* m	e·*ne*·ro
February	*febrero* m	fe·*bre*·ro
March	*marzo* m	*mar*·tho
April	*abril* m	a·*breel*
May	*mayo* m	*ma*·yo
June	*junio* m	*khoo*·nyo
July	*julio* m	*khoo*·lyo
August	*agosto* m	a·*gos*·to
September	*septiembre* m	sep·*tyem*·bre
October	*octubre* m	ok·*too*·bre
November	*noviembre* m	no·*vyem*·bre
December	*diciembre* m	dee·*thyem*·bre

> seasons

summer	*verano* m	ve·*ra*·no
autumn	*otoño* m	o·*to*·nyo
winter	*invierno* m	een·*vyer*·no
spring	*primavera* f	pree·ma·*ve*·ra

dates

las fechas

What date?
¿Qué día?　　　　ke *dee*·a

What date is it today?
¿Qué día es hoy?　　ke *dee*·a es oy

It's (18 October).
Es (el dieciocho de　es (el dye·thee·o·cho de
octubre).　　　　ok·*too*·bre)

TOOLS

present

now	*ahora*	a·o·ra
right now	*ahora mismo*	a·o·ra *mees*·mo
this ...		
afternoon	*esta tarde*	es·ta *tar*·de
month	*este mes*	es·te mes
morning	*esta mañana*	es·ta ma·*nya*·na
week	*esta semana*	es·ta se·*ma*·na
year	*este año*	es·te a·nyo
today	*hoy*	oy
tonight	*esta noche*	es·ta *no*·che

past

... ago	*hace ...*	a·the ...
(three) days	*(tres) días*	(tres) dee·as
half an hour	*media hora*	me·dya o·ra
a while	*un rato*	un ra·to
(five) years	*(cinco) años*	(theen·ko) a·nyos
day before	*anteayer*	an·te·a·*yer*
yesterday		
last ...		
month	*el mes pasado*	el mes pa·*sa*·do
night	*anoche*	a·*no*·che
week	*la semana pasada*	la se·*ma*·na pa·*sa*·da
year	*el año pasado*	el a·nyo pa·*sa*·do
since (May)	*desde (mayo)*	*des*·de (ma·yo)
yesterday	*ayer*	a·*yer*
yesterday ...	*ayer por la ...*	a·*yer* por la ...
afternoon	*tarde*	*tar*·de
evening	*noche*	*no*·che
morning	*mañana*	ma·*nya*·na

future

in ...	dentro de ...	den·tro de ...
(six) days	(seis) días	(seys) dee·as
an hour	una hora	oo·na o·ra
(five) minutes	(cinco)	(theen·ko)
	minutos	mee·noo·tos
a month	un mes	oon mes
next ...	... que viene	... ke vye·ne
month	el mes	el mes
week	la semana	la se·ma·na
year	el año	el a·nyo
tomorrow	mañana	ma·nya·na
day after tomorrow	pasado mañana	pa·sa·do ma·nya·na
tomorrow ...	mañana por la ...	ma·nya·na por la ...
afternoon	tarde	tar·de
evening	noche	no·che
morning	mañana	ma·nya·na
until (June)	hasta (junio)	as·ta (khoo·nyo)

during the day

durante el día

afternoon	tarde f	tar·de
dawn	madrugada f	ma·droo·ga·da
day	día m	dee·a
evening	noche f	no·che
midday	mediodía m	me·dyo·dee·a
midnight	medianoche f	me·dya·no·che
morning	mañana f	ma·nya·na
night	noche f	no·che
sunrise	amanecer m	a·ma·ne·ther
sunset	puesta f del sol	pwes·ta del sol

Where's the nearest ATM?

¿Dónde está el cajero
automático más
cercano?

don·de es·ta el ka·khe·ro
ow·to·ma·tee·ko mas
ther·ka·no

Can I use my credit card to withdraw money?

¿Puedo usar mi tarjeta
de crédito para sacar
dinero?

pwe·do oo·sar mee tar·khe·ta
de kre·dee·to pa·ra sa·kar
dee·ne·ro

What's the exchange rate?

¿Cuál es el tipo de cambio?

kwal es el tee·po de kam·byo

What's the charge for that?

¿Cuánto hay que pagar
por eso?

kwan·to ai ke pa·gar
por e·so

How much is this?

¿Cuánto cuesta esto?

kwan·to kwes·ta es·to

The price is too high.

Cuesta demasiado.

kwes·ta de·ma·sya·do

Can you lower the price?

¿Podría bajar un
poco el precio?

po·dree·a ba·khar oon
po·ko el pre·thyo

I'd like to change ...	Me gustaría cambiar ...	me goos·ta·ree·a kam·byar ...
money	dinero	dee·ne·ro
a travellers cheque	un cheque de viajero	oon che·ke de vya·khe·ro

I'd like to ...	Me gustaría …	me goos·ta·ree·a …
arrange a transfer	hacer una transferencia	ha·ther oo·na trans·fe·ren·thya
cash a cheque	cambiar un cheque	kam·byar oon che·ke
get a cash advance	obtener un adelanto	ob·te·ner on a·de·lan·to
get change for this note	conseguir cambio para este billete	kon·se·geer kam·byo pa·ra es·te bee·lye·te
withdraw money	sacar dinero	sa·kar dee·ne·ro

Do you accept ...?	¿Aceptan ...?	a·thep·tan …
credit cards	tarjetas de crédito	tar·khe·tas de kre·dee·to
debit cards	tarjetas de débito	tar·khe·tas de de·bee·to
travellers cheques	cheques de viajero	che·kes de vya·khe·ro

Do I need to pay up front?
¿Necesito pagar por adelantado?
ne·the·see·to pa·gar por a·de·lan·ta·do

Could I have a receipt, please?
¿Podría darme un recibo, por favor?
po·dree·a dar·me oon re·thee·bo por fa·vor

I'd like my money back.
Quisiera que me devuelva el dinero.
kee·sye·ra ke me de·vwel·va el dee·ne·ro

I'd like my change, please.
Quisiera mi cambio, por favor.
kee·sye·ra mee kam·byo por fa·vor

There's a mistake in the bill.
Hay un error en la cuenta.
ai oon e·ror en la kwen·ta

For more money-related phrases, see **banking**, page 79.

listen for ...

kye·re feer·mar o een·tro·doo·theer soo peen
¿Quiere firmar o introducir su PIN?
Do you want to sign or use your PIN?

getting around

desplazándose

At what time does the ... leave/arrive?	*¿A qué hora sale/llega el ...?*	a ke o·ra sa·le/lye·ga el ...
boat	*barco*	bar·ko
bus (city)	*autobús*	ow·to·boos
bus (intercity)	*autocar*	ow·to·kar
plane	*avión*	a·vyon
train	*tren*	tren
tram	*tranvía*	tran·vee·a
At what time's the ... (bus)?	*¿A qué hora es el ... (autobús)?*	a ke o·ra es el ... (ow·to·boos)
first	*primer*	pree·mer
last	*último*	ool·tee·mo
next	*próximo*	prok·see·mo
I'd like a/an ... seat.	*Quisiera un asiento ...*	kee·sye·ra oon a·syen·to ...
aisle	*de pasillo*	de pa·see·lyo
non-smoking	*de no fumadores*	de no foo·ma·do·res
smoking	*de fumadores*	de foo·ma·do·res
window	*junto a la ventana*	khoon·to a la ven·ta·na

asking for an address

What's the/your address?
¿Cuál es la/su dirección? — kwal es la/soo dee·rek·thyon

avenue	*avenida* f	a·ve·nee·da
lane	*callejón* m	ka·lye·khon
street	*calle* f	ka·lye

Is there (a) …?	¿Hay …?	ai …
air-conditioning	aire acon-	ai·re a·kon·
	dicionado	dee·thyo·na·do
blanket	una manta	oo·na man·ta
toilet	servicios	ser·vee·thyos
video	vídeo	vee·de·o

How long will it be delayed?
¿Cuánto tiempo se
retrasará?
kwan·to tyem·po se
re·tra·sa·ra

Is this seat free?
¿Está libre este asiento?
es·ta lee·bre es·te a·syen·to

That's my seat.
Ése es mi asiento.
e·se es mee a·syen·to

Can you tell me when we get to (Valladolid)?
¿Me podría decir
cuándo lleguemos a
(Valladolid)?
me po·dree·a de·theer
kwan·do lye·ge·mos a
(va·lya·do·leeth)

I'd like to get off at (Aranjuez).
Me gustaría bajarme
en (Aranjuez).
me goos·ta·ree·a ba·khar·me
en (a·ran·khweth)

I want to get off here!
¡Quiero bajarme aquí!
kye·ro ba·khar·me a·kee

buying tickets

comprando billetes

Do I need to book?
¿Tengo que reservar?
ten·go ke re·ser·var

How much is it?
¿Cuánto cuesta?
kwan·to kwes·ta

Where can I buy a ticket?
¿Dónde puedo comprar
un billete?
don·de pwe·do kom·prar
oon bee·lye·te

es·ta pa·*ra*·da es ...
Esta parada es ...   This stop is ...

la *prok*·see·ma pa·*ra*·da es ...
La próxima parada es ...   The next stop is ...

es·ta kom·*ple*·to
Está completo.   It's full.

el ... es·ta re·tra·sa·do/kan·the·*la*·do
El ... está retrasado/   The ... is delayed/
cancelado.   cancelled.

How long does the trip take?
¿Cuánto se tarda?   kwan·to se tar·da

Is it a direct route?
¿Es un viaje directo?   es oon vya·khe dee·rek·to

Can I get a stand-by ticket?
¿Puede ponerme en la   pwe·de po·ner·me en la
lista de espera?   lees·ta de es·pe·ra

I'd like to ...	*Me gustaría ...*	me goos·ta·ree·a ...
my ticket.	*mi billete.*	mee bee·lye·te
cancel	*cancelar*	kan·the·lar
change	*cambiar*	kam·byar
collect	*recoger*	re·ko·kher
confirm	*confirmar*	kon·feer·mar

Two ... tickets,	*Dos billetes ...,*	dos bee·lye·tes ...
please.	*por favor.*	por fa·vor
1st-class	*de primera clase*	de pree·me·ra kla·se
2nd-class	*de segunda clase*	de se·goon·da kla·se
child's	*infantil*	een·fan·teel
return	*de ida y vuelta*	de ee·da ee vwel·ta
student's	*de estudiante*	de es·too·dyan·te

A one-way ticket to (Barcelona).
Un billete sencillo   oon bee·lye·te sen·thee·lyo
a (Barcelona).   a (bar·the·lo·na)

transport

39

luggage

el equipaje

My luggage has been ...	Mis maletas han sido ...	mees ma·*le*·tas an *see*·do ...
damaged	*dañadas*	da·*nya*·das
lost	*perdidas*	per·*dee*·das
stolen	*robadas*	ro·*ba*·das

My luggage hasn't arrived.
Mis maletas se han perdido.
mees ma·*le*·tas se an per·*dee*·do

I'd like a luggage locker.
Quisiera un casillero de consigna.
kee·*sye*·ra oon ka·see·*lye*·ro de kon·*seeg*·na

Can I have some coins/tokens?
¿Me podía dar monedas/fichas?
me po·*dee*·a dar mo·*ne*·das/*fee*·chas

plane

el avión

When's the next flight to (Barcelona)?
¿Cuándo sale el próximo vuelo para (Barcelona)?
kwan·do *sa*·le el *prok*·see·mo *vwe*·lo *pa*·ra (bar·*the*·*lo*·na)

What time do I have to check in?
¿A qué hora tengo que facturar mi equipaje?
a ke *o*·ra *ten*·go ke fak·too·*rar* mee e·kee·*pa*·khe

For phrases about getting through customs, see **border crossing**, page 50.

bus

Which bus goes to (Madrid)?
¿Qué autobús va a (Madrid)?   ke ow·to·boos va a (ma·dreeth)

Where's the bus stop?
¿Dónde está la parada   don·de es·ta la pa·ra·da
del autobus?   del ow·to·boos

What's the next stop?
¿Cuál es la próxima   kwal es la prok·see·ma
parada?   pa·ra·da

Bus number ...
El autobús número ...   el ow·to·boos noo·me·ro ...

Please tell me when we get to (Valladolid).
¿Puede avisarme cuando   pwe·de a·vee·sar·me kwan·do
lleguemos a (Valladolid)?   lye·ge·mos a (va·lya·do·leeth)

For bus numbers, see **numbers & amounts**, page 29.

train

What station is this?
¿Cuál es esta estación?   kwal es es·ta es·ta·thyon

What's the next station?
¿Cuál es la próxima   kwal es la prok·see·ma
estación?   es·ta·thyon

Does this train stop at (Valencia)?
¿Para el tren en (Valencia)?   pa·ra el tren en (va·len·thya)

Do I need to change trains?
¿Tengo que cambiar de tren?   ten·go ke kam·byar de tren

Which carriage is ...?	¿Cuál es el coche ...?	kwal es el ko·che ...
1st class	de primera clase	de pree·me·ra kla·se
for (Bilbao)	para (Bilbao)	pa·ra (beel·bow)
for dining	comedor	ko·me·dor

boat

el barco

Are there life jackets?
¿Hay chalecos salvavidas?   ai cha·*le*·kos sal·va·*vee*·das

What's the sea like today?
¿Cómo está el mar hoy?   *ko*·mo es·*ta* el mar oy

I feel seasick.
Estoy mareado.   es·*toy* ma·re·a·do

taxi

el taxi

I'd like a	*Quisiera un*	kee·*sye*·ra oon
taxi ...	*taxi ...*	*tak*·see ...
at (9am)	*a (las nueve de la mañana)*	a (las *nwe*·ve de la ma·*nya*·na)
tomorrow	*mañana*	ma·*nya*·na

Where's the taxi stand?
¿Dónde está la parada de taxis?   *don*·de es·*ta* la pa·*ra*·da de *tak*·sees

Is this taxi free?
¿Está libre este taxi?   es·*ta* lee·bre es·te *tak*·see

Please put the meter on.
Por favor, ponga el taxímetro.   por fa·*vor* pon·ga el tak·*see*·me·tro

How much is the flag fall/hiring charge?
¿Cuánto es la tasa de alquiler?   *kwan*·to es la *ta*·sa de al·kee·*ler*

How much is it (to the Prado)?
¿Cuánto cuesta ir (al Prado)?   *kwan*·to *kwes*·ta eer (al *pra*·do)

Please take me to (this address).
Por favor, lléveme a (esta dirección).   por fa·*vor* lye·ve·me a (es·ta dee·rek·*thyon*)

How much is the final fare?
¿Cuánto es en total?   *kwan*·to es en to·*tal*

Please ...	*Por favor ...*	por fa·vor ...
slow down	*vaya más*	va·ya mas
	despacio	des·pa·thyo
wait here	*espere aquí*	es·pe·re a·kee
Stop ...!	*¡Pare ...!*	pa·re ...
at the corner	*en la esquina*	en la es·kee·na
here	*aquí*	a·kee

For other useful phrases, see **directions**, page 61, and **money**, page 35.

car & motorbike hire

Where can I hire a ...?
¿Dónde se puede alquilar ...? don·de se pwe·de al·kee·lar ...

Does that include insurance/mileage?
¿Incluye el seguro/ een·kloo·ye el se·goo·ro/
kilometraje? kee·lo·me·tra·khe

I'd like to	*Quisiera*	kee·sye·ra
hire a/an ...	*alquilar ...*	al·kee·lar ...
4WD	*un todoterreno*	oon to·do·te·re·no
automatic car	*un coche*	oon ko·che
	automático	ow·to·ma·tee·ko
manual car	*un coche*	oon ko·che
	manual	ma·nwal
motorbike	*una moto*	oo·na mo·to

with ...	*con ...*	kon ...
air conditioning	*aire acon-*	ai·re a·kon·
	dicionado	dee·thyo·na·do
a driver	*chófer*	cho·fer

How much for	*¿Cuánto cuesta*	kwan·to kwes·ta
... hire?	*el alquiler por ...?*	el al·kee·ler por ...
daily	*día*	dee·a
hourly	*hora*	o·ra
weekly	*semana*	se·ma·na

on the road

Is this the road to (Seville)?
   ¿Se va a (Sevilla) por   se va a (se·vee·lya) por
   esta carretera?   es·ta ka·re·te·ra

Where's a petrol station?
   ¿Dónde hay una   don·de ai oo·na
   gasolinera?   ga·so·lee·ne·ra

What's the ...	*¿Cuál es el*	kwal es el
speed limit?	*límite de*	lee·mee·te de
	velocidad ...?	ve·lo·thee·da ...
city	*en la ciudad*	en la thyoo·da
country	*en el campo*	en el kam·po

signs

Acceso	ak·the·so	**Entrance**
Aparcamiento	a·par·ka·myen·to	**Parking**
Ceda el Paso	the·da el pa·so	**Give Way**
Desvío	des·vee·o	**Detour**
Dirección Única	dee·rek·thyon oo·nee·ka	**One Way**
Frene	fre·ne	**Slow Down**
Peaje	pe·a·khe	**Toll**
Peligro	pe·lee·gro	**Danger**
Prohibido Aparcar	pro·ee·bee·do a·par·kar	**No Parking**
Prohibido el Paso	pro·ee·bee·do el pa·so	**No Entry**
Stop	es·top	**Stop**
Vía de Acceso	vee·a de ak·the·so	**Exit Freeway**

Please fill it up.
 Por favor, lléneme el   por fa·*vor* *lye*·ne·me el
 depósito.   de·*po*·see·to

I'd like (20) litres of ...
 Quiero (veinte)   *kye*·ro (*veyn*·te)
 litros de ...   *lee*·tros de ...

petrol (gas)	*gasolina* f	ga·so·*lee*·na
diesel	*diesel*	*dye*·sel
leaded (regular)	*gasolina* f *normal*	ga·so·*lee*·na nor·*mal*
unleaded	*gasolina* f *sin plomo*	ga·so·*lee*·na seen *plo*·mo

Please check the ... *Por favor, revise ...* por fa·*vor* re·*vee*·se ...
 oil   *el nivel del*   el nee·*vel* del
        aceite   a·*they*·te
 tyre pressure *la presión de los* la pre·*syon* de los
        neumáticos   ne·oo·*ma*·tee·kos
 water   *el nivel del agua* *nee*·vel del a·gwa

petrol
gasolina f
ga·so·*lee*·na

windscreen
parabrisas m
pa·ra·*bree*·sas

battery
batería f
ba·ta·*ree*·a

engine
moteur m
mo·ter

headlight
faro m
fa·ro

tyre
rueda f
rwe·da

de ke *mar*·ka es
  ¿De qué marca es?   **What make/model is it?**

(How long) Can I park here?
  ¿(Por cuánto tiempo)   (por kwan·to tyem·po)
  Puedo aparcar aquí?   pwe·do a·par·kar a·kee

Where do I pay?
  ¿Dónde se paga?   don·de se pa·ga

problems

problemas

I need a mechanic.
  Necesito un/una   ne·the·see·to oon/oo·na
  mecánico/a. m/f   me·ka·nee·ko/a

The car has broken down (at Salamanca).
  El coche se ha averiado   el ko·che se a a·ve·rya·do
  (en Salamanca).   (en sa·la·man·ka)

I had an accident.
  He tenido un   e te·nee·do oon
  accidente.   ak·thee·den·te

The motorbike won't start.
  No arranca la moto.   no a·ran·ka la mo·to

I have a flat tyre.
  Tengo un pinchazo.   ten·go oon peen·cha·tho

I've lost my car keys.
  He perdido las llaves   e per·dee·do las lya·ves
  de mi coche.   de mee ko·che

I've locked my keys inside.
  He cerrado con las llaves   e the·ra·do kon las lya·ves
  dentro.   den·tro

I've run out of petrol.
Me he quedado sin gasolina.
me e ke·*da*·do seen ga·so·*lee*·na

Can you fix it (today)?
¿Puede arreglarlo (hoy)?
pwe·de a·re·*glar*·lo (oy)

How long will it take?
¿Cuánto tardará?
kwan·to tar·da·*ra*

bicycle

la bicicleta

Where can I hire a bicycle?
¿Dónde se puede alquilar una bicicleta?
don·de se *pwe*·de al·kee·*lar* *oo*·na bee·thee·*kle*·ta

Where can I buy a (second-hand) bike?
¿Dónde se puede comprar una bicicleta (de segunda mano)?
don·de se *pwe*·de kom·*prar* *oo*·na bee·thee·*kle*·ta (de se·*goon*·da *ma*·no)

How much is it per ...?	*¿Cuánto cuesta por ...?*	*kwan*·to *kwes*·ta por ...
afternoon	*una tarde*	*oo*·na *tar*·de
day	*un día*	oon *dee*·a
hour	*una hora*	*oo*·na *o*·ra
morning	*una mañana*	*oo*·na ma·*nya*·na

I have a puncture.
Se me ha pinchado una rueda.
se me a peen·*cha*·do *oo*·na *rwe*·da

I'd like to have my bicycle repaired.
Me gustaría arreglar mi bicicleta.
me goo·sta·*ree*·a a·reg·*lar* mee bee·thee·*kle*·ta

Are there cycling paths?
¿Hay carril bicicleta?
ai ka·*reel* bee·thee·*kle*·ta

Is there bicycle parking?
¿Hay aparcamiento de bicicletas?
ai a·par·ka·*myen*·to de bee·thee·*kle*·tas

Can I take my bike on the train?

¿Puedo llevar mi   *pwe*·do lye·*var* mee
bicicleta en el tren?   bee·thee·*kle*·ta en el tren

bicycle chain	*cadena* f *de bici*	ka·*de*·na de *bee*·thee
bicycle path map	*mapa* f *de carril*	*ma*·pa de ka·*reel*
	bicicleta	bee·thee·*kle*·ta
bicycle pump	*bomba* f *de bici*	*bom*·ba de *bee*·thee

local transport

el transporte local

People usually walk around cities and municipalities, but if you want to catch a bus, you could ask:

Are you waiting for more people?

¿Está esperando a   es·*ta* es·pe·*ran*·do a
más gente?   mas *khen*·te

Can you take us around the city, please?

¿Nos puede llevar por   nos *pwe*·de lye·*var* por
la ciudad?   la thyoo·*da*

For phrases on disabled access, see **senior & disabled travellers**, page 85.

signs		
Aduana	a·*dwa*·na	**Customs**
Artículos	ar·*tee*·koo·los	**Duty-Free**
Libres de	*lee*·bres de	**Goods**
Impuestos	eem·*pwes*·tos	
Control de	con·*trol* de	**Passport**
Pasaporte	pa·sa·*por*·te	**Control**
Salida	sa·*lee*·da	**Exit/Way Out**

passport control

control de pasaporte

I'm here ...	Estoy aquí ...	es·*toy* a·*kee* ...
on business	de negocios	de ne·*go*·thyos
on holiday	de vacaciones	de va·ka·*thyo*·nes
in transit	en tránsito	en *tran*·see·to
to study	estudiando	es·too·*dyan*·do

I'm here for ...	Estoy aquí por ...	es·*toy* a·*kee* por ...
days	días	*dee*·as
months	meses	*me*·ses
weeks	semanas	se·*ma*·nas

I'm going to (Salamanca).
Voy a (Salamanca).   voy a (sa·la·*man*·ka)

I'm staying at the ...
Me estoy alojando en ...   me es·*toy* a·lo·*khan*·do en ...

listen for ...

soo ... por fa·*vor*	Su ..., por favor.	Your ..., please.
pa·sa·*por*·te	pasaporte	passport
vee·*sa*·do	visado	visa
es·*ta*	¿Está	Are you
vya·*khan*·do ...	viajando ...?	travelling ...?
en oon *groo*·po	en un grupo	in a group
kon fa·*mee*·lya	con familia	with a family
so·lo	solo	on your own

customs

I have nothing to declare.
*No tengo nada que
declarar.*
no *ten*·go *na*·da ke
de·kla·*rar*

I have something to declare.
Quisiera declarar algo.
kee·*sye*·ra de·kla·*rar al*·go

That's (not) mine.
Eso (no) es mío.
e·so (no) es *mee*·o

I didn't know I had to declare it.
*No sabía que tenía
que declararlo.*
no sa·*bee*·a ke te·*nee*·a
ke de·kla·*rar*·lo

For phrases on payments and receipts, see **money**, page 35.

filling in forms		
Apellido(s)	a·pe·*lyee*·do(s)	surname(s) – many Spanish use two surnames, their father's and their mother's
Domicilio	do·mee·*thee*·lyo	address (residence)
Exp. en	eksp en	issued at
Fecha	*fe*·cha	date
Fecha de nacimiento	*fe*·cha de na·thee·*myen*·to	date of birth
Firma	*feer*·ma	signature
Lugar de nacimiento	loo·*gar* de na·thee·*myen*·to	place of birth
Nacionalidad	na·thyo·na·lee·*da*	nationality
Nombre	*nom*·bre	given name
Pasaporte	pa·sa·*por*·te	passport
Profesión	pro·fe·*syon*	occupation

finding accommodation

buscando alojamiento

Where's a ...?	¿Dónde hay ...?	don·de ai ...
bed & breakfast	una pensión con desayuno	oo·na pen·syon kon de·sa·yoo·no
camping ground	terreno de cámping	te·re·no de kam·peeng
guesthouse	una pensión	oo·na pen·syon
hotel	un hotel	oon o·tel
youth hostel	un albergue juvenil	oon al·ber·ge khoo·ve·neel

Can you recommend somewhere ...?	¿Puede recomendar algún sitio ...?	pwe·de re·ko·men·dar al·goon see·tyo ...
cheap	barato	ba·ra·to
luxurious	de lujo	de loo·kho
nearby	cercano	ther·ka·no
nice	agradable	a·gra·da·ble
romantic	romántico	ro·man·tee·ko

What's the address?
¿Cuál es la dirección? kwal es la dee·rek·thyon

For more on how to get there, see **directions**, page 61.

local talk

dive	tugurio m	too·goo·ryo
farm stay	casa f rural	ka·sa roo·ral
mountain hut	refugio m de montaña	re·foo·khyo de mon·ta·nya
rat-infested	plagado de ratas	pla·ga·do de ra·tas
spa	balneario m	bal·ne·a·ryo
top spot	lugar m guay	loo·gar gwai
wellness centre	centro m de salud y bienestar	then·tro de sa·loo ee bye·ne·star

booking ahead & checking in

I'd like to book a room, please.
Quisiera reservar una
habitación.
kee·sye·ra re·ser·var oo·na
a·bee·ta·thyon

I have a reservation.
He hecho una reserva.
e e·cho oo·na re·ser·va

My name's …
Me llamo …
me lya·mo …

For (three) nights/weeks.
Por (tres) noches/
semanas.
por (tres) no·ches/
se·ma·nas

From (July 2) to (July 6).
Desde (el dos de julio)
hasta (el seis de julio).
des·de (el dos de khoo·lyo)
as·ta (el seys de khoo·lyo)

Do I need to pay upfront?
¿Necesito pagar por
adelantado?
ne·the·see·to pa·gar por
a·de·lan·ta·do

Do you offer (long-stay) discounts?
¿Ofrecen descuentos
(por larga estancia)?
of·re·then des·kwen·tos
(por lar·ga es·tan·thya)

Is breakfast included?
¿El desayuno está
incluído?
el de·sa·yoo·no es·ta
een·kloo·ee·do

Is there parking?
¿Hay aparcamiento?
ai a·par·ka·myen·to

listen for …

lo syen·to es·ta kom·ple·to
Lo siento, está completo.   I'm sorry, we're full.

por kwan·tas no·ches
¿Por cuántas noches?   For how many nights?

soo pa·sa·por·te por fa·vor
Su pasaporte, por favor.   Your passport, please.

How much is it per ...?	*¿Cuánto cuesta por ...?*	kwan·to kwes·ta por ...
night	*noche*	*no*·che
person	*persona*	per·*so*·na
week	*semana*	se·*ma*·na
Can I pay by ...?	*¿Puedo pagar con ...?*	pwe·do pa·*gar* con ...
credit card	*tarjeta de crédito*	tar·*khe*·ta de *kre*·dee·to
travellers cheque	*cheques de viajero*	*che*·kes de vya·*khe*·ro

For other methods of payment, see **money**, page 35.

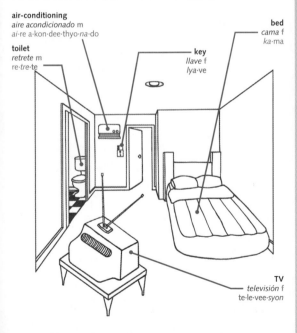

air-conditioning
aire acondicionado m
ai·re a·kon·dee·thyo·*na*·do

toilet
retrete m
re·*tre*·te

key
llave f
lya·ve

bed
cama f
ka·ma

TV
televisión f
te·le·vee·*syon*

Do you have a ... room?	¿Tiene una habitación ...?	tye·ne oo·na a·bee·ta·thyon ...
double	doble	do·ble
single	individual	een·dee·vee·dwal
twin	con dos camas	kon dos ka·mas

with/without (a) ...	con/sin ...	kon/seen ...
Can I see it?	¿Puedo verla?	pwe·do ver·la
It's fine, I'll take it.	Vale, la alquilo.	va·le la al·kee·lo

requests & queries

When/Where's breakfast served?
¿Cuándo/Dónde se sirve   kwan·do/don·de se seer·ve
el desayuno?   el de·sa·yoo·no

Please wake me at (seven).
Por favor, despiérteme   por fa·vor des·pyer·te·me
a (las siete).   a (las sye·te)

Can I get another ...?
¿Puede darme otro/a ...? m/f   pwe·de dar·me o·tro/a ...

Can I use the ...?	¿Puedo usar ...?	pwe·do oo·sar ...
Internet	el Internet	el een·ter·net
kitchen	la cocina	la ko·thee·na
laundry	el lavadero	el la·va·de·ro
telephone	el teléfono	el te·le·fo·no

Is there a/an ...?	¿Hay ...?	ai ...
lift (elevator)	ascensor	as·then·sor
message board	tablón de anuncios	ta·blon de a·noon·thyos
safe	una caja fuerte	oo·na ka·kha fwer·te
swimming pool	piscina	pees·thee·na

Do you ... here?	*¿Aquí ...?*	a·*kee* ...
arrange tours	*organizan*	or·ga·*nee*·than
	recorridos	re·ko·*ree*·dos
change money	*cambian*	*kam*·byan
	dinero	dee·*ne*·ro

signs

Centro Financiero	*then*·tro fee·nan·*thye*·ro	**Business Centre**
Recepción	re·thep·*thyon*	**Reception**
Salida de Emergencia	sa·*lee*·da de e·mer·*khen*·thya	**Emergency Exit**
Servicios	ser·*vee*·thyos	**Toilets**
Servicio de Lavandería	ser·*vee*·thyo de la·van·de·*ree*·a	**Laundry Service**

Can I leave a message for someone?
¿Puedo dejar un   *pwe*·do de·*khar* oon
mensaje para alguien?   men·*sa*·khe *pa*·ra al·gyen

Is there a message for me?
¿Tiene un mensaje   *tye*·ne oon men·*sa*·khe
para mí?   *pa*·ra mee

I'm locked out of my room.
Cerré la puerta y se me   the·*re* la *pwer*·ta y se me
olvidaron las llaves dentro.   ol·vee·*da*·ron las *lya*·ves *den*·tro

The (bathroom) door is locked.
La puerta (del baño) está   la *pwer*·ta (del *ba*·nyo) es·ta
cerrada.   the·*ra*·da

complaints

It's too ...	Es demasiado ...	es de·ma·sya·do ...
cold	fría f	free·a
dark	oscura f	os·koo·ra
expensive	cara f	ka·ra
light	clara f	kla·ra
noisy	ruidosa f	rwee·do·sa
small	pequeña f	pe·ke·nya

The ... doesn't work.	No funciona ...	no foon·thyo·na ...
air-conditioning	el aire acondicionado	el ai·re a·kon·dee·thyo·na·do
fan	el ventilador	el ven·tee·la·dor
heater	la estufa	la es·too·fa
toilet	el retrete	el re·tre·te
window	la ventana	la ven·ta·na

This ... isn't clean.
Éste/Ésta ... no está limpio/a. m/f   es·te/es·ta ... no es·ta leem·pyo/a

There's no hot water.
No hay agua caliente.   no ai a·gwa ka·lyen·te

a knock at the door

Who is it?	¿Quién es?	kyen es
Just a moment.	Un momento.	oon mo·men·to
Come in.	Adelante.	a·de·lan·te

Can you come back later, please?
¿Puede volver más tarde, por favor?   pwe·de vol·ver mas tar·de por fa·vor

checking out

What time is check out?
*¿A qué hora hay que dejar
libre la habitación?*
a ke o·ra ai ke de·*khar*
lee·bre la a·bee·ta·*thyon*

How much extra to stay until (6 o'clock)?
*¿Cuánto más cuesta
quedarse hasta (las seis)?*
kwan·to mas *kwes*·ta
ke·*dar*·se as·ta (las seys)

Can I have a late check out?
*¿Puedo dejar la
habitación más tarde?*
pwe·do de·*khar* la
a·bee·ta·*thyon* mas *tar*·de

Can I leave my bags here?
*¿Puedo dejar las
maletas aquí?*
pwe·do de·*khar* las
ma·*le*·tas a·*kee*

There's a mistake in the bill.
Hay un error en la cuenta.
ai oon e·*ror* en la *kwen*·ta

I'm leaving now.
Me voy ahora.
me voy a·*o*·ra

Can you call a taxi for me (for 11 o'clock)?
*¿Me puede pedir un
taxi (para las once)?*
me *pwe*·de pe·*deer* oon
tak·see (*pa*·ra las *on*·the)

Could I have my ..., please?	*¿Me puede dar ..., por favor?*	me *pwe*·de dar ... por fa·*vor*
deposit	*mi depósito*	mee de·*po*·see·to
passport	*mi pasaporte*	mee pa·sa·*por*·te
valuables	*mis objetos de valor*	mees ob·*khe*·tos de va·*lor*

I'll be back ...	*Volveré ...*	vol·ve·*re* ...
in (three) days	*en (tres) días*	en (tres) *dee*·as
next week	*la próxima semana*	la *prok*·see·ma se·*ma*·na
on (Tuesday)	*el (martes)*	el (*mar*·tes)

I had a great stay, thank you.
He tenido una estancia   e te·*nee*·do *oo*·na es·*tan*·thya
muy agradable, gracias.   mooy a·gra·*da*·ble *gra*·thyas

You've been terrific.
Han sido estupendos.   an *see*·do es·too·*pen*·dos

I'll recommend it to my friends.
Se lo recomendaré a   se lo re·ko·men·da·*re* a
mis amigos.   mees a·*mee*·gos

camping

Where's the nearest ...?	*¿Dónde está ...?*	*don*·de es·*ta* ...
camp site	*el terreno de cámping más cercano*	el te·*re*·no de *kam*·peeng mas ther·*ka*·no
shop	*la tienda más cercana*	la *tyen*·da mas ther·*ka*·na
I'm looking for the nearest ...	*Estoy buscando ...*	es·*toy* boos·*kan*·do ...
showers	*las duchas más cercanas*	las *doo*·chas mas ther·*ka*·nas
toilet block	*los servicios más cercanos*	los ser·*vee*·thyos mas ther·*ka*·nos

Is it coin-operated?
¿Funciona con monedas?   foon·*thyo*·na kon mo·*ne*·das

Is the water drinkable?
¿Se puede beber el agua?   se *pwe*·de *be*·ber el *a*·gwa

Can I ...?	*¿Se puede ...?*	se *pwe*·de ...
camp here	*acampar aquí*	a·kam·*par* a·*kee*
park next to	*aparcar al lado*	a·par·*kar* al *la*·do
my tent	*de la tienda*	de la *tyen*·da

Do you have ...?	¿Tiene ...?	tye·ne ...
electricity	electricidad	e·lek·tree·thee·da
shower facilities	duchas	doo·chas
a site	un sitio	oon see·tyo
tents for hire	tiendas de campaña para alquilar	tyen·das de kam·pa·nya pa·ra al·kee·lar

How much is it per ...?	¿Cuánto vale por ...?	kwan·to va·le por ...
caravan	caravana	ka·ra·va·na
person	persona	per·so·na
tent	tienda	tyen·da
vehicle	vehículo	ve·ee·koo·lo

Whom do I ask to stay here?

¿Con quién tengo que hablar kon kyen ten·go ke a·blar
para quedarme aquí? pa·ra ke·dar·me a·kee

Could I borrow ...?

¿Me puede prestar ...? me pwe·de pres·tar ...

For cooking utensils, see **self-catering**, page 157.

renting

Do you have a/an ... for rent?	¿Tiene ... para alquilar?	tye·ne ... pa·ra al·kee·lar
apartment	un piso	oon pee·so
cabin	una cabaña	oo·na ka·ba·nya
house	una casa	oo·na ca·sa
room	una habitación	oo·na a·bee·ta·thyon
villa	un chalet	oon cha·le

furnished	amueblado/a m/f	a·mwe·bla·do/a
partly furnished	semi amueblado/a m/f	se·mee a·mwe·bla·do/a
unfurnished	sin amueblar	seen a·mwe·blar

staying with locals

Can I stay at your place?
¿Me puedo quedar en me *pwe*·do ke·*dar* en
su/tu casa? pol/inf soo/too *ka*·sa

Can I help?
¿Puedo ayudar? *pwe*·do a·yoo·*dar*

Can I use your telephone?
¿Puedo usar su/tu *pwe*·do oo·*sar* soo/too
teléfono? pol/inf te·*le*·fo·no

Thanks for your hospitality.
Gracias por su/tu *gra*·thyas por soo/too
hospitalidad. pol/inf os·pee·ta·lee·*da*

I have my own ...	*Tengo mi propio ...*	*ten*·go mee *pro*·pyo ...
mattress	*colchón*	kol·*chon*
sleeping bag	*saco de dormir*	*sa*·ko de dor·*meer*

Can I ...?	*¿Puedo ...?*	*pwe*·do ...
bring anything for the meal	*traer algo para la comida*	tra·*er al*·go *pa*·ra la ko·*mee*·da
do the dishes	*lavar los platos*	la·*var* los *pla*·tos
set/clear the table	*poner/quitar la mesa*	po·*ner*/kee·*tar* la *me*·sa
take out the rubbish	*sacar la basura*	sa·*kar* la ba·*soo*·ra

For compliments to the chef, see **eating out**, page 147.

---

signs

Caballeros	ka·ba·*lye*·ros	**Men**
Caliente	ka·*lyen*·te	**Hot**
Dirección Prohibida	dee·rek·*thyon* pro·hee·*bee*·da	**No Entry**
Frío	*free*·o	**Cold**
Señoras	se·*nyo*·ras	**Women**

PRACTICAL

60

Excuse me.
Perdón.　　　　　　　per·*don*

Could you help me, please?
¿Perdón, puede　　　　per·*don* pwe·de
ayudarme, por favor?　a·yoo·*dar*·me por fa·*vor*

Where's ...?
¿Dónde está ...?　　　*don*·de es·*ta* ...

I'm looking for ...
Busco ...　　　　　　*boos*·ko ...

Which way is ...?
¿Por dónde se va a ...?　por *don*·de se va a ...

How can I get there?
¿Cómo se puede ir?　　*ko*·mo se *pwe*·de eer

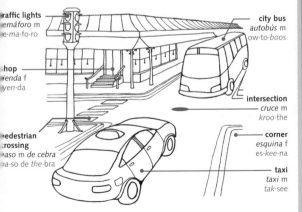

traffic lights
semáforo m
se·*ma*·fo·ro

shop
tienda f
tyen·da

pedestrian crossing
paso m *de cebra*
pa·so de *the*·bra

city bus
autobús m
ow·to·*boos*

intersection
cruce m
kroo·the

corner
esquina f
es·*kee*·na

taxi
taxi m
tak·see

How far is it?

¿A cuánta distancia   a kwan·ta dees·tan·thya
está?   es·ta

What's the address?

¿Cuál es la dirección?   kwal es la dee·rek·thyon

Can you show me (on the map)?

¿Me lo puede indicar   me lo pwe·de een·dee·kar
(en el mapa)?   (en el ma·pa)

It's ...	Está ...	es·ta ...
behind ...	detrás de ...	de·tras de ...
far away	lejos	le·khos
here	aquí	a·kee
in front of ...	enfrente de ...	en·fren·te de ...
left	por la izquierda	por la eeth·kyer·da
near	cerca	ther·ka
next to ...	al lado de ...	al la·do de ...
opposite ...	frente a ...	fren·te a ...
right	por la derecha	por la de·re·cha
straight ahead	todo recto	to·do rek·to
there	ahí	a·ee

Turn ...	Doble ...	do·ble ...
at the corner	en la esquina	en la es·kee·na
at the traffic lights	en el semáforo	en el se·ma·fo·ro
left/right	a la izquierda/	a la eeth·kyer·da/
	derecha	de·re·cha

It's ...	Está ...	es·ta ...
(two) kilometres	(dos) kilómetros	(dos) kee·lo·me·tros
(three) metres	(tres) metros	(tres) me·tros
(six) minutes	(seis) minutos	(seys) mee·noo·tos

by bus	por autobús	por ow·to·boos
by taxi	por taxi	por tak·see
by train	por tren	por tren
on foot	a pie	a pye

For locations and compass directions, see the **dictionary**.

looking for ...

buscando ...

Where's ...?
¿Dónde está ...?   don·de es·ta ...

Where can I buy ...?
¿Dónde puedo comprar ...?   don·de pwe·do kom·prar ...

camping store	*tienda f de provisiones de camping*	tyen·da de pro·vee·syo·nes de kam·peeng
(super)market	*(super)mercado* m	(soo·per·)mer·ka·do

For more on shops and how to get there, see **directions**, page 61, and the **dictionary**.

making a purchase

comprando algo

How much is this?
¿Cuánto cuesta esto?   kwan·to kwes·ta es·to

What is this made from?
¿De qué está hecho?   de ke es·ta e·cho

I'd like to buy ...
Quisiera comprar ...   kee·sye·ra kom·prar ...

I'm just looking.
Sólo estoy mirando.   so·lo es·toy mee·ran·do

Can I look at it?
¿Puedo verlo?   pwe·do ver·lo

Do you have any others?
¿Tiene otros?   tye·ne o·tros

Do you have something cheaper?
¿Tiene algo más barato?   tye·ne al·go mas ba·ra·to

Do you accept ...?	¿Aceptan ...?	a·thep·tan ...
credit cards	tarjetas de crédito	tar·khe·tas de kre·dee·to
debit cards	tarjetas de débito	tar·khe·tas de de·bee·to
travellers cheques	cheques de viajero	che·kes de vya·khe·ro
Could I have a ..., please?	¿Podría darme ..., por favor?	po·dree·a dar·me ... por fa·vor
bag	una bolsa	oo·na bol·sa
receipt	un recibo	oon re·thee·bo

I don't need a bag, thanks.
No necesito bolsa, gracias.
no ne·the·see·to bol·sa gra·thyas

Can you write down the price?
¿Puede escribir el precio?
pwe·de es·kree·beer el pre·thyo

Could I have it wrapped?
¿Me lo podría envolver?
me lo po·dree·a en·vol·ver

Does it have a guarantee?
¿Tiene garantía?
tye·ne ga·ran·tee·a

Can I have it sent overseas?
¿Pueden enviarlo por   pwe·den en·vee·*ar*·lo por
correo a otro país?   ko·*re*·o a *o*·tro pa·*ees*

Can you order it for me?
¿Me lo puede pedir?   me lo *pwe*·de pe·*deer*

Can I pick it up later?
¿Puedo recogerlo más   *pwe*·do re·ko·*kher*·lo mas
tarde?   *tar*·de

It's faulty.
Es defectuoso.   es de·fek·too·*o*·so

I'd like ...,	*Quisiera ...,*	kee·*sye*·ra ...
please.	*por favor.*	por fa·*vor*
my change	*mi cambio*	mee *kam*·byo
my money back	*que me devuelva*	ke me de·*vwel*·va
	el dinero	el dee·*ne*·ro
to return this	*devolver esto*	de·vol·*ver* es·to

local talk

bargain	*ganga* f	*gan*·ga
bargain	*cazador* m	ka·tha·*dor*
hunter	*de ofertas*	de o·*fer*·tas
rip-off	*estafa* f	es·*ta*·fa
sale	*ventas* f pl	*ven*·tas
specials	*rebajas* f pl	re·*ba*·khas

bargaining

el regateo

That's too expensive.
Es muy caro.   es mooy *ka*·ro

Can you lower the price?
¿Podría bajar un   po·*dree*·a ba·*khar* oon
poco el precio?   *po*·ko el *pre*·thyo

I'll give you ...
Le/Te daré ... pol/inf   le/te da·*re* ...

clothes

Can I try it on?
¿Me lo puedo probar? me lo *pwe*·do pro·bar

My size is ...
Uso la talla ... *oo*·so la *ta*·lya ...

It doesn't fit.
No me queda bien. no me *ke*·da byen

small	pequeño/a m/f	pe·*ke*·nyo/a
medium	mediano/a m/f	me·*dya*·no/a
large	grande m&f	*gran*·de

For clothing items see the **dictionary**, and for sizes see **numbers & amounts**, page 29.

repairs

reparaciones

Can I have my	*¿Puede reparar mi*	*pwe*·de re·pa·*rar* mee
... repaired here?	*... aquí?*	... a·*kee*
backpack	mochila	mo·*chee*·la
camera	cámara	*ka*·ma·ra
computer	ordenador	or·de·na·*dor*

When will my	*¿Cuándo estarán*	*kwan*·do es·ta·*ran*
... be ready?	*listos/as mis ...?* m/f	*lees*·tos/as mees ...
(sun)glasses	gafas (de sol) f	*ga*·fas (de sol)
shoes	zapatos m	tha·*pa*·tos

darn holes		
buttons	botónes m pl	bo·*to*·nes
needle	aguja f	a·*goo*·kha
scissors	tijeras f pl	tee·*khe*·ras
thread	hilo m	*ee*·lo

hairdressing

I'd like (a) ...	Quisiera ...	kee·sye·ra ...
blow wave	un secado a mano	oon se·ka·do a ma·no
colour	un tinte de pelo	oon teen·te de pe·lo
haircut	un corte de pelo	oon kor·te de pe·lo
highlights	reflejos	re·fle·khos
my beard	que me recorte	ke me re·kor·te
trimmed	la barba	la bar·ba
shave	que me afeite	ke me a·fey·te
trim	que me recorte	ke me re·kor·te
	el pelo	el pe·lo

Don't cut it too short.
No me lo corte no me lo kor·te
demasiado corto. de·ma·sya·do kor·to

Shave it all off!
¡Aféitelo todo! a·fey·te·lo to·do

Please use a new blade.
Por favor, use una por fa·vor oo·se oo·na
cuchilla nueva. koo·chee·lya nwe·va

For colours, see the **dictionary**.

worth a read

Spanish literature has a long history (dating from the 12th century), resulting in a thriving writing industry today. Look out for authors Ana María Matute, Jorge Luis Borges, Miguel de Unamuno, Carmen Martín Gaite, Juan Goytisolo, Miguel Delibes, Gabriel García Márquez and the 1989 Nobel Prize winner, Camilo José Cela.

books & reading

libros & lectura

Is there a/an (English-language) …?	*¿Hay algún/ alguna … (en inglés)?* m/f	ai al·*goon*/ al·*goo*·na … (en een·*gles*)
bookshop	*librería* m	lee·bre·*ree*·a
section	*sección* f	sek·*thyon*

I (don't) like …
(No) Me gusta/gustan … sg/pl (no) me *goos*·ta/*goos*·tan …

Do you have Lonely Planet guidebooks?
¿Tiene libros de Lonely Planet? tye·ne *lee*·bros de *lon*·lee *pla*·net

I'm looking for something by (Javier Marías).
Estoy buscando algo de (Javier Marías). es·*toy* boos·*kan*·do al·go de (kha·*vyer* ma·*ree*·as)

For more on books and reading, see **interests**, page 109.

---

listen for …

en ke le *pwe*·do ser·*veer* *¿En qué le puedo servir?*	**Can I help you?**
al·go mas *¿Algo más?*	**Anything else?**
no *ten*·go *No tengo.*	**I don't have any.**

---

music & DVD

música & DVD

I heard a band called …
Escuché a un grupo que se llama … es·koo·*che* a oon *groo*·po ke se *lya*·ma …

What's their best recording?
¿Cuál es su mejor disco? kwal es soo me·*khor dees*·ko

Can I listen to this?
¿Puedo escuchar esto?
pwe·do es·koo·char es·to

Is this a pirated copy?
¿Es copia pirata?
es ko·pya pee·ra·ta

Will this work on any DVD player?
¿Esto puede funcionar
en cualquier reproductor
de DVD?
es·to pwe·de foon·thyo·nar
en kwal·kyer re·pro·dook·tor
de de oo·ve de

What region is this DVD for?
¿Para qué región es este DVD?
pa·ra ke re·khyon es es·te
de oo·ve de

I'd like (a) ...	Quisiera ...	kee·sye·ra ...
CD	un cómpact	oon kom·pak
DVD	un DVD	oon de oo·ve de
headphones	unos	oo·nos
	auriculares	ow·ree·koo·la·res

video & photography

Can you ...?	¿Podría ...?	po·dree·a ...
print digital	imprimir	eem·pree·meer
photos	fotos digitales	fo·tos dee·khee·ta·les
recharge the	recargar la	re·kar·gar la
battery for my	batería de mi	ba·te·ree·a de mee
digital camera	cámara digital	ka·ma·ra dee·khee·tal
transfer my	pasar las fotos	pa·sar las fo·tos
photos from	de mi cámara	de mee ka·ma·ra
camera to CD	a un cómpact	a oon kom·pak

How much is it to develop this film?
¿Cuánto cuesta revelar
este carrete?
kwan·to kwes·ta re·ve·lar
es·te ka·re·te

Can you load my film?
¿Puede cargar el carrete?
pwe·de kar·gar el ka·re·te

Do you have slide film?
¿Tiene diapositivas?
tye·ne dya·po·see·tee·vas

I need a passport photo taken.
Necesito fotos de pasaporte.
ne·the·*see*·to *fo*·tos de pa·sa·*por*·te

I'd like double copies.
Quisiera dos copias.
kee·*sye*·ra dos *ko*·pyas

I need a cable to connect my camera to a computer.
Necesito un cable para conectar mi cámara al ordenador.
ne·the·*see*·to oon *ka*·ble *pa*·ra ko·nek·*tar* mee *ka*·ma·ra al or·de·na·*dor*

I need a cable to recharge this battery.
Necesito un cable para recargar esta batería.
ne·the·*see*·to oon *ka*·ble *pa*·ra re·kar·*gar* es·ta ba·te·*ree*·a

I need a video cassette for this camera.
Necesito una cinta de vídeo para esta cámara.
ne·the·*see*·to *oo*·na *theen*·ta de *vee*·de·o *pa*·ra es·ta *ka*·ma·ra

Do you have (a) ... for this camera?	*¿Tiene ... para esta cámara?*	*tye*·ne ... *pa*·ra es·ta *ka*·ma·ra
batteries	*pilas*	*pee*·las
flash (bulb)	*una bombilla de flash*	*oo*·na bom·*bee*·lya de flesh
light meter	*un fotómetro*	oon fo·*to*·me·tro
memory cards	*tarjetas de memoria*	tar·*khe*·tas de me·*mo*·rya
zoom (lens)	*un lente zoom*	oon *len*·te thoom

I need a/an ... film for this camera.	*Necesito película ... para esta cámara.*	ne·the·*see*·to pe·*lee*·koo·la ... *pa*·ra es·ta *ka*·ma·ra
B&W	*en blanco y negro*	en *blan*·ko y *ne*·gro
colour	*en color*	en ko·*lor*
(400) speed	*de sensibilidad (cuatrocientos)*	de sen·see·bee·lee·*da* (kwa·tro·*thyen*·tos)

... camera	*cámara ...*	*ka*·ma·ra ...
digital	*digital*	dee·khee·*tal*
disposable	*desechable*	de·se·*cha*·ble
underwater	*submarina*	soob·ma·*ree*·na
video	*de vídeo*	de *vee*·de·o

post office

correos

I want to send a ...	*Quisiera enviar ...*	kee·*sye*·ra en·vee·*ar* ...
parcel	*un paquete*	oon pa·*ke*·te
postcard	*una postal*	oo·na pos·*tal*
I want to buy ...	*Quisiera comprar ...*	kee·*sye*·ra kom·*prar* ...
an envelope	*un sobre*	oon *so*·bre
stamps	*sellos*	*se*·lyos
airmail	*por vía aérea*	por *vee*·a a·*e*·re·a
customs declaration	*declaración* f *de aduana*	de·kla·ra·*thyon* de a·*dwa*·na
domestic	*nacional*	na·thyo·*nal*
express mail	*correo* m *urgente*	ko·*re*·o oor·*khen*·te
fragile	*frágil*	*fra*·kheel
glue	*pegamento* m	pe·ga·*men*·to
international	*internacional*	een·ter·na·thyo·*nal*
mail box	*buzón* m	boo·*thon*
PO box	*apartado* m *de correos*	a·par·*ta*·do de ko·*re*·os
postal address	*dirección* f *postal*	dee·rek·*thyon* pos·*tal*
postcode	*código* m *postal*	*ko*·dee·go pos·*tal*
registered mail	*correo* m *certificado*	ko·*re*·o ther·tee·fee·*ka*·do
sea mail	*correo* m *marítimo*	ko·*re*·o ma·*ree*·tee·mo
surface mail	*por vía terrestre*	por *vee*·a te·*res*·tre

Please send it by air/surface mail to ...
 Por favor, mándelo por vía aérea/terrestre a ...
 por fa·*vor man*·de·lo por *vee*·a a·*e*·re·a/te·*res*·tre a ...

It contains ...
 Contiene ...
 kon·*tye*·ne ...

Where's the poste restante section?

¿Dónde está la lista de correos?	don·de es·ta la lees·ta de ko·re·os

Is there any mail for me?

¿Hay alguna carta para mí?	ai al·goo·na kar·ta pa·ra mee

phone

el teléfono

I want to make ...	Quiero hacer ...	kye·ro a·ther ...
a call to (Singapore)	una llamada a (Singapur)	oo·na lya·ma·da a (seen·ga·poor)
an Internet call	una llamada por Internet	oo·na lya·ma·da por een·ter·net
a local call	una llamada local	oo·na lya·ma·da lo·kal
a reverse-charge/ collect call	una llamada a cobro revertido	oo·na lya·ma·da a ko·bro re·ver·tee·do
I want to ...	Quiero ...	kye·ro ...
buy a phone card	comprar una tarjeta telefónica	kom·prar oo·na tar·khe·ta te·le·fo·nee·ka
speak for (three) minutes	hablar por (tres) minutos	ab·lar por (tres) mee·noo·tos
How much is ...?	¿Cuánto cuesta ...?	kwan·to kwes·ta...
a (three)-minute call	una llamada de (tres) minutos	oo·na lya·ma·da de (tres) mee·noo·tos
each extra minute	cada minuto extra	ka·da mee·noo·to ek·stra

What's your phone number?

¿Cuál es su/tu número de teléfono? pol/inf	kwal es too noo·me·ro de te·le·fo·no

Where's the nearest public phone?

¿Dónde hay una cabina telefónica?	don·de ai oo·na ka·bee·na te·le·fo·nee·ka

For telephone numbers, see **numbers & amounts**, page 29.

The number is …
El número es … el *noo*·me·ro es …

I'd like to know the number for …
Quisiera saber el número kee·*sye*·ra sa·*ber* el *noo*·me·ro
para … *pa*·ra …

Can I look at a phone book?
¿Puedo mirar la guía de *pwe*·do mee·*rar* la *gee*·a de
teléfonos? te·*le*·fo·nos

What's the area code for …?
¿Cuál es el prefijo de kwal es el pre·*fee*·kho de
la zona ...? la *tho*·na ...

What's the country code for …?
¿Cuál es el prefijo kwal es el pre·*fee*·kho
del país ...? del pa·*ees* ...

Do you have international prepaid phone cards?
¿Tiene tarjetas de teléfono *tye*·ne tar·*khe*·tas de te·*le*·fo·no
de prepago de pre·*pa*·go
internacionales? een·ter·na·thyo·*na*·les

It's engaged.
Está comunicando. es·*ta* ko·moo·nee·*kan*·do

The connection's bad.
Es mala conexión. es *ma*·la ko·nek·*syon*

listen for ...

de *par*·te de kyen
¿De parte de quién? **Who's calling?**

kon kyen *kye*·re a·*blar*
¿Con quién quiere **Who do you want to**
hablar? **speak to?**

lo *syen*·to *pe*·ro a·*o*·ra no es·*ta*
Lo siento, pero ahora **I'm sorry, he/she is**
no está. **not here.**

lo *syen*·to *tye*·ne el *noo*·me·ro e·kee·vo·*ka*·do
Lo siento, tiene el **Sorry, you have got**
numero equivocado. **the wrong number.**

see a·*kee* es·*ta*
Sí, aquí está. **Yes, he/she is here.**

communications

73

Hello. (calling)	Hola.	o·la
Hello? (answering)	¿Diga?	dee·ga
Can I speak to ...?	¿Está ...?	es·ta ...
It's ...	Soy ...	soy ...

I've been cut off.
  Me han cortado. me an kor·ta·do

Can I leave a message?
  ¿Puedo dejar un mensaje? pwe·do de·khar oon men·sa·khe

Please tell him/her I called.
  Sí, por favor, dile que he see por fa·vor dee·le ke e
  llamado. lya·ma·do

I'll call back later.
  Ya llamaré más tarde. ya lya·ma·re mas tar·de

mobile/cell phone

el teléfono móvil

I'd like a/an ...	Quisiera ...	kee·sye·ra ...
adaptor plug	un adaptador	oon a·dap·ta·dor
charger for	un cargador	oon kar·ga·dor
my phone	para mi	pa·ra mee
	teléfono	te·le·fo·no
mobile/cell	un móvil para	oon mo·veel pa·ra
phone for hire	alquilar	al·kee·lar
prepaid phone	una tarjeta	oo·na tar·khe·ta
	prepagada	pre·pa·ga·da
prepaid recharge	una tarjeta de	oo·na tar·khe·ta de
card	recarga de	re·kar·ga de
	prepago	pre·pa·go
SIM card for	una tarjeta	oo·na tar·khe·ta
your network	SIM para su red	seem pa·ra soo red

What are the rates?
  ¿Cuál es la tarifa? kwal es la ta·ree·fa

(30c) per (30) seconds.
  (Treinta centavos) por (treyn·ta then·ta·vos) por
  (treinta) segundos. (treyn·ta) se·goon·dos

the internet

Where's the local Internet cafe?
¿Dónde hay un cibercafé
cercano?
*don·de ai oon thee·ber·ka·fe
ther·ka·no*

Do you have public Internet access here?
¿Tiene acceso público
a Internet?
*tye·ne ak·the·so poo·blee·ko
a een·ter·net*

Is there wireless Internet access here?
¿Hay acceso inalámbrico
a Internet aquí?
*ai ak·the·so een·a·lam·bree·ko
a een·ter·net a·kee*

Can I connect my laptop here?
¿Puedo conectar mi
ordenador portátil aquí?
*pwe·do ko·nek·tar mee
or·de·na·dor por·ta·teel a·kee*

Do you have headphones (with a microphone)?
¿Tiene auriculares
(con micrófono)?
*tye·ne ow·ree·koo·la·res
(kon mee·kro·fo·no)*

I'd like to buy a card/USB for prepaid mobile Internet.
Quisiera comprar una
tarjeta/USB para
Internet móvil de prepago.
*kee·sye·ra kom·prar oo·na
tar·khe·ta/oo·e·se·be pa·ra
een·ter·net mo·veel de pre·pa·go*

I'd like to ...	Quisiera ...	kee·sye·ra ...
burn a CD	copiar un disco	ko·pyar oon dees·ko
check my email	revisar mi correo electrónico	re·vee·sar mee ko·re·o e·lek·tro·nee·ko
download my photos	descargar mis fotos	des·kar·gar mees fo·tos
get Internet access	usar el Internet	oo·sar el een·ter·net
use a printer	usar una impresora	oo·sar oo·na eem·pre·so·ra
use a scanner	usar un escáner	oo·sar oon es·ka·ner
use Skype	usar Skype	oo·sar es·kaip

How much per ...?	¿Cuánto cuesta por ...?	kwan·to kwes·ta por ...
hour	hora	o·ra
page	página	pa·khee·na

Do you have Macs/PCs?
¿Tiene Apples/PCs?   tye·ne *a*·pels/*pe*·thes

How do I log on?
¿Cómo entro al sistema?   *ko*·mo en·tro al sees·*te*·ma

What's the password?
¿Cúal es la contraseña?   kwal es la kon·tra·*se*·nya

It's crashed.
Se ha quedado colgado.   se a ke·*da*·do kol·*ga*·do

I've finished.
He terminado.   e ter·mee·*na*·do

Can I connect my	*¿Puedo conectar*	*pwe*·do ko·nek·*tar*
... to this computer?	*mi... a este*	mee ... a *es*·te
	ordenador?	or·de·na·*dor*
camera	*cámara*	*ka*·ma·ra
media player (MP3)	*MP3*	e·me·pe·tres
portable hard	*disco duro*	*dees*·ko *doo*·ro
drive	*portátil*	por·*ta*·teel
PSP	*PSP*	pe·e·se·pe
USB flash drive	*memoria*	me·*mo*·rya
(memory stick)	*USB*	oo·e·se·be

a spangled web

Nowhere is the spread of 'Spanglish' more evident than on the Internet. Here are some Spanish substitutes for common net-related terms.

chat	*charlar*	*char*·lar
cyberspace	*ciberespacio* m	see·ber·e·*spa*·thyo
download	*descargar*	des·kar·*gar*
homepage	*página* f *Web*	*pa*·jee·na web
	inicial	ee·nee·*thyal*
online	*en línea*	en *lee*·ne·a
search engine	*sistema* f *de*	sees·*te*·ma de
	búsqueda	*boos*·ke·da
surf	*correr tabla*	ko·*rer ta*·bla
	por la red	por la re
username	*nombre* m *de*	*nom*·bre de
	usuario	oo·*swa*·ryo
website	*sitio* m *Web*	*see*·tyo web

People usually shoot the breeze for a while before they get down to business. For titles and addressing people, see **meeting people**, page 90.

I'm attending a ...	Asisto a …	a·sees·to a ...
conference	un congreso	oon kon·gre·so
course	un curso	oon koor·so
meeting	una reunión	oo·na re·oo·nyon
trade fair	una feria de muestras	oo·na fe·rya de mwes·tras

I'm with ...	Estoy con …	es·toy kon ...
my company	mi compañía	mee kom·pa·nyee·a
my colleagues	mis colegas	mees ko·le·gas
(two) others	otros (dos)	ot·ros (dos)

using your manners

If you're in a formal situation or you want to show respect to someone much older than yourself, you should use the polite form of address (see below). The best approach is to take the lead from how people address you and respond in the same way. It's always a good idea to use the polite form in business, and also with any service providers (be they kiosk attendants or doctors).

you sg pol	Usted	oo·ste
you pl pol	Ustedes	oo·ste·des

What's your name?
¿Cómo se llama Usted? sg pol — ko·mo se lya·ma oos·te

How are you?
¿Cómo esta Usted? sg pol — ko·mo es·ta oos·te

For more on polite forms, see **personal pronouns** in the **grammar** chapter, page 19.

Where's the ...?	¿Dónde está ...?	don·de es·ta ...
business centre	el centro	el *then*·tro
	financiero	fee·nan·*thye*·ro
conference	el congreso	el kon·*gre*·so

Where's the meeting?
¿Dónde es a reunión?　　don·de es la re·oo·*nyon*

I'm alone.
Estoy solo/a. m/f　　es·*toy* so·lo/a

Let me introduce my colleague.
¿Puedo presentarle a mi　　pwe·do pre·sen·*tar*·le a mee
compañero/a? m/f　　kom·pa·*nye*·ro/a

I'm staying at ..., room ...
Me estoy alojando en ...,　　me es·*toy* a·lo·*khan*·do en ...
la habitación ...　　la a·bee·ta·*thyon* ...

I'm here for ... days/weeks.
Estoy aquí por ... días/　　es·*toy* a·*kee* por ... *dee*·as/
semanas.　　se·*ma*·nas

Here's my business card.
Aquí tiene mi tarjeta　　a·*kee* tye·ne mee tar·*khe*·ta
de visita.　　de vee·*see*·ta

Can I have your business card?
¿Puede darme su tarjeta　　pwe·de *dar*·me soo tar·*khe*·ta
de visita?　　de vee·*see*·ta

I have an appointment with ...
Tengo una cita con ...　　ten·go oo·na *thee*·ta kon ...

That went very well.
Eso fue muy bien.　　e·so fwe mooy byen

Thank you for your interest/time.
Gracias por su interés/　　gra·thyas por soo een·te·*res*/
tiempo.　　*tyem*·po

Shall we go for a drink/meal?
¿Vamos a tomar/　　va·mos a to·*mar*/
comer algo?　　ko·*mer* al·go

It's on me.
Invito yo.　　een·*vee*·to yo

bank

el banco

Where can I ...?	¿Dónde puedo ...?	don·de pwe·do ...
I'd like to ...	Me gustaría ...	me goos·ta·ree·a ...
arrange a transfer	hacer una transferencia	ha·ther oo·na trans·fe·ren·thya
cash a cheque	cambiar un cheque	kam·byar oon che·ke
change money	cambiar dinero	kam·byar dee·ne·ro
change travellers cheques	cobrar cheques de viajero	ko·brar che·kes de vya·khe·ro
get a cash advance	obtener un adelanto	ob·te·ner on a·de·lan·to
get change for this note	conseguir cambio para este billete	kon·se·geer kam·byo pa·ra es·te bee·lye·te
withdraw money	sacar dinero	sa·kar dee·ne·ro

What time does the bank open?
¿A qué hora abre el banco?   a ke o·ra a·bre el ban·ko

Where's the nearest foreign exchange office?
¿Dónde está la oficina   don·de es·ta la o·fee·thee·na
de cambio más cercano?   de kam·byo mas ther·ka·no

The ATM took my card.
El cajero automático   el ka·khe·ro ow·to·ma·tee·ko
se ha tragado mi tarjeta.   se a tra·ga·do mee tar·khe·ta

I've forgotten my PIN.
Me he olvidado del NPI.   me e ol·vee·da·do del e·ne pe ee

Can I have smaller notes?
¿Me lo puede dar en   me lo pwe·de dar en
billetes más pequeños?   bee·lye·tes mas pe·ke·nyos

What's the charge for that?
¿Cuánto hay que pagar   kwan·to ai ke pa·gar
por eso?   por e·so

What's the exchange rate?
  ¿Cuál es el tipo de cambio?   kwal es el *tee*·po de *kam*·byo

Has my money arrived yet?
  ¿Ya ha llegado mi dinero?   ya a lye·*ga*·do mee dee·*ne*·ro

How long will it take to arrive?
  ¿Cuánto tiempo tardará   *kwan*·to *tyem*·po tar·da·*ra*
  en llegar?   en lye·*gar*

For more useful phrases, see **money**, page 35.

---

listen for ...

ai oon pro·*ble*·ma kon soo *kwen*·ta
  Hay un problema   **There's a problem with**
  con su cuenta.   **your account.**

no le *ke*·dan *fon*·dos
  No le quedan fondos.   **You have no funds left.**

no po·*de*·mos a·*ther* e·so
  No podemos hacer eso.   **We can't do that.**

por fa·*vor* feer·me a·*kee*
  Por favor firme aquí.   **Please sign here.**

pwe·de es·kree·*beer*·lo
  ¿Puede escribirlo?   **Could you write it down?**

pwe·do ver soo ee·den·tee·fee·ka·*thyon*/
pa·sa·*por*·te por fa·*vor*
  ¿Puedo ver su   **Can I see some ID/your**
  identificación/   **passport, please?**
  pasaporte, por favor?

tye·ne oon des·koo·*byer*·to
  Tiene un descubierto.   **You're overdrawn.**

en ...   En ...   In ...
  (*kwa*·tro) *dee*·as   *(cuatro) días*   **(four) working**
  la·bo·*ra*·bles   *laborables*   **days**
  oo·na se·*ma*·na   *una semana*   **one week**

I'd like a/an ...	*Quisiera ...*	kee·*sye*·ra ...
audio set	*un equipo audio*	oon e·*kee*·po ow·dyo
catalogue	*un catálogo*	oon ka·*ta*·lo·go
guidebook in English	*una guía turística en inglés*	*oo*·na *gee*·a too·*rees*·tee·ka en een·*gles*
(local) map	*un mapa (de la zona)*	oon *ma*·pa (de la *tho*·na)

Do you have information on ... sights?	*¿Tiene información sobre los lugares de interés ...?*	*tye*·ne een·for·ma·*thyon* *so*·bre los loo·*ga*·res de een·te·*res* ...
architectural	*arquitectónico*	ar·kee·tek·*to*·nee·ko
cultural	*cultural*	kool·too·*ral*
historical	*histórico*	ees·*to*·ree·ko
local	*local*	lo·*kal*
natural	*natural*	na·too·*ral*
religious	*religioso*	re·lee·*khyo*·so
unique	*único*	*oo*·nee·ko

Can we hire a guide?
¿Podemos alquilar un guía?　po·*de*·mos al·kee·*lar* oon *gee*·a

I'd like to hire a local guide.
Me gustaría contratar a un guía local.　me goos·ta·*ree*·a kon·tra·*tar* a oon *gee*·a lo·*kal*

I'd like to see ...
Me gustaría ver ...　me goos·ta·*ree*·a ver ...

Could you take a photograph of me?
¿Me puede hacer una foto?　me *pwe*·de a·*ther* *oo*·na *fo*·to

Can I take photographs (of you)?
¿(Le/Te) Puedo tomar fotos? pol/inf　(le/te) *pwe*·do to·*mar* *fo*·tos

I'll send you the photograph.
Le/Te mandaré la foto. pol/inf　le/te man·da·*re* la *fo*·to

What's that?	¿Qué es eso?	ke es e·so
Who made it?	¿Quién lo hizo?	kyen lo ee·tho
How old is it?	¿De qué época es?	de ke e·po·ka es

getting in

la entrada

What time does it open/close?
¿A qué hora abren/cierran?   a ke o·ra ab·ren/thye·ran

What's the admission charge?
¿Cuánto cuesta la entrada?   kwan·to kwes·ta la en·tra·da

Is there a discount for ...?	¿Hay descuentos para ...?	ai des·kwen·tos pa·ra ...
children	niños	nee·nyos
families	familias	fa·mee·lee·as
groups	grupos	groo·pos
older people	gente mayor	khen·te ma·yor
pensioners	pensionistas	pen·syo·nees·tas
students	estudiantes	es·too·dyan·tes

signs		
Abierto	a·byer·to	**Open**
Cerrado	the·ra·do	**Closed**
Prohibido	pro·ee·bee·do	**Prohibited**

tours

recorridos

Are there organised walking tours?
¿Organizan recorridos a pie?   or·ga·nee·than re·ko·ree·dos a pye

I'd like to do cooking/language classes.
Me gustaría ir a clases de cocina/idiomas.   me goos·ta·ree·a eer a kla·ses de ko·thee·na/ee·dyo·mas

Can you recommend a ...?	¿Puede recomendar algún/alguna ...? m/f	pwe·de re·ko·men·dar al·goon/al·goo·na ...
When's the next ...?	¿Cuándo es el/la próximo/a ...? m/f	kwan·do es el/la prok·see·mo/a ...
boat trip	paseo m en barca	pa·se·o en bar·ka
day trip	excursión f de un día	eks·koor·syon de oon dee·a
excursion	excursión f	eks·koor·syon
tour	recorrido m	re·ko·ree·do

Do I need to take ... with me?	¿Necesito llevar ...?	ne·the·see·to lye·var ...
Is ... included?	¿Incluye ...?	een·kloo·ye ...
equipment	equipo	e·kee·po
food	comida	ko·mee·da
transport	transporte	trans·por·te

The guide will pay.
El guía va a pagar.
el gee·a va a pa·gar

The guide has paid.
El guía ha pagado.
el gee·a a pa·ga·do

How long is the tour?
¿Cuánto dura el recorrido?
kwan·to doo·ra el re·ko·ree·do

What time should I be back?
¿A qué hora tengo que volver?
a ke o·ra ten·go ke vol·ver

Be back here at ...
Vuelva ...
vwel·va ...

I'm with them.
Voy con ellos.
voy kon e·lyos

I've lost my group.
He perdido a mi grupo.
e per·dee·do a mee groo·po

the royal lisp

According to a popular legend, one of the Spanish kings – some say Felipe IV, others Ferdinand I – had a slight speech impediment. Unable to pronounce the sound *s* properly, he lisped his way through conversation. In an epic act of flattery, the entire court, and eventually all of Spain, mimicked his lisp. This story provides a colourful explanation as to why Spaniards pronounce the word *cerveza* (beer) as ther·ve·tha, while Latin Americans continue to pronounce it ser·ve·sa.

It so happens, the story of the lisping king is a myth. After all, only the letters *c* and *z* are pronounced th (when they precede an *i* or an *e*), while the letter *s* remains the same as in English. The reason for this selectiveness is due to the way Spanish evolved from Latin and has nothing to do with lisping monarchs at all. In fact, when you hear someone say *gracias*, gra·thyas, they are no more lisping as when you say 'thank you' in English.

senior & disabled travellers
viajeros mayores & minusválidos

I have a disability.
Soy minusválido/a. m/f — soy mee·noos·va·lee·do/a

I'm deaf.
Soy sordo/a. m/f — soy sor·do/a

I'm hard of hearing.
Tengo problemas de audición. — ten·go pro·ble·mas de ow·dee·thyon

Speak more loudly, please.
Hable más alto, por favor. — ab·le mas al·to por fa·vor

My companion is blind.
Mi compañero/a es ciego/a. m/f — mee kom·pa·nye·ro/a es thye·go/a

I need assistance.
Necesito asistencia. — ne·the·see·to a·sees·ten·thya

Are guide dogs permitted?
¿Se permite la entrada a los perros lazarillos? — se per·mee·te la en·tra·da a los pe·ros la·tha·ree·lyos

What services do you have for people with a disability?
¿Qué servicios tienen para minusválidos? — ke ser·vee·thyos tye·nen pa·ra mee·noos·va·lee·dos

Is there wheelchair access?
¿Hay acceso para la silla de ruedas? — ai ak·the·so pa·ra la see·lya de rwe·das

Are there parking spaces for people with a disability?
¿Tiene aparcamiento para minusválidos? — tye·ne a·par·ka·myen·to pa·ra mee·noos·va·lee·dos

Are there rails in the bathroom?
¿Hay pasamanos en el baño? — ai pa·sa·ma·nos en el ba·nyo

Are there toilets for people with a disability?
¿Hay aseos para minusválidos? — ai a·se·os pa·ra mee·noos·va·lee·dos

Is there somewhere I can sit down?

¿Hay algun sitio dónde   ai al·*goon* see·tyo *don*·de
me pueda sentar?   me *pwe*·da sen·*tar*

Could you help me cross this street?

¿Me puede ayudar a   me *pwe*·de a·yoo·*dar* a
cruzar la calle?   kroo·*thar* la *ka*·lye

Could you call me a taxi for the disabled?

¿Podría llamar a un taxi   po·*dree*·a lya·*mar* a oon *tak*·see
para minusválidos?   *pa*·ra mee·noos·va·lee·dos

Braille library	*biblioteca* f *Braille*	bee·blee·o·*te*·ka *brai*·lye
crutches	*muletas* f pl	moo·*le*·tas
guide dog	*perro* m *lazarillo*	*pe*·ro la·tha·*ree*·lyo
person with a disability	*persona* f *minusválida*	per·*so*·na mee·noos·va·lee·da
ramp	*rampa* f	*ram*·pa
senior person	*persona* f *mayor*	per·*so*·na ma·*yor*
space	*espacio* m	es·*pa*·thyo
walking frame	*andador* m	an·da·*dor*
walking stick	*bastón* m	ba·*ston*
wheelchair	*silla* f *de ruedas*	*see*·lya de *rwe*·das

signs

Acceso para Sillas de Ruedas	ak·*the*·so *pa*·ra *thee*·lyas de ru·*e*·das	**Wheelchair Entrance**
Ascensor	as·then·*sor*	**Elevator/Lift**
Aseos para Minusválidos	a·*the*·os *pa*·ra mee·nus·va·lee·dos	**Toilets for the Disabled**
Carros de Minusválidos	*ka*·ros de mee·nus·va·lee·dos	**Trolleys for the Disabled (in major supermarkets)**

Is there a/an ...?	¿Hay ...?	ai ...
baby change room	una sala en la que cambiarle el pañal al bebé	oo·na sa·la en la ke kam·byar·le el pa·nyal al be·be
(English-speaking) babysitter	canguro (de habla inglésa)	kan·goo·ro (de ab·la een·gle·sa)
child discount	descuento para niños	des·kwen·to pa·ra nee·nyos
child-minding service	servicio de cuidado de niños	ser·vee·thyo de kwee·da·do de nee·nyos
children's menu	menú infantil	me·noo een·fan·teel
family discount	descuento familiar	des·kwen·to fa·mee·lyar
highchair	trona	tro·na

I need a ...	Necesito ...	ne·the·see·to ...
baby seat	un asiento de seguridad para bebés	oon a·syen·to de se·goo·ree·da pa·ra be·bes
child seat	un asiento de seguridad para niños	oon a·syen·to de se·goo·ree·da pa·ra nee·nyos
cot	una cuna	oo·na koo·na
potty	un orinal de niños	oon o·ree·nal de nee·nyos
stroller	un cochecito	oon ko·che·thee·to

If your child is sick, see **health**, page 179.

Do you sell ...?	¿Vende ...?	ven·de ...
baby wipes	toallitas	to·a·lyee·tas
	para bebés	pa·ra be·bes
disposable nappies/ diapers	pañales de usar y tirar	pa·nya·les de oo·sar ee tee·rar
milk formula	leche en polvo	le·che en pol·vo
painkillers for infants	analgésicos para bebés	a·nal·khe·see·kos pa·ra be·bes

Do you mind if I breastfeed here?

¿Le molesta que dé de pecho aquí?	le mo·les·ta ke de de pe·cho a·kee

Are children allowed?

¿Se admiten niños?	se ad·mee·ten nee·nyos

Is this suitable for (three)-year-old children?

¿Es apto para niños de (tres) años?	es ap·to pa·ra nee·nyos de (tres) a·nyos

What's your name?

¿Cómo te llamas? inf	ko·mo te lya·mas

How old are you?

¿Cuántos años tienes? inf	kwan·tos a·nyos tye·nes

For more on talking to children, see **meeting people**, page 96.

creche	guardería f	gwar·de·ree·a
park	parque m	par·ke
playground	parque m infantil	par·ke een·fan·teel
slide	tobogán m	to·bo·gan
swimming pool	piscina f	pees·thee·na
swings	columpios m pl	ko·loom·pyos
theme park	parque m de atracciones	par·ke de a·trak·thyo·nes
toyshop	juguetería f	khoo·ge·te·ree·a

---

bless you!

In Spain, a polite way to respond to someone sneezing is by saying ¡Salud! sa·loo (health) or ¡Jesús! khe·soos (literally 'Jesus').

SOCIAL > meeting people

conociendo a la gente

basics

lo básico

Yes.	*Sí.*	see
No.	*No.*	no
Please.	*Por favor.*	por fa·*vor*
Thank you (very much).	*(Muchas) Gracias.*	(*moo*·chas) *gra*·thyas
You're welcome.	*De nada.*	de *na*·da
Excuse me.	*Perdón/*	per·*don*/
	Discúlpeme.	dees·*kool*·pe·me
Sorry.	*Lo siento.*	lo *syen*·to

greetings

los saludos

In Spain people are often quite casual in their interactions. It's fine to use the following expressions in both formal and informal situations.

Hello/Hi.	*Hola.*	o·la
Good morning.	*Buenos días.*	*bwe*·nos *dee*·as
Good afternoon. (until 8pm)	*Buenas tardes.*	*bwe*·nas *tar*·des
Good evening/ night.	*Buenas noches.*	*bwe*·nas *no*·ches
See you later.	*Hasta luego.*	*as*·ta *lwe*·go
Goodbye/Bye.	*Adiós.*	a·*dyos*
How are you?	*¿Qué tal?*	ke tal
Fine, thanks.	*Bien, gracias.*	byen *gra*·thyas

What's your name?

¿Cómo se llama Usted? pol	*ko*·mo se *lya*·ma oos·*te*
¿Cómo te llamas? inf	*ko*·mo te *lya*·mas

My name is …

Me llamo …	me *lya*·mo …

I'd like to introduce you to …

Quisiera presentarle a … pol	kee·*sye*·ra pre·sen·*tar*·le a …
Quisiera presentarte a … inf	kee·*sye*·ra pre·sen·*tar*·te a …

I'm pleased to meet you.

Mucho gusto.	*moo*·cho *goos*·to

titles & addressing people

dirigiéndose a la gente

Señor and *Señora* tend to be used in everyday speech. *Doña*, although rare, is used as a mark of respect towards older women, while *Don* is sometimes used to address men. An elderly neighbour, for example, might be called *Doña Lola*. For more on polite forms, see also the box **using your manners**, page 77, and **personal pronouns** in the **grammar** chapter, page 19.

Mr	*Señor*	se·*nyor*
Sir	*Don*	don
Miss	*Señorita*	se·nyo·*ree*·ta
Ms/Mrs	*Señora*	se·*nyo*·ra
Madam	*Doña*	*do*·nya

call a friend

You may hear friends calling each other *tío* m, *tee*·o, or *tía* f, *tee*·a, but these words are usually used when talking about others. They're a bit crass (a little like using 'sheila' to describe a girl in Australia). Guys use *colega*, ko·*le*·ga, and *hombre*, *om*·bre, to address their workmates or male friends. In the south, people call their friends *pixas*, *pee*·chas or *xoxos*, *cho*·chos.

making conversation

Spain is known for its distinct regional areas. A great conversation starter in Spain is to ask someone where they come from. Other good topics are sport, politics, history and travel.

Do you live here?
¿Vives aquí?　　　　　vee·ves a·kee

Where are you going?
¿Adónde vas?　　　　　a·don·de vas

What are you doing?
¿Qué haces?　　　　　ke a·thes

Are you waiting (for a city bus)?
¿Estás esperando　　　es·tas es·pe·ran·do
(un autobús)?　　　　　(oon ow·to·boos)

Can I have a light, please?
¿Tienes fuego, por favor?　tye·nes fwe·go por fa·vor

Do you like this?
¿Te gusta esto?　　　　te goos·ta es·to

I love this.
Me encanta esto.　　　me en·kan·ta es·to

I'm here ...	*Estoy aquí ...*	es·toy a·kee ...
for a holiday	*de vacaciones*	de va·ka·thyo·nes
on business	*en viaje de*	en vya·khe de
	negocios	ne·go·thyos
to study	*estudiando*	es·tu·dyan·do
with my family	*con mi familia*	kon mee fa·mee·lya
with my partner	*con mi pareja*	kon mee pa·re·kha

listen for ...

es·tas a·kee de va·ka·thyo·nes
¿Estás aquí de　　　　**Are you here on**
vacaciones?　　　　　**holiday?**

What's this called?
¿Cómo se llama esto?   ko·mo se *lya*·ma es·to

What do you think (about ...)?
¿Qué piensas (de ...)?   ke *pyen*·sas (de ...)

What a gorgeous baby!
¡Qué niño/a más   ke *nee*·nyo/a mas
precioso/a! m/f   pre·*thyo*·so/a

Can I take a photo?
¿Puedo hacer una foto?   pwe·do a·*ther* oo·na fo·to

That's (beautiful), isn't it?
¿Es (precioso), no?   es (pre·*thyo*·so) no

How long are you here for?
¿Cuánto tiempo te vas   kwan·to *tyem*·po te vas
a quedar?   a ke·*dar*

I'm here for ... weeks/days.
Estoy aquí por ...   es·toy a·kee por ...
semanas/días.   se·*ma*·nas/*dee*·as

This is my ...	*Éste/a es mi ...* m/f	es·te/a es mee ...
child	*hijo/a* m/f	ee·kho/a
colleague	*colega* m&f	ko·*le*·ga
friend	*amigo/a* m/f	a·*mee*·go/a
husband	*marido*	ma·*ree*·do
partner	*pareja* m&f	pa·*re*·kha
wife	*esposa*	es·*po*·sa

---

local talk

Drop a few casual expressions into your Spanish and see the difference it makes in interacting with locals:

Great!	*¡Cojonudo!*	ko·kho·*noo*·do
Congratulations!	*¡Enhorabuena!*	e·no·ra·*bwe*·na
How cool!	*¡Qué guay!*	ke gwai
How interesting!	*¡Qué interesante!*	ke een·te·re·*san*·te
Really?	*¿De veras?*	de *ve*·ras
That's fantastic!	*¡Estupendo!*	es·too·*pen*·do
What's up?	*¿Qué hay?*	ke ai
You don't say!	*¡No me digas!*	no me *dee*·gas

nationalities

You'll find that many country names are similar to English, so even if you don't know the Spanish name, it's more than likely you'll be understood. For more countries, see the **dictionary**.

Where are you from?

¿De dónde es Usted? pol	de don·de es oos·te
¿De dónde eres? inf	de don·de e·res

I'm from ...	Soy de ...	soy de ...
Australia	Australia	ow·stra·lya
Canada	Canadá	ka·na·da
England	Inglaterra	een·gla·te·ra
New Zealand	Nueva Zelanda	nwe·va the·lan·da
the USA	los Estados Unidos	los es·ta·dos oo·nee·dos

age

How old ...?	¿Cuántos años ...?	kwan·tos a·nyos ...
are you	tienes	tye·nes
is your	tiene su/tu	tye·ne soo/too
daughter	hija pol/inf	ee·kha
is your son	tiene su/tu	tye·ne soo/too
	hijo pol/inf	ee·kho

I'm ... years old.
Tengo ... años. ten·go ... a·nyos

He's/She's ... years old.
Tiene ... años. tye·ne ... a·nyos

I'm younger than I look.
Soy más joven de lo soy mas kho·ven de lo
que parezco. ke pa·reth·ko

Too old!
¡Demasiado viejo! de·ma·sya·do vye·kho

For your age, see **numbers & amounts**, page 29.

occupations & study

What do you do?
¿A qué te dedicas? a ke te de·*dee*·kas

What are you studying?
¿Qué estudias? ke es·*too*·dyas

I'm self-employed.
Soy trabajador/ soy tra·ba·kha·*dor*/
trabajadora tra·ba·kha·*do*·ra
autónomo/a. m/f ow·*to*·no·mo/a

I work in education/hospitality.
Trabajo en enseñanza/ tra·*ba*·kho en en·se·*nyan*·tha/
hostelería. os·te·le·*ree*·a

I'm a/an …	*Soy …*	soy …
architect	*arquitecto/a* m/f	ar·kee·*tek*·to/a
mechanic	*mecánico/a* m/f	me·*ka*·nee·ko/a
student	*estudiante* m&f	es·too·*dyan*·te
teacher	*profesor/*	pro·fe·*sor*/
	profesora m/f	pro·fe·*so*·ra
writer	*escritor/*	es·kree·*tor*/
	escritora m/f	es·kree·*to*·ra
I'm …	*Estoy …*	es·*toy* …
retired	*jubilado/a* m/f	khoo·bee·*la*·do/a
unemployed	*en el paro*	en el *pa*·ro
I'm studying …	*Estudio …*	es·*too*·dyo …
business	*comercio*	ko·*mer*·thyo
humanities	*humanidades*	oo·ma·nee·*da*·des
languages	*idiomas*	ee·*dyo*·mas
science	*ciencias*	*thyen*·thyas

I'm studying at ...	Estudio en ...	es·too·dyo en ...
college	el instituto	el eens·tee·too·to
school	el colegio	el ko·le·khyo
trade school	el instituto	el eens·tee·too·to
	de formación	de for·ma·thyon
	profesional	pro·fe·syo·nal
university	la universidad	la oo·nee·ver·see·da

For more occupations and studies, see the **dictionary**.

family

la familia

Do you have	¿Tiene ...? pol	tye·ne ...
(a) ...?	¿Tienes ...? inf	tye·nes ...
I (don't) have (a) ...	(No) Tengo ...	(no) ten·go ...
brother	un hermano	oon er·ma·no
children	hijos	ee·khos
family	una familia	oo·na fa·mee·lya
partner	una pareja m&f	oo·na pa·re·kha
sister	una hermana	oo·na er·ma·na

Do you live with your ...?
¿Vives con tu ...? vee·ves kon too ...

I live with my ...
Vivo con mi ... vee·vo kon mee ...

This is my ...
Éste/a es mi ... m/f es·te/a es mee ...

Are you married?
¿Estás casado/a? m/f es·tas ka·sa·do/a

I'm single.
Soy soltero/a. m/f soy sol·te·ro/a

I live with someone.
Vivo con alguien. vee·vo kon al·gyen

I'm ...	Estoy ...	es·toy ...
married	casado/a m/f	ka·sa·do/a
separated	separado/a m/f	se·pa·ra·do/a

children

When's your birthday?
  ¿Cuándo es tu   kwan·do es too
  cumpleaños?   koom·ple·a·nyos

Do you go to school or kindergarten?
  ¿Vas al colegio o a la   vas al ko·le·khyo o a la
  guardería?   gwar·de·ree·a

What grade are you in?
  ¿En qué curso estás?   en ke koor·so es·tas

Do you like ...?	*¿Te gusta ...?*	te goos·ta ...
school	*el colegio*	el ko·le·khyo
sport	*el deporte*	el de·por·te
your teacher	*tu profesor/*	too pro·fe·sor/
	profesora m/f	pro·fe·so·ra

What do you do after school?
  ¿Qué haces después del   ke a·thes des·pwes del
  colegio?   ko·le·khyo

Do you learn English?
  ¿Aprendes inglés?   a·pren·des een·gles

I come from very far away.
  Vengo de muy lejos.   ven·go de mooy le·khos

Are you lost?
  ¿Estás perdido/a? m/f   es·tas per·dee·do/a

Show me how to play.
  Dime cómo se juega.   dee·me ko·mo se khwe·ga

Well done!
  ¡Muy bien!   mooy byen

farewells

Tomorrow is my last day here.
*Mañana es mi último
día aquí.*
ma·*nya*·na es mee *ool*·tee·mo
dee·a a·*kee*

It's been great meeting you.
*Me ha encantado
conocerte.*
me a en·kan·*ta*·do
ko·no·*ther*·te

Keep in touch!
*¡Nos mantendremos en
contacto!*
nos man·ten·*dre*·mos en
kon·*tak*·to

Are you on Facebook?
¿Estás en Facebook?
es·*tas* en *feys*·book

I'll send you copies of the photos.
*Te enviaré copias de
las fotos.*
te en·vee·a·*re* ko·pyas de
las *fo*·tos

---

spanish grannies

Even idioms translate across languages. Here are a few
golden oldies:

It's like casting pearls before swine.
*Es como echar
margaritas a los
cerdos.*
es *ko*·mo e·*char*
ma·ga·*ree*·tas a los
ther·dos

(lit: it's like feeding daisies to the pigs)

When it rains, it pours.
*Éramos pocos y
parió la abuela.*
e·ra·mos *po*·kos y
pa·ree·o la a·*bwe*·la

(lit: there were a few of us and then granny gave birth)

This is like watching grass grow.
*Es más largo que un
día sin pan.*
es mas *lar*·go ke oon
dee·a seen pan

(lit: it's longer than a day without bread)

meeting people

If you ever visit (Scotland), you can …	Si algún día visitas (Escocia), …	see al·*goon* dee·a vee·*see*·tas (es·ko·thya) …
come and visit	ven a visitarnos	ven a vee·see·*tar*·nos
stay with me	te puedes quedar conmigo	te *pwe*·des ke·*dar* kon·*mee*·go

Here's my …	Éste/Ésta es mi … m/f	es·te/es·ta es mee …
What's your …?	¿Cuál es tu …?	kwal es too …
address	dirección f	dee·rek·*thyon*
email address	dirección f de email	dee·rek·*thyon* de ee·mayl
fax number	número m de fax	*noo*·me·ro de faks
mobile number	número m de móvil	*noo*·me·ro de *mo*·veel
work number	número m de teléfono en el trabajo	*noo*·me·ro de te·*le*·fo·no en el tra·*ba*·kho

For more on addresses, see **directions**, page 61.

For more on addresses, see **directions**, page 61.

brave new world

With Columbus' discovery of the New World in 1492 began an era of Spanish expansion in America, which is also reflected in the language. *Patata*, *tomate*, *cacao* and *chocolate* are just a few examples of words that entered Spanish (and consequently English) from the indigenous American languages. Bear in mind that Spanish has evolved differently and it's a good idea to take Lonely Planet's *Latin American Spanish* phrasebook with you, rather than this one, if you're travelling there.

SOCIAL

writing to people

If you want to impress your new friends by writing to them in Spanish, here are some useful expressions:

Dear ...
Querido/a ... m/f — ke·*ree*·do/a

I'm sorry it's taken me so long to write.
Siento haber tardado — *syen*·to a·*ber* tar·*da*·do
tanto en escribir. — *tan*·to en es·kree·*beer*

It was great to meet you.
Me encantó conocerte. — me en·kan·*to* ko·no·*ther*·te

Thank you so much for your hospitality.
Muchísimas gracias — moo·*chee*·see·mas *gra*·thyas
por tu hospitalidad. — por too os·pee·ta·lee·*da*

I miss you a lot.
Te echo mucho de menos. — te e·cho *moo*·cho de *me*·nos

I had a fantastic time in ...
Me lo pasé genial en ... — me lo pa·*se* khe·*nyal* en ...

My favourite place was ...
Mi lugar preferido — mee loo·*gar* pre·fe·*ree*·do
fue ... — fwe ...

I hope to visit ... again.
Espero visitar otra vez ... — es·*pe*·ro vee·see·*tar* ot·ra veth

Say 'hi' to ... (and ...) for me.
Saluda a ... (y a ...) — sa·*loo*·da a ... (ee a ...)
de mi parte. — de mee *par*·te

I'd love to see you again.
Tengo ganas de verte — *ten*·go *ga*·nas de *ver*·te
otra vez. — *ot*·ra veth

Write soon!
¡Escríbeme pronto! — es·*kree*·be·me *pron*·to

With love,
Un beso, — oon *be*·so

Regards,
Saludos, — sa·*loo*·dos

basque

Basque, or *Euskara*, is spoken at the western end of the Pyrenees and along the Bay of Biscay – from Bayonne in France to Bilbao in Spain, and then inland, almost to Pamplona.

No one quite knows its origin. Some have related it to the Sioux language, to Japanese, and even to the language of the Atlanteans. To complicate matters, dialects are also spoken in the Basque country, including Bizkaian, Gipuzkoan, High Navarrese, Aezkoan, Salazarese, Lapurdian, Low Navarrese and Suberoan. The most likely theory is that Basque is the lone survivor of a language family which once extended across Europe, and was wiped out by the languages of the Celts, the Germanic tribes and the Romans. It's amazing that Basque has survived so close to its original form.

Speaking Spanish in the Basque-speaking towns might be expected from a foreigner, but is not as warmly received as an attempt at one of the most ancient languages of Europe.

> greetings & civilities

Hi!	*Kaixo!*	kai·sho
Good morning.	*Egun on.*	e·goo non
Good afternoon/ evening.	*Arratsalde on.*	a·ra·chyal·de on
Goodbye.	*Agur.*	a·goor
Take care.	*Ondo ibili.*	on·do ee·beel·ee
How are you?	*Zer moduz?*	ser mo·doos
Fine, thank you.	*Ongi, eskerrik asko.*	on·gee e·ske·reek as·ko
Excuse me.	*Barkatu.*	bar·ka·too
Please.	*Mesedez.*	me·se·des
Thank you.	*Eskerrik asko.*	es·ke·reek kas·ko
You're welcome.	*Ez horregatik.*	es o·re·ga·teek

> language difficulties

Do you speak English?
> *Ingelesez ba al dakizu?*
> een·ge·le·ses ba al da·kee·*soo*

I know a little Basque.
> *Euskara apur bat badakit.*
> e·*oos*·ka·ra a·*poor* bat ba·da·*keet*

I don't understand.
> *Ez dut ulertzen.*
> es toot oo·*ler*·tzen

Could you speak in Castillian, please?
> *Erdaraz egingo al didazu, mesedez?*
> er·da·ras e·*geen*·go al dee·*da*·soo me·*se*·des

How do you say that in Basque?
> *Nola esaten da hori euskaraz?*
> *no*·la e·*sa*·ten da o·ree e·oo·ska·*ras*

catalan

Catalan is spoken by up to 10 million people in the north-east of Spain, a territory that comprises Catalonia, coastal Valencia and the Balearic Islands (Majorca, Minorca and Ibiza). Outside Spain, Catalan is also spoken in Andorra, the south of France and the town of Alguer in Sardinia.

Many famous creative types have been Catalan speakers: painters like Dalí, Miró and Picasso, architects like Gaudí and writers like Mercé Rodoreda.

Despite the fact that almost all Catalan speakers from Spain are bilingual, they appreciate it when visitors attempt to communicate, if even in the simplest way, in Catalan.

> greetings & civilities

Hello!	Hola!	o·la
Good morning.	Bon dia.	bon dee·a
Good afternoon.	Bona tarda.	bo·na tar·da
Good evening.	Bon vespre.	bon bes·pra
Goodbye.	Adéu.	a·the·oo
How are you?	Com estàs?	kom as·tas
(Very) Well.	(Molt) Bé.	(mol) be
Excuse me.	Perdoni.	par·tho·nee
Sorry.	Ho sento.	oo sen·to
Please.	Sisplau.	sees·pla·oo
Thank you.	Gràcies.	gra·see·as
Yes/No.	Sí/No.	see/no

> language difficulties

Do you speak English?
Parla anglès?
par·la an·*gles*

Could you speak in Castilian, please?
*Pot parlar castellà
sisplau?*
pot par·*la* kas·ta·*lya*
sees·*pla*·oo

I (don't) understand.
(No) Ho entenc.
(no) oo an·teng

How do you say ...?
Com es diu ...?
kom az *dee*·oo

local talk

No problem!
Això rai!
a·*sho* ra·ee

What a laugh!
Quin tip de riure!
kin tip da ri·a·oo·ra

galician

Galician, or *Galego*, is an official language of the Autonomous Community of Galicias and is also widely understood in neighbouring regions Asturias and Castilla-Léon. It's very similar to Portuguese, as the two languages have roots in Vulgar Latin.

Galicians are likely to revert to Spanish when addressing a stranger, especially a foreigner, but making a small effort to communicate in Galician will always be welcomed.

> greetings & civilities

Hello!	*Ola!*	o·la
Good day.	*Bon dia.*	bon *dee*·a
Good afternoon/ evening.	*Boa tarde.*	bo·a *tar*·de
Goodbye.	*Adeus.*	a·*de*·oos
	Até logo.	a·*te* lo·go
Excuse me.	*Perdón.*	per·*don*
Please.	*Por favor.*	por fa·*vor*
Thank you.	*Grácias.*	gra·see·as
Many thanks.	*Moitas grácias.*	moy·tas gra·see·as
That's fine.	*De nada.*	de na·da
Yes/No.	*Si/Non.*	see/non

> language difficulties

Do you speak English?
Fala inglés?   fa·la een·*gles*

Could you speak in Castilian, please?
Pode falar en español,   po·de fa·la en e·spa·*nyol*
por favor?   por fa·*bor*

I (don't) understand.
(Non) Entendo.   (non) en·*ten*·do

What's this called in Galician?
Como se chama iso en   ko·mo se *cha*·ma ee·so en
galego?   ga·*le*·go

common interests

los intereses en común

What do you do in your spare time?
¿Qué te gusta hacer en tu tiempo libre?
ke te *goos*·ta a·*ther* en too *tyem*·po *lee*·bre

Do you like (travelling)?
¿Te gusta (viajar)?
te *goos*·ta (vya·*khar*)

I (don't) like …	(No) Me gusta …	(no) me *goos*·ta …
art	el arte	el *ar*·te
computer games	videojuegos	vee·de·o·*khwe*·gos
cooking	cocinar	ko·thee·*nar*
dancing	ir a bailar	eer a bai·*lar*
fashion	la moda	la *mo*·da
films	el cine	el *thee*·ne
gardening	jardinería	kha·dee·ne·*ree*·a
hiking	el excursionismo	el eks·koor·syo·*nees*·mo
movies	el cine	el *thee*·ne
music	la música	la *moo*·see·ka
painting	la pintura	la peen·*too*·ra
photography	la fotografía	la fo·to·gra·*fee*·a
pub crawls	ir de bar en bar	eer de bar en bar
reading	leer	le·*er*
shopping	ir de compras	eer de *kom*·pras
socialising	salir	sa·*leer*
sport	el deporte	el de·*por*·te
surfing the Internet	navegar por internet	na·ve·*gar* por een·ter·*net*
travelling	viajar	vya·*khar*
watching TV	ver la televisión	ver la te·le·vee·*syon*

For sporting interests, see **sports**, page 129, and the dictionary.

music

Do you like to ...?	¿Te gusta ...?	te *goos*·ta ...
dance	*ir a bailar*	eer a bai·*lar*
go to concerts	*ir a conciertos*	eer a kon·*thyer*·tos
listen to music	*escuchar música*	es·koo·*char* moo·see·ka
play an instrument	*tocar algún instrumento*	to·kar al·*goon* eens·troo·*men*·to
sing	*cantar*	kan·tar

What ... do you like?	¿Qué ... te gusta/ gustan? sg/pl	ke ... te *goos*·ta/ *goos*·tan
bands	*grupos* pl	*groo*·pos
music	*música* sg	moo·see·ka
singers	*cantantes* pl	kan·*tan*·tes

classical music	*música* f *clásica*	moo·see·ka *kla*·see·ka
electronic music	*música* f *electrónica*	moo·see·ka e·lek·*tro*·nee·ka
jazz	*jazz* m	khath
metal	*metal* m	me·*tal*
pop	*música* f *pop*	moo·see·ka pop
punk	*música* f *punk*	moo·see·ka poonk
rock	*música* f *rock*	moo·see·ka rok
traditional music	*música* f *popular*	moo·see·ka po·pu·*lar*
world music	*música* f *étnica*	moo·see·ka *et*·nee·ka

art

When's the gallery open?
  ¿A qué hora abre la galería?   a ke *o*·ra *a*·bre la ga·le·*ree*·a

What's in the collection?
  ¿Qué hay en la colección?   ke ai en la ko·lek·*thyon*

What kind of art are you interested in?
¿Qué tipo de arte te interesa?
ke *tee*·po de *ar*·te te een·te·*re*·sa

I'm interested in …
Me interesa/ interesan … sg/pl
me een·te·*re*·sa/ een·te·*re*·san …

What do you think of …?
¿Qué piensas de …?
ke *pyen*·sas de …

It's a/an … exhibition.
Es una exposición de …
es *oo*·na eks·po·see·*thyon* de …

I like the works of …
Me gustan las obras de …
me *goos*·tan las *o*·bras de …

It reminds me of …
Me recuerda a …
me re·*kwer*·da a …

… art	*arte* m …	*ar*·te …
graphic	*gráfico*	*gra*·fee·ko
impressionist	*impresionista*	eem·pre·syo·*nees*·ta
modernist	*modernista*	mo·der·*nees*·ta
Renaissance	*renacentista*	re·na·then·*tees*·ta

cinema & theatre

I feel like going to (a comedy).
Tengo ganas de ir
a (una comedia).
ten·go ga·nas de eer
a (oo·na ko·me·dya)

What's showing at the cinema (tonight)?
¿Qué película dan en el
cine (esta noche)?
ke pe·lee·koo·la dan en el
thee·ne (es·ta no·che)

Is it in English?
¿Es en inglés?
es en een·gles

Is it dubbed?
¿Está doblada?
es·ta dob·la·da

Does it have (English) subtitles?
¿Tiene subtítulos
(en inglés)?
tye·ne soob·tee·too·los
(en een·gles)

I want to sell this ticket.
Quiero vender esta entrada.
kye·ro ven·der es·ta en·tra·da

Are those seats taken?
¿Están ocupados estos
asientos?
es·tan o·koo·pa·dos es·tos
a·syen·tos

Have you seen ...?
¿Has visto ...?
as vees·to ...

Who's in it?
¿Quién actúa?
kyen ak·too·a

It stars ...
Actúa ...
ak·too·a ...

Did you like the ...? *¿Te gustó el ...?*   te goos·to el ...
  ballet   *ballet*   ba·le
  film   *cine*   thee·ne
  play   *teatro*   te·a·tro

I (don't) like ...	*(No) Me gusta/*	(no) me *goos*·ta/
	gustan ... sg/pl	*goos*·tan ...
I thought it was ...	*Pienso que fue ...*	*pyen*·so ke fwe ...
excellent	*excelente*	eks·the·*len*·te
long	*largo*	*lar*·go
OK	*regular*	re·goo·*lar*
animated films	*películas* f pl *de*	pe·*lee*·koo·las de
	dibujos	dee·*boo*·khos
	animados	a·nee·*ma*·dos
comedy	*comedia* f	ko·*me*·dya
documentary	*documentales* m pl	do·koo·men·*ta*·les
drama	*drama* m	*dra*·ma
film noir	*cine* m *negro*	*thee*·ne *ne*·gro
(Spanish) cinema	*cine* m *(español)*	*thee*·ne (es·pa·*nyol*)
horror movies	*cine* m *de terror*	*thee*·ne de te·*ror*
sci-fi	*cine* m *de*	*thee*·ne de
	ciencia ficción	*thyen*·thya feek·*thyon*
short films	*cortos* m pl	*kor*·tos
thrillers	*cine* m *de*	*thee*·ne de
	suspenso	soos·*pen*·so

Off to a show? See **buying tickets**, page 38, and **going out**, page 115.

reading

la lectura

What kind of books do you read?
¿Qué tipo de libros lees? ke *tee*·po de *lee*·bros *le*·es

Which (Spanish) author do you recommend?
¿Qué autor (español) ke ow·*tor* (es·pa·*nyol*)
recomiendas? re·ko·*myen*·das

Have you read ...?
¿Has leído ...? as le·*ee*·do ...

On this trip I'm reading …
En este viaje estoy   en *es*·te *vya*·khe es·*toy*
leyendo …   le·*yen*·do …

I'd recommend …
Recomiendo a …   re·ko·*myen*·do a …

Where can I exchange books?
¿Dónde puedo cambiar   *don*·de *pwe*·do kam·*byar*
libros?   *lee*·bros

For more on books and reading, see **shopping**, page 68.

---

dog in the manger

Proverbs are big in Spain. The Marques de Santilllana compiled a national collection in the second half of the 15th century, and one of the characters in *Don Qixote*, Sancho Panza, speaks almost entirely in proverbs.

The author Cervantes described these popular sayings as 'short sentences based on long experience', or is that long-windedness?

ser como el perro del hortelano, que ni come las berzas, ni las deja comer al amo
ser *ko*·mo el *pe*·ro del or·te·*la*·no ke nee *ko*·me las *ber*·thas nee las *de*·kha ko·*mer* al *a*·mo

(lit: to be like the market gardener's dog who doesn't eat the cabbages and won't let his master eat them either)

feelings

los sentimientos

Feelings are described with either nouns or adjectives: the nouns use 'have' in Spanish (eg, 'I have hunger') and the adjectives use 'be' (like in English).

I'm (not) ...	(No) Tengo ...	(no) ten·go ...
Are you ...?	¿Tienes ...?	tye·nes ...
cold	frío	free·o
hot	calor	ka·lor
hungry	hambre	am·bre
in a hurry	prisa	pree·sa
thirsty	sed	se

I'm (not) ...	(No) Estoy ...	(no) es·toy ...
Are you ...?	¿Estás ...?	es·tas ...
annoyed	fastidiado/a m/f	fas·tee·dya·do/a
embarrassed	avergonzado/a m/f	a·ver·gon·tha·do/a
happy	feliz m&f	fe·leeth
sad	triste m&f	trees·te
tired	cansado/a m/f	kan·sa·do/a
well	bien m&f	byen

If you're not feeling well, see **health**, page 182.

opinions

las opiniones

Did you like it?
¿Te gustó?   te goos·to

What did you think of it?
¿Qué pensaste de eso?   ke pen·sas·te de e·so

I thought it was ...	Pienso que fue ...	pyen·so ke fwe ...
It's ...	Es ...	es ...
beautiful	bonito/a m/f	bo·nee·to/a
bizarre	raro/a m/f	ra·ro/a
crap	un coñazo/a m/f	oon ko·nya·tho/a
crazy	loco/a m/f	lo·ko/a
entertaining	entretenido/a m/f	en·tre·te·nee·do/a
excellent	fantástico/a m/f	fan·tas·tee·ko/a
full on	heavy m&f	khe·vee
horrible	horrible m&f	o·ree·ble

mixed feelings

a little	un poco	oon po·ko
I'm a little sad.	Estoy un poco triste. m&f	es·toy oon po·ko trees·te
quite	bastante	bas·tan·te
I'm quite disappointed.	Estoy bastante decepcionado/a. m/f	es·toy bas·tan·te de·thep·thyo·na·do/a
very	muy	mooy
I feel very lucky.	Me siento muy afortunado/a. m/f	me syen·to mooy a·for·too·na·do/a

politics & social issues

la política & los temas sociales

Who do you vote for?
¿A quién votas?   a kyen vo·tas

I support the ... party.
Apoyo al partido ...   a·po·yo al par·tee·do ...

Did you hear about ...?
¿Has oído que ...?   as o·ee·do ke ...

Are you in favour of ...?
¿Estás a favor de ...?   es·*tas* a fa·*vor* de ...

How do people feel about ...?
¿Cómo se siente la   *ko*·mo se *syen*·te la
gente de ...?   *khen*·te de ...

corruption	*corrupción* f	ko·roop·*thyon*
crime	*crimen* m	*kree*·men
drugs	*drogas* f pl	*dro*·gas
the economy	*economía* f	e·ko·no·*mee*·a
EU expansion	*expansión* f *de la*	eks·pan·*syon* de la
	Unión Europea	oon·*yon* e·oo·ro·*pe*·a
globalisation	*globalización* f	glo·ba·lee·tha·*thyon*
health care	*seguro* m *médico*	se·*goo*·ro *me*·dee·ko
immigration	*inmigración* f	een·mee·gra·*thyon*
monarchy	*monarquía* f	mo·nar·*kee*·a
racism	*racismo* m	ra·*thees*·mo
terrorism	*terrorismo* m	te·ro·*rees*·mo
unemployment	*desempleo* m	de·sem·*ple*·o
war in ...	*guerra* f en ...	*ge*·ra en ...

---

octopus in the garage

Keeping the attention of your audience can be a challenge in a foreign language. Try emphasising your opinion with some of these colourful expressions:

He's/She's the best.
Es un trozo de pan.   es oon *tro*·tho de pan
(lit: he's/she's a piece of bread)

You can't make a silk purse out of a sow's ear.
Aunque el mono se vista   *own*·ke el *mo*·no se *vees*·ta
de seda, mono se queda.   de *se*·da *mo*·no se *ke*·da
(lit: though the monkey may wear silk, it's still a monkey)

He's/She's a fish out of water.
Se encuentra   se en·koo·*en*·tra
como un pulpo en   *ko*·mo oon *pool*·po en
un garaje.   oon ga·*ra*·khe
(lit: he's/she's like an octopus in a garage)

the environment

Is there an environmental problem here?

¿Aquí hay un problema   a·*kee* ai oon pro·*ble*·ma
con el medio ambiente?   kon el *me*·dyo am·*byen*·te

Is this (forest) protected?

¿Está este (bosque)   es·*ta* es·te (*bos*·ke)
protegido?   pro·te·*khee*·do

alternative energy sources	*recursos* m pl *de energía alternativa*	re·*koor*·sos de e·ner·*khee*·a al·ter·na·*tee*·va
animal rights	*derechos* m pl *de los animales*	de·*re*·chos de los a·nee·*ma*·les
carbon dioxide emissions	*emisiones* f pl *de dióxido de carbono*	e·mee·*syo*·nes de dee·*ok*·see·do de kar·*bo*·no
climate change	*cambio* m *climático*	*kam*·byo klee·*ma*·tee·ko
deforestation	*deforestación* f	de·fo·res·ta·*thyon*
global warming	*calentamiento* m *global*	ka·len·ta·*myen*·to glo·*bal*
hunting	*caza* f	*ka*·tha
oil spill	*fuga* f *de petróleo*	*foo*·ga de pe·*tro*·le·o
pollution	*contaminación* f	kon·ta·mee·na·*thyon*
sustainable energy	*energía* f *sostenible*	e·ner·*khee*·a sos·te·*nee*·ble

perhaps, perhaps, perhaps

Maybe.	*Quizás.*	kee·*thas*
OK.	*Vale.*	*va*·le
No way!	*¡De ningún modo!*	de neen·*goon mo*·do
It's/I'm OK.	*Está/Estoy bien.*	es·*ta*/es·*toy* byen
Just a minute.	*Un momento.*	oon mo·*men*·to
No problem.	*Sin problema.*	seen pro·*ble*·ma
Of course!	*¡Claro que sí!*	*kla*·ro ke see
Sure.	*Claro.*	*kla*·ro
You bet!	*¡Ya lo creo!*	ya lo *kre*·o
Just joking.	*Era broma.*	e·ra *bro*·ma

where to go

adónde ir

What's there to do in the evenings?

¿Qué se puede hacer		ke se *pwe*·de a·*ther*
por las noches?		por las *no*·ches

What's on ...?   ¿Qué hay ...?   ke ai ...

locally	*en la zona*	en la *tho*·na
this weekend	*este fin de*	*es*·te feen de
	semana	se·*ma*·na
today	*hoy*	oy
tonight	*esta noche*	*es*·ta *no*·che

Where are ...?   ¿Dónde hay ...?   *don*·de ai ...

gay venues	*lugares gay*	loo·*ga*·res gai
places to eat	*lugares para*	loo·*ga*·res *pa*·ra
	comer	ko·*mer*
pubs	*pubs*	poobs

Is there a local ...   ¿Hay una guía ...   ai *oo*·na *gee*·a ...

guide?	*de la zona?*	de la *tho*·na
entertainment	*del ocio*	del *o*·thyo
film	*de cine*	de *thee*·ne
gay	*de lugares gay*	de loo·*ga*·res gai
music	*de música*	de *moo*·see·ka

read my lips

Foreign movies are usually dubbed into Spanish, but in bigger cities you'll find that some films have Spanish subtitles. Look out for *v.o.* (*version original* ver·*syon* o·ree·khee·*nal*, 'original version') or *v.o.s.* (*version original subtitulada* ver·*syon* o·ree·khee·*nal* soob·tee·too·*la*·da, 'original version with subtitles') in listings.

I feel like going to a/the ...	Tengo ganas de ir ...	ten·go ga·nas de eer ...
ballet	al ballet	al ba·le
bar	a un bar	a oon bar
cafe	a un café	a oon ka·fe
concert	a un concierto	a oon kon·thyer·to
karaoke bar	a un bar de karaoke	a oon bar de ka·ra·o·ke
movies	al cine	al thee·ne
nightclub	a una discoteca	a oo·na dees·ko·te·ka
party	a una fiesta	a oo·na fyes·ta
restaurant	a un restaurante	a oon res·tow·ran·te
theatre	al teatro	al te·a·tro

invitations

What are you doing this evening?
¿Qué haces esta noche? ke a·thes es·ta no·che

What are you up to (right now)?
¿Qué haces (ahora)? ke a·thes (a·o·ra)

Would you like to go for a ...?	¿Quieres que vayamos a ...?	kye·res ke va·ya·mos a ...
coffee	tomar un café	to·mar oon ka·fe
drink	tomar algo	to·mar al·go
meal	comer	ko·mer
walk	pasear	pa·se·ar

I feel like going ...	Me apetece ir a ...	me a·pe·te·the eer a ...
dancing	bailar	bai·lar
out somewhere	salir	sa·leer

My round.
   Invito yo.   een·*vee*·to yo

Do you know a good restaurant?
   ¿Conoces algún buen   ko·*no*·thes al·*goon* bwen
   restaurante?   res·tow·*ran*·te

Do you want to come to the (...) concert with me?
   ¿Quieres venir conmigo   *kye*·res ve·*neer* kon·*mee*·go
   al concierto (de ...)?   al kon·*thyer*·to (de ...)

We're having a party.
   Vamos a dar una fiesta.   *va*·mos a dar *oo*·na *fyes*·ta

Do you want to come?
   ¿Por qué no vienes?   por ke no *vye*·nes

Are you ready?
   ¿Estás listo/a? m/f   es·*tas lees*·to/a

---

are you my type?

If professions, age and nationality don't really cut it when trying to describe yourself (and others), see if these words help:

activist	*activista* m&f	ak·tee·*vees*·ta
alcoholic	*alcohólico/a* m/f	al·ko·o·*lee*·ko/a
artistic	*artísticó/a* m/f	ar·*tees*·tee·ko/a
creative	*creador/*	kre·a·*dor/*
	creadora m/f	kre·a·*do*·ra
daggy/dorky	*hortera* m&f	or·*te*·ra
goth	*siniestra* m&f	see·*nye*·stra
heavy	*heavy* m&f	*khe*·vee
intellectual	*intelectual* m&f	een·te·*lek*·twal
progressive	*progre* m&f	*pro*·gre
sporty	*deportivo/a* m/f	de·por·*tee*·vo/a
trendy/stylish	*moderno/a* m/f	mo·*der*·no/a
workaholic	*adícto/a* m/f	a·*deek*·to/a
	al trabajo	al tra·*ba*·kho
yuppie	*yupi* m&f	*yoo*·pee

responding to invitations

Sure!
¡Por supuesto!   por soo·*pwes*·to

Yes, I'd love to.
Me encantaría.   me en·kan·ta·*ree*·a

Where will we go?
¿A dónde vamos?   a *don*·de va·*mos*

That's very kind of you.
Es muy amable por   es mooy a·*ma*·ble por
tu parte.   *too par*·te

No, I'm afraid I can't.
Lo siento pero no puedo.   lo *syen*·to *pe*·ro no *pwe*·do

Sorry, I can't sing/dance.
Lo siento, no sé cantar/bailar.   lo *syen*·to no se kan·*tar*/bai·*lar*

What about tomorrow?
¿Qué tal mañana?   ke tal ma·*nya*·na

arranging to meet

What time shall we meet?
¿A qué hora quedamos?   a ke *o*·ra ke·*da*·mos

Where will we meet?
¿Dónde quedamos?   *don*·de ke·*da*·mos

Let's meet ...   *Quedamos ...*   ke·*da*·mos ...
  at (eight) o'clock   a *(las ocho)*   a (las *o*·cho)
  at the (entrance)   en *(la entrada)*   en (la en·*tra*·da)

I'll pick you up.
Paso a recogerte.   pa·so a re·ko·*kher*·te

I'll be coming later.
Iré más tarde.   ee·*re* mas *tar*·de

Where will you be?
¿Dónde estarás?   *don*·de es·ta·*ras*

If I'm not there by (nine), don't wait for me.
Si no estoy a (las nueve),   see no es·*toy* a (las *nwe*·ve)
no me esperes/esperéis. sg/pl   no me es·*pe*·res/es·pe·*reys*

OK!
¡Hecho!   e·cho

I'll see you then.
Nos vemos.   nos *ve*·mos

See you later/tomorrow.
Hasta luego/mañana.   *as*·ta *lwe*·go/ma·*nya*·na

I'm looking forward to it.
Tengo muchas ganas   *ten*·go *moo*·chas *ga*·nas
de ir.   de eer

Sorry I'm late.
Siento llegar tarde.   *syen*·to lye·*gar tar*·de

Never mind.
No pasa nada.   no *pa*·sa *na*·da

---

attention-getter

Hey!	*¡Eh, tú!*	e too
Look!	*¡Mira!*	*mee*·ra
Listen (to this)!	*¡Escucha (esto)!*	es·*koo*·cha (*es*·to)

nightclubs & bars

Where can we go (salsa) dancing?
¿Dónde podemos ir a   *don*·de po·*de*·mos eer a
bailar (la salsa)?   bai·*lar* (la *sal*·sa)

How do I get there?
¿Cómo se llega?   *ko*·mo se *lye*·ga

What type of music do you like?
¿Qué tipo de música   ke *tee*·po de *moo*·see·ka
prefieres?   pre·*fye*·res

I really like (reggae).
Me encanta (el reggae).   me en·*kan*·ta (el *re*·gai)

Come on!
¡Vamos!   *va*·mos

This place is great!
¡Este lugar me encanta!   *es*·te loo·*gar* me en·*kan*·ta

For more on bars, drinks and partying, see **eating out**, page 150.

drugs

I don't take drugs.
No consumo ningún   no kon·*soo*·mo neen·*goon*
tipo de drogas.   *tee*·po de *dro*·gas

I take ... occasionally.
Tomo ... de vez en cuando.   *to*·mo ... de veth en *kwan*·do

Do you want to have a smoke?
¿Nos fumamos un porro?   nos foo·*ma*·mos oon *po*·ro

Do you have a light?
¿Tienes fuego?   *tye*·nes *fwe*·go

If the police are talking to you about drugs, see **police**, page 176, for useful phrases.

romance
romance

asking someone out

saliendo con alguien

Don't be surprised if invitations come late in the day. Social life in Spain continues well into the night: sometimes people begin to eat dinner at 10pm and many clubs open at midnight.

Would you like to do something (tonight)?
¿Quieres hacer algo (esta noche)? — kye·res a·ther al·go (es·ta no·che)

Yes, I'd love to.
Me encantaría. — me en·kan·ta·ree·a

I'm busy.
Estoy ocupado/a. m/f — es·toy o·koo·pa·do/a

local talk

He's/She's hot.
Él/Ella es cachondo/a. m/f — el/e·lya es ka·chon·do/a

What a babe.
Vaya hembra. — va·ya em·bra

He/She gets around.
Se va a la cama con cualquiera. — se va a la ka·ma kon kwal·kye·ra

pick-up lines

frases para ligar

Would you like a drink?
¿Te apetece una copa? — te a·pe·te·the oo·na ko·pa

Do you have a light?
¿Tienes fuego? — tye·nes fwe·go

romance

121

You're great.

Eres estupendo/a. m/f   e·res es·too·*pen*·do/a

You mustn't come here much, because
I would have noticed you sooner.

No debes venir mucho   no de·bes ve·*neer* moo·cho
por aquí porque me habría   por a·*kee* por·ke me a·*bree*·a
fijado en ti antes.   fee·*kha*·do en tee *an*·tes

I've been watching you for a while, and
you're (the best-looking girl) here.

Hace rato que te observo y a·the *ra*·to ke te ob·*ser*·vo ee
eres (la chica mas guapa)   e·res (la *chee*·ka mas *gwa*·pa)
aqui.   a·*kee*

rejections

I'm here with my boyfriend/girlfriend.

Estoy aquí con mi   es·*toy* a·*kee* kon mee
novio/a. m/f   *no*·vyo/a

Excuse me, I have to go now.

Lo siento, pero me tengo   lo *syen*·to *pe*·ro me *ten*·go
que ir.   ke eer

Leave me alone!

¡Déjame en paz!   *de*·kha·me en path

Go away!

¡Vete!   ve·te

Hey, I'm not interested in talking to you.

Mira tío/a, es que no me   *mee*·ra *tee*·o/a es ke no me
interesa hablar   een·te·*re*·sa ab·*lar*
contigo. m/f   kon·*tee*·go

getting closer

Can I kiss you?
  ¿Te puedo besar?   te *pwe*·do be·*sar*

Do you want to come inside for a drink?
  ¿Quieres entrar a   kye·res en·*trar* a
  tomar algo?   to·*mar* al·go

Do you want a massage?
  ¿Quieres un masaje?   kye·res oon ma·*sa*·khe

Let's go to bed!
  ¡Vámonos a la cama!   va·mo·nos a la *ka*·ma

sex

Kiss me!
  ¡Dame un beso!   *da*·me oon *be*·so

I want you.
  Te deseo.   te de·*se*·o

I want to make love to you.
Quiero hacerte el amor.
kye·ro a·ther·te el a·mor

Do you have a condom?
¿Tienes un condón?
tye·nes oon kon·don

Touch me here.
Tócame aquí.
to·ka·me a·kee

Do you like this?
¿Esto te gusta?
es·to te goos·ta

I (don't) like that.
Eso (no) me gusta.
e·so (no) me goos·ta

I think we should stop now.
Pienso que deberíamos parar.
pyen·so ke de·be·ree·a·mos pa·rar

Oh yeah!
¡Así!
a·see

That was amazing.
Eso fue increíble.
e·so fwe een·kre·ee·ble

Are you sleepy?
¿Tienes sueño?
tye·nes swe·nyo

Can I stay over?
¿Puedo quedarme?
pwe·do ke·dar·me

I love you.
Te quiero.
te kye·ro

I think we're good together.
Creo que estamos muy bien juntos.
kre·o ke es·ta·mos mooy byen khoon·tos

endearments

heart	*corazon* m&f	ko·ra·thon
little love	*amorcito/a* m/f	a·mor·thee·to/a
my life	*mi vida* m&f	mee vee·da
my love	*mi amor* m&f	mee a·mor
sky	*cielo* m&f	thye·lo
treasure	*tesoro* m&f	te·so·ro

In this book, masculine forms appear before the feminine forms. If you see a word ending in *-o/a*, it means the masculine form ends in *-o* and the feminine form ends in *-a* (ie you replace the *-o* ending with the *-a* ending to make it feminine), eg *hijo/a* ee·kho/a m/f (son/daughter). The same goes for the plural endings *-os/as*, eg *hijos/as* ee·khos/as m/f (sons/daughters). If you see an *(a)* between brackets at the end of a word, it means you have to add it in order to make that word feminine, eg *español(a)* es·pa·nyol/es·pa·nyo·la m/f (Spanish). In other cases we spell out the whole word, eg *actor/actriz* ak·tor/ak·treeth m/f (actor/actress).

See also **gender** in the **grammar** chapter, page 17.

problems

los problemas

Are you seeing someone else?
  ¿Me estás engañando   me es·*tas* en·ga·*nyan*·do
  con alguien?   kon al·*gyen*

I never want to see you again.
  No quiero volver a verte.   no *kye*·ro vol·*ver* a *ver*·te

He's just a friend.
  Es un amigo nada más.   es oon a·*mee*·go *na*·da mas

She's just a friend.
  Es una amiga   es *oo*·na a·*mee*·ga
  nada más.   *na*·da mas

I want to stay friends.
  Me gustaría que   me goos·ta·*ree*·a ke
  quedáramos como amigos.   ke·*da*·ra·mos *ko*·mo a·*mee*·gos

It's not you, it's me.
 No eres tu, soy yo.   no e·res too soy yo

We'll work it out.
 Lo resolveremos.   lo re·sol·ve·re·mos

passionate language

That's not true!
 ¡Eso no es verdad!   e·so no es ver·da

In your dreams!
 ¡En sueños!   en swe·nyos

Come off it!
 ¡No me jodas!   no me kho·das

Damn!
 ¡Hostia!   os·tya

Shit!
 ¡Mierda!   myer·da

beliefs & cultural differences

creencias & diferencias culturales

religion

la religión

What's your religion?
    ¿Cuál es su/tu religión? pol/inf   kwal es soo/too re·lee·*khyon*

Can I pray here?
    ¿Puedo rezar aquí?   *pwe*·do re·*thar* a·*kee*

I'm (not) ...	(No) Soy ...	(no) soy ...
agnostic	*agnóstico/a* m/f	ag·*nos*·tee·ko/a
Buddhist	*budista* m&f	boo·*dees*·ta
Catholic	*católico/a* m/f	ka·*to*·lee·ko/a
Christian	*cristiano/a* m/f	krees·*tya*·no/a
Hindu	*hindú* m&f	een·*doo*
Jewish	*judío/a* m/f	khoo·*dee*·o/a
Muslim	*musulmán* m	moo·sool·*man*
	musulmána f	moo·sool·*ma*·na
(Eastern) Orthodox	*ortodoxo/a* m/f	or·to·*dok*·so/a
practising	*practicante* m&f	prak·tee·*kan*·te
religious	*religioso/a* m/f	re·lee·*khyo*·so/a

I (don't) believe in ...	(No) Creo en ...	(no) *kre*·o en ...
God	*Dios*	dyos
destiny/fate	*el destino*	el des·*tee*·no

cultural differences

las diferencias culturales

Is this a local or national custom?
    ¿Esto es una costumbre   es·to es *oo*·na kos·*toom*·bre
    local o nacional?   lo·*kal* o na·thyo·*nal*

This is (very) ...	Esto es (muy) ...	es·to es (mooy) ...
fun	*divertido*	dee·ver·tee·do
interesting	*interesante*	een·te·re·san·te
different	*diferente*	dee·fe·ren·te

I'm not used to this.
No estoy acostumbrado/a   no es·toy a·kos·toom·bra·do/a
a esto. m/f   a es·to

I'm sorry, it's against my beliefs.
Lo siento, eso va en contra   lo syen·to e·so va en kon·tra
de mis creencias.   de mees kre·en·thyas

I don't mind watching, but I'd rather not join in.
No me importa mirar,   no me eem·por·ta mee·rar
pero prefiero no   pe·ro pre·fye·ro no
participar.   par·tee·thee·par

I'll try it.
Lo probaré.   lo pro·ba·re

Sorry, I didn't mean to do/say anything wrong.
Lo siento, lo hice/dije   lo syen·to lo ee·the/dee·khe
sin querer.   seen ke·rer

sporting interests

los intereses deportivos

What sport do you play?
¿Qué deporte practicas?   ke de·*por*·te prak·*tee*·kas

What sport do you follow?
¿A qué deporte eres   a ke de·*por*·te e·res
aficionado/a? m/f   a·fee·thyo·*na*·do/a

I play/do ...
Practico ...   prak·*tee*·ko ...

I follow ...
Soy aficionado/a al ... m/f   soy a·fee·thyo·*na*·do/a al ...

basketball	*baloncesto* m	ba·lon·*thes*·to
cycling	*ciclismo* m	thee·*klees*·mo
football (soccer)	*fútbol* m	*foot*·bol
tennis	*tenis* m	*te*·nis
volleyball	*voleibol* m	bo·*lei*·bol

For more sports, see the **dictionary**.

Do you like sport?
¿Te gustan los deportes?   te *goos*·tan los de·*por*·tes

Yes, very much.
Me encantan.   me en·*kan*·tan

Not really.
En realidad, no mucho.   en re·a·lee·*da* no *moo*·cho

I like watching it.
Me gusta mirar.   me *goos*·ta mee·*rar*

Who's your favourite sportsperson?

¿Quién es tu deportista   kyen es too de·por·*tees*·ta
favorito/a? m/f   fa·vo·*ree*·to/a

What's your favourite team?

¿Cuál es tu equipo   kwal es too e·*kee*·po
favorito?   fa·vo·*ree*·to

going to a game

ir al partido

Would you like to go to a (basketball) game?

¿Te gustaría ir   te goos·ta·*ree*·a eer
a un partido de   a oon par·*tee*·do de
(baloncesto)?   (ba·lon·*thes*·to)

Who are you supporting?

¿Con qué equipo vas?   kon ke e·*kee*·po vas

How much time is left?

¿Cuánto tiempo queda de   *kwan*·to *tyem*·po *ke*·da de
partido?   par·*tee*·do

Who's ...?	*¿Quién ...?*	kyen ...
playing	*juega*	*khwe*·ga
winning	*va ganando*	va ga·*nan*·do

That was a ...	*¡Ese partido*	e·se par·*tee*·do
game!	*fue ...!*	fwe ...
boring	*aburrido*	a·boo·*ree*·do
great	*cojonudo*	ko·kho·*noo*·do

scoring		
What's the score?	*¿Cómo van?*	*ko*·mo van
draw/even	*empatados*	em·pa·*ta*·dos
love (zero)	*cero*	*the*·ro
match-point	*match point*	mach poyn
nil (zero)	*cero*	*the*·ro

playing sport

Do you want to play?
¿Quieres jugar?
kye·res khoo·gar

Can I join in?
¿Puedo jugar?
pwe·do khoo·gar

Yeah, that'd be great.
Sí, me encantaría.
see me en·kan·ta·ree·a

Not at the moment, thanks.
Ahora mismo no, gracias.
a·o·ra mees·mo no gra·thyas

I have an injury.
Tengo una lesión.
ten·go oo·na le·syon

Where's the best place to run around here?
¿Cuál es el mejor sitio
para hacer footing por
aquí cerca?
kwal es el me·khor see·tyo
pa·ra a·ther foo·teen por
a·kee ther·ka

Do I have to be a member to attend?
¿Hay que ser socio/a
para entrar? m/f
ai ke ser so·thyo/a
pa·ra en·trar

Is there a women-only pool?
¿Hay alguna piscina
sólo para mujeres?
ai al·goo·na pees·thee·na
so·lo pa·ra moo·khe·res

Where are the change rooms?
¿Dónde están los
vestuarios?
don·de es·tan los
ves·twa·ryos

Can I have a locker?
¿Puedo usar una
taquilla?
pwe·do oo·sar oo·na
ta·kee·lya

Where's the	*¿Dónde está …*	*don·de es·ta …*
nearest …?	*más cercano/a?* m/f	mas ther·ka·no/a
gym	*el gimnasio* m	el kheem·na·syo
swimming pool	*la piscina* f	la pees·thee·na
tennis court	*la pista* f *de tenis*	la pees·ta de te·nees

sports

131

What's the charge per ...?	¿Cúanto cobran por ...?	kwan·to ko·bran por ...
day	día	dee·a
game	partida	par·tee·da
hour	hora	o·ra
visit	visita	vee·see·ta
Can I hire a ...?	¿Es posible alquilar una ...?	es po·see·ble al·kee·lar oo·na ...
ball	pelota	pe·lo·ta
bicycle	bicicleta	bee·thee·kle·ta
court	cancha	kan·cha
racquet	raqueta	ra·ke·ta

fair play?

I disagree!	No estoy de acuerdo!	no es·toy de a·kwer·do
Yeah, sure!	Sí hombre!	see om·bre
Yes, but ...	Sí, pero ...	see pe·ro ...
Whatever.	Lo que sea.	lo ke se·a

diving

el buceo

I'd like to (go) ...	Me gustaría ...	me goos·ta·ree·a ...
explore wrecks	explorar naufragios	eks·plo·rar now·fra·khyos
learn to dive	aprender a bucear	a·pren·der a boo·the·ar
scuba diving	hacer submarinismo	a·ther soob·ma·ree·nees·mo
snorkelling	bucear con tubo	boo·the·ar kon too·bo

Where are some good diving sites?

¿Dónde hay buenos lugares   don·de ai bwe·nos loo·ga·res
para bucear?   pa·ra boo·the·ar

Are there jellyfish?

¿Hay medusas?   ai me·doo·sas

Where can we hire ...?

¿Dónde se puede alquilar ...?   don·de se pwe·de al·kee·lar ...

diving course	*curso* m *de buceo*	koor·so de boo·the·o
diving equipment	*equipo* m *de buceo*	e·kee·po de boo·the·o
flippers	*aletas* f pl	a·le·tas
mask	*gafas* f pl	ga·fas
wetsuits	*trajes* m pl	tra·khes
	isotérmicos	ee·so·ter·mee·kos

extreme sports

los deportes extremos

Are you sure this is safe?

¿De verdad que esto es   de ver·da ke es·to es
seguro?   se·goo·ro

Is the equipment secure?

¿Está seguro el equipo?   es·ta se·goo·ro el e·kee·po

This is insane!

¡Esto es una locura!   es·to es oo·na lo·koo·ra

abseiling	*rappel* m	ra·pel
bungy-jumping	*puenting* m	pwen·teen
caving	*espeleología* f	es·pe·le·o·lo·khee·a
game fishing	*pesca* f *deportiva*	pes·ka de·por·tee·va
mountain biking	*ciclismo* m *de*	thee·klees·mo de
	montaña	mon·ta·nya
rock-climbing	*escalada* f	es·ka·la·da

For phrases on hiking, see **outdoors**, page 137, and **camping**, page 58.

soccer/football

el fútbol

Who plays for (Real Madrid)?
*¿Quién juega en el
(Real Madrid)?*
kyen *khwe*·ga en el
(re·*al* ma·*dree*)

What a terrible team!
¡Qué equipo más espantoso!
ke e·*kee*·po mas es·pan·*to*·so

He's a great player.
Es un gran jugador.
es oon gran khoo·ga·*dor*

**He played brilliantly in the match
against (Italy).**
*Jugó de fenomenal
en el partido contra
(Italia).*
khoo·*go* de fe·no·me·*nal*
en el par·*tee*·do *kon*·tra
(ee·*ta*·lya)

Which team is at the top of the league?
*¿Qué equipo está en
primera posición en
la liga?*
ke e·*kee*·po es·*ta* en
pree·*me*·ra po·see·*thyon* en
la *lee*·ga

corner	saque m de esquina	sa·ke de es·kee·na
free kick	tiro m libre	tee·ro lee·bre
goalkeeper	portero m	por·te·ro
offside	fuera de juego	fwe·ra de khwe·go
penalty	penalty m	pe·nal·tee

sports talk

What a ...!	¡Qué ...!	ke ...
goal	gol	gol
pass	pase	pa·se

Your/My point.
Tu/Mi punto. too/mee *poon*·to

Kick it to me!
¡Pásamelo! pa·sa·me·lo

You're a good player.
Juegas bien. khwe·gas byen

Thanks for the game.
Gracias por el partido. gra·thyas por el par·tee·do

tennis

el tenis

Would you like to play tennis?
¿Quieres jugar al tenis? kye·res khoo·gar al te·nees

Can we play at night?
¿Se puede jugar de noche? se pwe·de khoo·gar de no·che

Game, set, match.
Juego, set y partido. khwe·go set ee par·tee·do

ace	ace m	eys
advantage	ventaja f	ven·ta·kha
fault	falta f	fal·ta
play doubles	jugar dobles	khoo·gar do·bles
(against)	(contra)	(kon·tra)
serve	saque m	sa·ke

water sports

Can I book a lesson?
¿Puedo reservar una clase? pwe·do re·ser·var oo·na kla·se

Is safety gear provided?
¿Proporcionan el equipo pro·por·thyo·nan el e·kee·po
de seguridad? de se·goo·ree·da

Are there any ...?	¿Hay ...?	ai ...
reefs	*arrecifes*	a·re·thee·fes
rips	*corrientes*	ko·ryen·tes
water hazards	*peligros en*	pe·lee·gros en
	el agua	el a·gwa

motorboat	*lancha* f *motora*	*lan*·cha mo·*to*·ra
sail	*vela* f	*ve*·la
surfboard	*tabla* f *de surf*	*ta*·bla de soorf
surfing	*surf* m	soorf
water-skis	*esquís* m pl *acuáticos*	es·*kees* a·kwa·tee·kos
wave	*ola* f	*o*·la

local sports

If you hear the sounds of bat, ball and exertion, it may be *pelotari*, pelota players, enjoying the traditional game of *pelota vasca*, a type of handball. It's also known as *jai-alai* in Basque.

ball	*pelota* f	pe·*lo*·ta
striker	*delantero/a* m/f	de·lan·*te*·ro/a
wall	*frontón* m	fron·*ton*

hiking

el excursionismo

There's plenty of walking, hiking and mountaineering to do in Spain. A recognised cross-country walking trail is known as *Gran Recorrido* (*GR*), gran re·ko·*ree*·do, while the shorter walking paths scattered throughout the country are called *Pequeños Recorridos* (*PR*), pe·*ke*·nyos re·ko·*ree*·dos.

Where can I ...?	¿Dónde puedo ...?	don·de pwe·do ...
buy supplies	comprar viveres	kom·prar vee·ver·es
find someone	encontrar a	en·kon·trar a
who knows	alguien que	al·gyen ke
this area	conozca el área	ko·noth·ka el a·re·a
get a map	obtener un mapa	ob·te·ner oon ma·pa
hire hiking gear	alquilar un equipo para ir de excursion	al·kee·lar oon e·kee·po pa·ra eer de eks·koor·syon

signs

Por Aquí a ...	por a·kee a ...	**This Way To ...**
Prohibido Acampar	pro·ee·bee·do a·kam·par	**No Camping**
Terreno de Cámping	te·re·no de kam·peen	**Camping Ground**

Where can I find out about hiking trails?

¿Dónde hay información
sobre caminos rurales de
la zona?

don·de ai een·for·ma·*thyon*
so·bre ka·*mee*·nos roo·*ra*·les
de la *tho*·na

How long is the trail?

¿Cuántos kilómetros
tiene el camino?

kwan·tos kee·*lo*·me·tros
tye·ne el ka·*mee*·no

How high is the climb?

¿A qué altura se escala?

a ke al·*too*·ra se es·*ka*·la

Do we need a guide?

¿Se necesita un guía?

se ne·the·*see*·ta oon *gee*·a

Are there guided treks?

¿Se organizan
excursiones guiadas?

se or·ga·*nee*·than
eks·koor·*syo*·nes gee·*a*·das

Do we need to take ...?	¿Se necesita llevar ...?	se ne·the·*see*·ta lye·*var* ...
bedding	algo en que dormir	al·go en ke dor·*meer*
food	comida	ko·*mee*·da
water	agua	a·gwa

Is the track ...?	¿Es ... el sendero?	es ... el sen·*de*·ro
(well-)marked	(bien) marcado	(byen) mar·*ka*·do
open	abierto	a·*byer*·to
scenic	pintoresco	peen·to·*res*·ko

Which is the ... route?	¿Cuál es el camino más ...?	kwal es el ka·*mee*·no mas ...
easiest	fácil	*fa*·theel
most interesting	interesante	een·te·re·*san*·te
shortest	corto	*kor*·to

Where's a ...?	¿Dónde hay ...?	don·de ai ...
camping site	un cámping	oon kam·peen
village	un pueblo	oon pwe·blo

Where are the ...?	¿Dónde hay ...?	don·de ai ...
showers	duchas	doo·chas
toilets	servicios	ser·vee·thyos

Where have you come from?
¿De dónde vienes?   de don·de vye·nes

How long did it take?
¿Cuánto ha tardado?   kwan·to a tar·da·do

Does this path go to ...?
¿Este camino va a ...?   es·te ka·mee·no va a ...

Can we go through here?
¿Se puede pasar por aquí?   se pwe·de pa·sar por a·kee

Is the water OK to drink?
¿Se puede beber el agua?   se pwe·de be·ber el a·gwa

I'm lost.
Estoy perdido/a. m/f   es·toy per·dee·do/a

Is it safe?
¿Es seguro?   es se·goo·ro

Is there a hut there?
¿Hay una cabaña allí?   ai oo·na ka·ba·nya a·lyee

When does it get dark?
¿A qué hora oscurece?   a ke o·ra os·koo·re·the

signs

| ¡Prohibido | pro·ee·bee·do | **No Swimming!** |
| Nadar! | na·dar | |

outdoors

139

at the beach

en la playa

Where's the ... beach?	*¿Dónde está la playa ...?*	*don·de es·ta la pla·ya ...*
best	*mejor*	me·*khor*
nearest	*más cercana*	mas ther·*ka*·na
nudist	*nudista*	noo·*dees*·ta

Is it safe to dive/swim here?
¿Es seguro bucear/ nadar aquí?
es se·*goo*·ro boo·the·*ar*/ na·*dar* a·*kee*

What time is high/low tide?
¿A qué hora es la marea alta/baja?
a ke o·ra es la ma·*re*·a *al*·ta/*ba*·kha

Do we have to pay?
¿Hay que pagar?
ai ke pa·*gar*

How much to rent ...?	*¿Cuánto por alquilar ... ?*	*kwan*·to por al·kee·*lar* ...
a chair	*una silla*	*oo*·na *see*·lya
a hut	*una cabaña*	*oo*·na ka·*ba*·nya
an umbrella	*un parasol*	oon pa·ra·*sol*

listen for ...

kwee·*da*·do kon la re·*sa*·ka
Cuidado con la resaca.
Be careful of the undertow.

es pe·lee·*gro*·so
¡Es peligroso!
It's dangerous!

e·res mo·*de*·lo
¿Eres modelo?
Are you a model?

SOCIAL

140

weather

What's the weather like?
¿Qué tiempo hace?   ke *tyem*·po *a*·the

What's the weather forecast?
¿Cuál es el pronóstico   kwal es el pro·*nos*·tee·ko
del tiempo?   del *tyem*·po

(Today) It's raining.
(Hoy) Está lloviendo.   (oy) es·*ta* lyo·*vyen*·do

(Today) It's snowing.
(Hoy) Está nevando.   (oy) es·*ta* ne·*van*·do

(Tomorrow) It will be raining.
(Mañana) Lloverá.   (ma·*nya*·na) lyo·ve·*ra*

Today it's ...	*Hoy hace ...*	oy *a*·the ...
Will it be ...	*Mañana*	ma·*nya*·na
tomorrow?	*hará ...?*	a·*ra* ...
cold	*frío*	*free*·o
freezing	*un frío que pela*	oon *free*·o ke *pe*·la
hot	*calor*	ka·*lor*
sunny	*sol*	sol
warm	*calor*	ka·*lor*
windy	*viento*	*vyen*·to

Where can I	*¿Dónde puedo*	*don*·de *pwe*·do
buy ...?	*comprar ...?*	kom·*prar* ...
a rain	*un*	oon
jacket	*impermeable*	eem·per·me·*a*·ble
sunblock	*crema solar*	*kre*·ma so·*lar*
an umbrella	*un paraguas*	oon pa·*ra*·gwas

hail	*granizo* m	gra·*nee*·tho
storm	*tormenta* f	tor·*men*·ta
sun	*sol* m	sol

flora & fauna

What ... is that?	¿Qué ... es ése/ésa? m/f	ke ... es e·se/e·sa
animal	animal m	a·nee·mal
bird	pájaro m	pa·kha·ro
flower	flor f	flor
plant	planta f	plan·ta
tree	árbol m	ar·bol

What's it used for?
¿Para qué se usa?　　　　　pa·ra ke se oo·sa

Can you eat the fruit?
¿Se puede comer la fruta?　se pwe·de ko·mer la froo·ta

Is it endangered?
¿Está en peligro　　　　　es·ta en pe·lee·gro
de extinción?　　　　　　de eks·teen·thyon

Is it ...?	¿Es ...?	es ...
common	común m&f	ko·moon
dangerous	peligroso/a m/f	pe·lee·gro·so/a
poisonous	venenoso/a m/f	ve·ne·no·so/a
protected	protegido/a m/f	pro·te·khee·do/a

For geographical and agricultural terms, and names of animals and plants, see the **dictionary**.

key language

lenguaje clave

The main meal in Spain, 'lunchtime' is called *la hora de comer*, la o·ra de ko·mer. It's served between 1.30pm and 4.30pm.

breakfast	*desayuno* m	de·sa·yoo·no
lunch	*comida* f	ko·mee·da
dinner	*cena* f	the·na
snack	*tentempié* m	ten·tem·pye
eat	*comer*	ko·mer
drink	*beber*	be·ber
daily special	*especial* m *del día*	es·pe·thyal del dee·a
set menu	*menú* m *del día*	me·noo del dee·a
I'd like ...	*Quisiera ...*	kee·sye·ra ...
Enjoy your meal!	*¡Buen provecho!*	bwen pro·ve·cho
I'm starving!	*¡Estoy*	es·toy
	hambriento/a! m/f	am·bryen·to/a

finding a place to eat

buscando un lugar para comer

Can you recommend a ...?	*¿Puede recomendar un/una ...?* m/f	pwe·de re·ko·men·dar oon/oo·na ...
bar	*bar* m	bar
cafe	*café* m	ka·fe
coffee bar	*cafetería* f	ka·fe·te·ree·a
restaurant	*restaurante* m	res·tow·ran·te

Are you still serving food?

| *¿Siguen sirviendo comida?* | see·gen seer·vyen·do ko·mee·da |

How long is the wait?

¿Cuánto hay que esperar?   kwan·to ai ke es·pe·rar

Where would you go for (a) ...?	*¿Adónde se va para ...?*	a·don·de se va pa·ra ...
celebration	*celebrar*	sel·e·brar
cheap meal	*comer barato*	ko·mer ba·ra·to
local specialities	*comer comida típica*	ko·mer ko·mee·da tee·pee·ka

I'd like to reserve a table for ...	*Quisiera reservar una mesa para ...*	kee·sye·ra re·ser·var oo·na me·sa pa·ra ...
(two) people	*(dos) personas*	(dos) per·so·nas
(eight) o'clock	*las (ocho)*	las (o·cho)

---

listen for ...

lo *syen*·to e·mos the·*ra*·do
Lo siento, hemos cerrado.   **Sorry, we're closed.**

no te·*ne*·mos *me*·sa
No tenemos mesa.   **We have no tables.**

oon mo·*men*·to
Un momento.   **One moment.**

I'd like ..., please.	*Quisiera ..., por favor.*	kee·sye·ra ... por fa·vor
a table for (five)	*una mesa para (cinco)*	oo·na me·sa pa·ra (theen·ko)
the (non-) smoking section	*(no) fumadores*	(no) foo·ma·do·res
the drink list	*la lista de bebidas*	la lees·ta de be·bee·das
the menu	*el menú*	el me·noo

Do you have ... ?	*¿Tienen ... ?*	tye·nen ...
children's meals	*comidas para niños*	ko·mee·das pa·ra nee·nyos
a menu in English	*un menú en inglés*	oon me·noo en een·gles

at the restaurant

Is it self-serve?
¿Es de autoservicio?
es de ow·to·ser·vee·thyo

Is service included in the bill?
¿La cuenta incluye servicio?
la kwen·ta een·kloo·ye ser·vee·thyo

What would you recommend?
¿Qué recomienda?
ke re·ko·myen·da

I'll have what they're having.
Tomaré lo mismo que ellos.
to·ma·re lo mees·mo ke e·lyos

Does it take long to prepare?
¿Tarda mucho en prepararse?
tar·da moo·cho en pre·pa·rar·se

What's in that dish?
¿Que lleva ese plato?
ke lye·va e·se pla·to

I'd like a local speciality.
Quisiera un plato típico.
kee·sye·ra oon pla·to tee·pee·ko

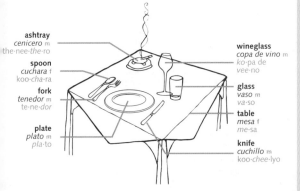

ashtray
cenicero m
the·nee·the·ro

spoon
cuchara f
koo·cha·ra

fork
tenedor m
te·ne·dor

plate
plato m
pla·to

wineglass
copa de vino m
ko·pa de vee·no

glass
vaso m
va·so

table
mesa f
me·sa

knife
cuchillo m
koo·chee·lyo

Are these complimentary?
¿Éstos son gratis? es·tos son gra·tees

We're just having drinks.
Sólo queremos tomar algo. so·lo ke·re·mos to·mar al·go

signs

Abierto	ab·yer·to	**Open**
Caliente	kal·yen·te	**Hot**
Cerrado	the·ra·do	**Closed**
Frío	free·o	**Cold**
Reservado	re·ser·va·do	**Reserved**
Servicios	ser·vee·thyos	**Toilets**

at the table

a la mesa

Please bring ...	*Por favor*	por fa·vor
	nos trae ...	nos tra·e ...
the bill	*la cuenta*	la kwen·ta
a glass	*un vaso*	oon va·so
a serviette	*una servilleta*	oo·na ser·vee·lye·ta
a wineglass	*una copa*	oo·na ko·pa
	de vino	de vee·no

I didn't order this.
Yo no he pedido esto. yo no e pe·dee·do es·to

listen for ...

le *goos·ta ...*
   ¿Le gusta ...? **Do you like ...?**

re·ko·*myen·do ...*
   Recomiendo ... **I suggest the ...**

*ko·*mo lo *kye·re pre·pa·ra·do*
   *¿Cómo lo quiere
   preparado?* **How would you like
that cooked?**

Aperitivos	a·pe·ree·*tee*·vos	Appetisers
Caldos	*kal*·dos	Soups
Cervezas	ther·*ve*·thas	Beers
De Entrada	de en·*tra*·da	Entrees
Digestivos	dee·khes·*tee*·vos	Digestifs
Ensaladas	en·sa·*la*·das	Salads
Licores	lee·*ko*·res	Spirits
Postres	*pos*·tres	Desserts
Refrescos	re·*fres*·kos	Soft Drinks
Segundos Platos	se·*goon*·dos *pla*·tos	Main Courses
Vinos Blancos	*vee*·nos *blan*·kos	White Wines
Vinos Dulces	*vee*·no *dool*·thes	Dessert Wines
Vinos	*vee*·nos	Sparkling
Espumosos	es·poo·*mo*·sos	Wines
Vinos Tintos	*vee*·nos *teen*·tos	Red Wines

talking food

hablando de comida

I love this dish.
Me encanta este plato. me en·*kan*·ta *es*·te *pla*·to

We love the local cuisine.
Nos encanta la comida nos en·*kan*·ta la ko·*mee*·da
típica de la zona. *tee*·pee·ka de la *tho*·na

That was delicious!
¡Estaba buenísimo! es·*ta*·ba bwe·*nee*·see·mo

My compliments to the chef.
Mi enhorabuena al mee en·o·ra·*bwe*·na al
cocinero. ko·thee·*ne*·ro

I'm full. *Estoy lleno/a.* m/f es·*toy* lye·no/a

This is ... *Esto está ...* *es*·to es·ta ...
  burnt *quemado* ke·*ma*·do
  (too) cold *(muy) frío* (mooy) *free*·o
  superb *exquisito* eks·kee·*see*·to

meals

> breakfast

What's a typical Spanish breakfast?

¿Cómo es un típico   ko·mo es oon tee·pee·ko
desayuno español?   de·sa·yoo·no es·pa·nyol

When's the breakfast served?

¿Cuándo se sirve   kwan·do se seer·ve
el desayuno?   el de·sa·yoo·no

omelette	*tortilla* f	tor·tee·lya
muesli	*muesli* m	mwes·lee
toast	*tostadas* f pl	tos·ta·das

> light meals

What's that called?	*¿Cómo se llama eso?*	ko·mo se lya·ma e·so
I'd like ..., please.	*Quisiera ..., por favor.*	kee·sye·ra ... por fa·vor
a piece	*un trozo*	oon tro·tho
a sandwich	*un sándwich*	oon san·weech
one slice	*una loncha*	oo·na lon·cha
that one	*ése/ésa* m/f	e·se/e·sa
two	*dos*	dos

For typical dishes see the **culinary reader**, page 161, and for other food items see the **dictionary**.

> condiments

Is there any ...?	¿Hay ...?	ai ...
chilli sauce	salsa de guindilla	sal·sa de geen·dee·lya
pepper	pimienta	pee·myen·ta
salt	sal	sal
tomato sauce/ ketchup	salsa de tomate	sal·sa de to·ma·te
vinegar	vinagre	vee·na·gre

methods of preparation

los métodos de cocción

I'd like it ...	Lo quiero ...	lo kye·ro ...
I don't want it ...	No lo quiero ...	no lo kye·ro ...
deep-fried	frito en aceite abundante	free·to en a·they·te a·boon·dan·te
medium	no muy hecho	no mooy e·cho
rare	vuelta y vuelta	vwel·ta ee vwel·ta
re-heated	recalentado	re·ka·len·ta·do
steamed	al vapor	al va·por
well-done	muy hecho	mooy e·cho
with the dressing on the side	con el aliño aparte	kon el a·lee·nyo a·par·te
without ...	sin ...	seen ...

For other specific meal requests, see **vegetarian & special meals**, page 159.

in the bar

Excuse me!	*¡Oiga!*	oy·ga
I'm next.	*Ahora voy yo.*	a·o·ra voy yo
I'll have ...	*Para mí ...*	pa·ra mee ...

Same again, please.
Otra de lo mismo.   o·tra de lo mees·mo

No ice, thanks.
Sin hielo, gracias.   seen ye·lo gra·thyas

I'll buy you a drink.
Te invito a una copa.   te een·vee·to a oo·na ko·pa

What would you like?
¿Qué quieres tomar?   ke kye·res to·mar

It's my round.
Es mi ronda.   es mee ron·da

You can get the next one.
La próxima la pagas tú.   la prok·see·ma la pa·gas too

How much is that?
¿Cuánto es eso?   kwan·to es e·so

How much alcohol does this contain?
¿Cuánto alcohol contiene?   kwan·to al·ko·ol kon·tye·ne

Do you serve meals here?
¿Sirven comidas aquí?   seer·ven ko·mee·das a·kee

listen for ...

a·kee tye·ne
¡Aquí tiene! — **Here you go!**

don·de le gus·ta·ree·a sen·tar·se
¿Dónde le gustaría sentarse? — **Where would you like to sit?**

en ke le pwe·do ser·veer
¿En qué le puedo servir? — **What can I get for you?**

kye·re to·mar al·go myen·tras es·pe·ra
¿Quiere tomar algo mientras espera? — **Would you like a drink while you wait?**

tapas

Tapas are scrumptious cooked bar snacks, available pretty much around the clock at bars and some clubs. You'll find they're free in some places, laid out in the bar for you to choose from. This follows village tradition at the turn of the century in the whole of Andalusia, as well as in Extremadura, Low Castile, Murcia and the working-class districts of Madrid and Barcelona.

Other places will rotate the dishes. Listen for ...

da·me oo·na pree·*me*·ra
¡Dame una primera!   **Give me a starter!**

oo·na se·*goon*·da
¡Una segunda!   **Give me a main dish!**

... as the bar attendant orders a different speciality each time from the cook. See if you can stay on your stool long enough to get back to number one again.

• how hungry are you?

banderilla f/	ban·de·ree·lya/	small tapa serving
moruno m/	mo·roo·no/	on bread or a
pinchito m	peen·chee·to	toothpick
ración f	ra·thyon	large tapa serving

• common tapas

montadito m	mon·ta·deet·o	bread-topped tapa
pan tumaca m	pan too·ma·ka	tapa of toasted bread rubbed with tomatoes & garlic, served with oil
queso m *en aceite*	ke·soh en a·say·tay	cheese in olive oil, served as a tapa

• regional tapas

naveganta f	na·ve·gan·ta	in Burgos
pintxo m	peen·cho	in Basque Country

nonalcoholic drinks

las bebidas no alcohólicas

I don't drink alcohol.
No bebo alcohol.   no *be*·bo al·ko·*ol*

(cup of) coffee ...	*(taza de) café ...*	*(ta*·tha de) ka·*fe* ...
(cup of) tea ...	*(taza de) té ...*	*(ta*·tha de) te ...
with milk	*con leche*	kon *le*·che
without sugar	*sin azúcar*	seen a·*thoo*·kar
soft drink	*refresco* m	re·*fres*·ko
... water	*agua ...*	*a*·gwa ...
boiled	*hervida*	er·*vee*·da
mineral	*mineral*	mee·ne·*ral*
(sparkling)	*(con gas)*	(kon gas)

alcoholic drinks

las bebidas alcohólicas

beer	*cerveza* f	ther·*ve*·tha
brandy	*coñac* m	ko·*nyak*
champagne	*champán* m	cham·*pan*
cocktail	*combinado* m	kom·bee·*na*·do
sangria (red-wine punch)	*sangría* f	san·*gree*·a
a shot of ...	*un chupito de ...*	oon choo·*pee*·to de ...
gin	*ginebra*	khee·*ne*·bra
rum	*ron*	ron
tequila	*tequila*	te·*kee*·la
vodka	*vodka*	*vod*·ka
whisky	*güisqui*	gwees·*kee*

Many Spanish bars provide massive plastic beakers of beer to cater for young revellers. It's cut with water and average tasting – but cheap and free flowing! These fountains of froth are called *minis*.

Other words you'll need when ordering a brew:

cerveza ...	ther·*ve*·tha ...	... beer
de barril	de ba·*ril*	draught
negra	*neg*·ra	dark
rubia	*roo*·bee·a	light
sin alcohol	sin al·*kol*	nonalcoholic
botellín m	bo·tel·*yin*	small bottle of beer (250 ml)
litrona f	lee·*tro*·na	litre bottle of beer
mediana f	me·dee·*a*·na	bottle of beer (300 ml)

a bottle/glass of	*una botella/*	*oo*·na bo·*te*·lya/
... wine	*copa de vino ...*	*ko*·pa de *vee*·no ...
dessert	*dulce*	*dool*·the
red	*tinto*	*teen*·to
rose	*rosado*	ro·*sa*·do
sparkling	*espumoso*	es·poo·*mo*·so
white	*blanco*	*blan*·ko
a ... of beer	*una ... de cerveza*	*oo*·na ... de ther·*ve*·tha
glass	*caña*	*ka*·nya
jug	*jarra*	*kha*·ra
pint	*pinta*	*peen*·ta

one too many?

Cheers!
¡Salud!
sa·*loo*

Thanks, but I don't feel like it.
Lo siento, pero no me apetece.
lo *syen*·to *pe*·ro no me a·pe·*te*·the

No thanks, I'm driving.
No gracias, tengo que conducir.
no *gra*·thyas *ten*·go ke kon·doo·*theer*

This is hitting the spot.
Me lo estoy pasando muy bien.
me lo es·*toy* pa·*san*·do mooy byen

I'm tired, I'd better go home.
Estoy cansado/a, mejor me voy a casa. m/f
es·*toy* kan·*sa*·do/a me·*khor* me voy a *ka*·sa

Where's the toilet?
¿Dónde está el lavabo?
don·de es·*ta* el la·*va*·bo

I'm feeling drunk.
Esto me está subiendo mucho.
es·to me es·*ta* soo·*byen*·do *moo*·cho

I feel fantastic!
¡Me siento fenomenal!
me *syen*·to fe·no·me·*nal*

I think I've had one too many.
Creo que he tomado demasiado.
kre·o ke e to·*ma*·do de·ma·*sya*·do

Can you call a taxi for me?
¿Me puedes pedir un taxi?
me *pwe*·des pe·*deer* oon *tak*·see

I don't think you should drive.
No creo que deberías conducir.
no *kre*·o ke de·be·*ree*·as kon·doo·*theer*

I'm pissed.
Estoy borracho/a. m/f
es·*toy* bo·*ra*·cho/a

I feel ill.
Me siento mal.
me *syen*·to mal

key language

A piece.	*Un trozo.*	oon *tro*·tho
A slice.	*Una loncha.*	oo·na *lon*·cha
That one.	*Ése.*	e·se
This.	*Esto.*	es·to
A bit more.	*Un poco más.*	oon *po*·ko mas
Less.	*Menos.*	me·nos
Enough!	*¡Basta!*	ba·sta
cooked	*cocido/a* m/f	ko·*thee*·do/a
dried	*seco/a* m/f	se·ko/a
fresh	*fresco/a* m/f	fres·ko/a
frozen	*congelado/a* m/f	kon·khe·*la*·do/a
raw	*crudo/a* m/f	*kroo*·do/a
smoked	*ahumado/a* m/f	a·oo·*ma*·do/a

buying food

How much?
  ¿Cuánto?　　　　　　kwan·to

How many?
  ¿Cuántos/as? m/f　　kwan·tos/as

How much is (a kilo of cheese)?
  ¿Cuánto vale (un kilo　kwan·to va·le (oon kee·lo
  de queso)?　　　　　de ke·so)

What's the local speciality?
  ¿Cuál es la especialidad　kwal es la es·pe·thya·lee·da
  de la zona?　　　　　de la tho·na

What's that?
  ¿Qué es eso?　　　　ke es e·so

en ke le *pwe*·do ser·*veer*
  ¿En qué le puedo servir?   **Can I help you?**

ke ke·*ree*·as
  ¿Qué querías?   **What would you like?**

no *ten*·go
  No tengo.   **I don't have any.**

Can I taste it?
  ¿Puedo probarlo/a? m/f   *pwe*·do pro·*bar*·lo/a

I'd like ...	*Póngame ...*	*pon*·ga·me ...
(three) pieces	*(tres) piezas*	(tres) *pye*·thas
(six) slices	*(seis) lonchas*	(seys) *lon*·chas
(two) kilos	*(dos) kilos*	(dos) *kee*·los
(200) grams	*(doscientos) gramos*	(dos·*thyen*·tos) *gra*·mos

Do you have ...?	*¿Tiene ...?*	*tye*·ne ...
anything cheaper	*algo más barato*	*al*·go mas ba·*ra*·to
any other kinds	*otros tipos*	*ot*·ros *tee*·pos

Where can I find the ... section?	*¿Dónde está la sección de ...?*	*don*·de es·*ta* la sek·*thyon* de ...
dairy	*productos lácteos*	pro·*dook*·tos *lak*·te·os
frozen goods	*productos congelados*	pro·*dook*·tos kon·khe·*la*·dos
fruit and vegetable	*frutas y verduras*	*froo*·tas ee ver·*doo*·ras
meat	*carne*	*kar*·ne
poultry	*aves*	*a*·ves

Where's the health-food section/store?
  ¿Dónde esta la sección/   *don*·de es·*ta* la sek·*thyon*/
  tienda de comida   *tyen*·da de ko·*mee*·da
  dietética?   dye·*te*·tee·ka

For food items, see the **culinary reader**, page 161, and the **dictionary**.

cooking utensils

Could I please borrow a/an ...?
¿Me puede prestar ...?   me *pwe*·de pres·*tar* ...

Where's a/an ...?
¿Dónde hay ...?   *don*·de ai ...

bottle opener	*abrebotellas* m	a·bre·bo·*te*·lyas
bowl	*bol* m	bol
can opener	*abrelatas* m	a·bre·*la*·tas
chopping board	*tabla* f *para cortar*	*tab*·la *pa*·ra *kor*·tar
cup	*taza* f	*ta*·tha
corkscrew	*sacacorchos* m	sa·ka·*kor*·chos
fork	*tenedor* m	ten·ne·*dor*
fridge	*nevera* m	ne·*ve*·ra
frying pan	*sartén* f	sar·*ten*
glass	*vaso* m	*va*·so
knife	*cuchillo* m	koo·*chee*·lyo
oven	*horno* m	*or*·no
plate	*plato* m	*pla*·to
saucepan	*cazo* m	*ka*·tho
spoon	*cuchara* f	koo·*cha*·ra
toaster	*tostadora* f	tos·ta·*do*·ra

For more cooking terminology, see the **dictionary**.

listen for ...

e·so es (oon man·*che*·go)
Eso es (un manchego).   **That's (a manchego).**

no *ke*·da mas
No queda más.   **There's none left.**

e·so es (*theen*·ko e·*oo*·ros)
Eso es (cinco euros).   **That's (five euros).**

al·go mas
¿Algo más?   **Anything else?**

useful amounts

Please give me ...	Por favor, deme ...	por fa·vor de·me ...
(100) grams	(cien) gramos	(thyen) gra·mos
half a dozen	una media docena	oo·na me·dya do·the·na
half a kilo	un medio kilo	oon me·dyo kee·lo
a kilo	un kilo	oon kee·lo
a bottle (of ...)	una botella (de ...)	oo·na bo·te·lya (de ...)
a jar	una jarra	oo·na kha·ra
a packet	un paquete	oon pa·ke·te
a tin	una lata	oo·na la·ta
(just) a little	(sólo) un poquito	(so·lo) oon po·kee·to
many	muchos/as m/f	moo·chos/as
more	más	mas
some	algunos/as m/f	al·goo·nos/as
less	menos	me·nos

ordering food

I'm vegetarian.
Soy vegetariano/a. m/f   soy ve·khe·ta·*rya*·no/a

Is there a (vegetarian) restaurant near here?
¿Hay un restaurante   ai oon res·tow·*ran*·te
(vegetariano) por aquí?   (ve·khe·ta·*rya*·no) por a·*kee*

Do you have ...   *¿Tienen comida ...?*   tye·nen ko·*mee*·da ...
food?
     halal   *halal*   a·*lal*
     kosher   *kosher*   ko·sher
     vegan   *vegetariana*   ve·khe·ta·*rya*·na
         estricta   es·*trik*·ta

I don't eat red meat.
No como carne roja.   no *ko*·mo *kar*·ne *ro*·kha

Is it cooked in/with butter?
¿Esta cocinado   es·ta ko·thee·*na*·do
en/con mantequilla?   en/kon man·te·*kee*·lya

Could you   *¿Me puede*   me *pwe*·de
prepare a meal   *preparar una*   pre·pa·*rar* oo·na
without ...?   *comida sin ...?*   ko·*mee*·da seen ...
     eggs   *huevo*   we·vo
     fish   *pescado*   pes·*ka*·do
     meat/fish   *caldo de carne/*   *kal*·do de *kar*·ne/
      stock   *pescado*   pes·*ka*·do
     pork   *cerdo*   *ther*·do
     poultry   *aves*   a·ves

Is this ...?	¿Esto es ...?	es·to es ...
free of animal produce	sin productos de animales	seen pro·dook·tos de a·nee·ma·les
free-range	de corral	de ko·ral
genetically modified	transgénico	trans·khe·nee·ko
gluten-free	sin gluten	seen gloo·ten
low in sugar	bajo en azúcar	ba·kho en a·thoo·kar
low-fat	bajo en grasas	ba·kho en gra·sas
organic	orgánico	or·ga·nee·ko
salt-free	sin sal	seen sal

special diets & allergies

regímenes especiales & alergias

I'm on a special diet.
Estoy a régimen especial.   es·toy a re·khee·men es·pe·thyal

I'm allergic to ...	Soy alérgico/a ... m/f	soy a·ler·khee·ko/a ...
dairy produce	a los productos lácteos	a los pro·dook·tos lak·te·os
honey	al miel	al myel
MSG	al glutamato monosódico	al gloo·ta·ma·to mo·no·so·dee·ko
nuts	a las nueces	a las nwe·thes
seafood	a los mariscos	a los ma·rees·kos
shellfish	a los crustáceos	a los kroos·ta·thyos

listen for ...

le pre·goon·ta·re al ko·thee·ne·ro
Le preguntaré
al cocinero.   **I'll check with the cook.**

pwe·de ko·mer ...
¿Puede comer ...?   **Can you eat ...?**

to·do lye·va (kar·ne)
Todo lleva (carne).   **It all has (meat) in it.**

This miniguide to Spanish cuisine lists dishes and ingredients in Spanish alphabetical order (see **alphabet**, page 11). Spanish nouns have their gender indicated by ⓜ or ⓕ. If it's a plural noun, you'll also see pl.

A

acebuche ⓜ a·the·*boo*·che *wild olive*
acedía ⓕ a·the·*dee*·a *plaice/flounder*
aceite ⓜ a·*they*·te *oil*
— **de girasol** de khee·ra·*sol*
sunflower oil
— **de oliva** de o·*lee*·va *olive oil*
— **de oliva virgen extra** de o·*lee*·va
veer·khen eks·tra *extra virgin olive oil*
aceituna ⓕ a·they·*too*·na *olive*
— **negra** ne·gra *black olive*
— **verde** ver·de *green olive*
ácido/a ⓜ/ⓕ a·thee·do/a *tart (of fruit)*
adobo ⓜ a·*do*·bo *marinade*
agrios ⓜ pl a·gryos *citrus fruits*
aguacate ⓜ a·gwa·*ka*·te *avocado*
aguaturma ⓕ a·gwa·*toor*·ma
Jerusalem artichoke
ajiaco ⓜ a·*khya*·ko *spicy potato dish*
ajoaceite ⓜ a·kho·a·*they*·te *garlic &*
oil sauce • garlic mayonnaise
ajoharina ⓕ a·kho·a·*ree*·na
potatoes stewed in garlic sauce
ajoarriero (al) a·kho·a·*rye*·ro (al) '*mule-*
driver's garlic' - *anything cooked in a*
sauce of onions, garlic & chilli
ala ⓕ a·la *(chicken) wing*
alajú ⓜ a·la·*khoo* *honey & almond cake*
albaricoque ⓜ al·ba·ree·*ko*·ke *apricot*
— **seco** se·ko *dried apricot*
albóndigas ⓕ pl al·*bon*·dee·gas
meatballs
— **de pescado** de pes·*ka*·do *fish balls*
alcachofas ⓕ pl al·ka·cho·fas *artichokes*
— **guisadas a la española** gee·*sa*·das
a la es·pa·*nyo*·la *artichokes in wine*
— **rellenas** re·*lye*·nas *stuffed artichokes*
alcaparra ⓕ al·ka·*pa*·ra *caper*

alioli ⓜ a·lee·o·*lee* *garlic mayonnaise*
almejas ⓕ pl al·*me*·khas
clams – superb eaten raw
— **a la marinera** a la ma·ree·*ne*·ra
clams in white wine
— **al horno** al or·no *baked clams*
almendrado ⓜ al·men·*dra*·do
almond cake or biscuit • chocolate
covered ice cream bar
almendras ⓕ pl al·*men*·dras *almonds*
alubia ⓕ a·*loo*·bya *haricot bean*
anacardo ⓜ a·na·*kar*·do *cashew nut*
anchoas ⓕ pl an·*cho*·as *anchovies –*
mostly eaten fresh, grilled or fried
angelote ⓜ an·khe·*lo*·te *monkfish*
anguila ⓕ an·*gee*·la *adult eel*
angulas ⓕ pl an·*goo*·las
baby eels – prized as a delicacy, they
resemble vermicelli
— **en all i pebre** en al ee *pe*·bre
baby eels with pepper & garlic
apio ⓜ a·pyo *celery*
arándano ⓜ a·ran·da·no *blueberry*
arenque ⓜ a·ren·ke *herring*
— **ahumado** a·oo·ma·do *kipper*
arroz ⓜ a·*roth* *rice*
— **a la Alcireña** a la al·thee·re·*nya*
baked rice dish
— **abanda (de València)** a·*ban*·da
(de va·*len*·thya) *fish paella*
— **con leche** kon *le*·che *rice pudding*
— **con pollo** kon po·lyo *chicken & rice*
— **integral** een·te·*gral* *brown rice*
— **marinera** ma·ree·*ne*·ra
seafood & rice
— **salvaje** sal·va·khe *wild rice*
asadillo ⓜ a·sa·*dee*·lyo
roasted red capsicums

asados ⓜ pl a·sa·dos *roast meats*

atún ⓜ a·toon
tuna – often served marinated & raw
— **al horno** al or·no *baked tuna*

avellana ⓕ a·ve·lya·na *hazelnut*

aves ⓕ pl a·ves *poultry*

azúcar ⓜ a·thoo·kar *sugar*

B

bacalao ⓜ ba·ka·low
cod – usually salted & dried
— **a la vizcaína** a la veeth·ka·ee·na
cod with chillies & capsicums
— **del convento** del kon·ven·to
cod with potatoes & spinach in broth

bacón ⓜ ba·kon *bacon*

barbo ⓜ bar·bo *red mullet*

barra ⓕ ba·ra *long stick of bread*

batata ⓕ ba·ta·ta *sweet potato*

beicon ⓜ bey·kon *streaky bacon rashers*

berberechos ⓜ pl ber·be·re·chos *cockles*
— **en vinagre** en vee·na·gre
cockles in vinegar

berenjenas ⓕ pl be·ren·khe·nas
eggplants
— **a la mallorquina** a la ma·lyor·kee·na
eggplants with garlic mayonnaise
— **con setas** kon se·tas
eggplants with mushrooms

berza ⓕ ber·tha *cabbage*
— **a la andaluza** a la an·da·loo·tha
cabbage & meat hotpot

besugo ⓜ be·soo·go *red bream*
— **a la Donostiarra** a la do·nos·tya·ra
barbecued red bream with garlic & paprika
— **estilo San Sebastián** es·tee·lo san se·bas·tyan *barbecued red bream with garlic & paprika*

bienmesabe ⓜ byen·me·sa·be *sponge cake, egg & almond confection*

bisbe ⓜ bees·be
black & white blood sausage

bistec ⓜ bees·tek *steak*
— **con patatas** kon pa·ta·tas
steak with chips

bizcocha ⓕ **manchega** beeth·ko·cha
man·che·ga *cake soaked in milk, sugar, vanilla & cinnamon*

bizcocho ⓜ beeth·ko·cho *sponge cake*
— **de almendra** de al·men·dra
almond cake
— **de avellana** de a·ve·lya·na
hazelnut cake

bizcochos ⓜ pl **borrachos** beeth·ko·chos
bo·ra·chos *cake soaked in liqueur*

bocadillo ⓜ bo·ka·dee·lyo
bread roll with a filling

bocas ⓕ pl **de la isla** bo·kas de la ees·la
large crab claws

bogavante ⓜ bo·ga·van·te *lobster*

bollo ⓜ bo·lyo *crusty bread roll*

bonito ⓜ bo·nee·to *white fleshy tuna*

boquerón ⓜ bo·ke·ron *whitebait*

boquerones ⓜ pl bo·ke·ro·nes
anchovies marinated in wine vinegar
— **fritos** free·tos *fried anchovies*

brama ⓕ bra·ma *sea bream*

bróculi ⓜ bro·ko·lee *broccoli*

budín ⓜ **de atún** boo·deen de a·toon
baked tuna pudding

bull ⓜ **de atún** bool de a·toon *rabbit with garlic & tuna boiled with potatoes*

buñuelitos ⓜ pl boo·nywe·lee·tos
small cheese or ham fritters
— **de San José** de san kho·se
lemon & vanilla crepes

buñuelo ⓜ boo·nywe·lo *fried pastry*

burrida ⓕ **de ratjada** boo·ree·da de
rat·kha·da *fish soup with almonds*

butifarra ⓕ **(blanca)** boo·tee·fa·ra
(blan·ka) *cured pork sausage*
— **con setas** kon se·tas
Catalan sausage with mushrooms

C

caballa ⓕ ka·ba·lya *mackerel*

cabra ⓕ ka·bra *goat*

cabracho ⓜ ka·bra·cho
scorpion fish • mullet

cacahuete ⓜ ka·ka·we·te *peanut*

cachelos ⓜ pl ka·che·los
potatoes with spicy sausage & pork

cádiz ⓕ ka·deeth
fresh goats' milk cheese

calabacín ⓜ ka·la·ba·theen zucchini

calabaza ⓕ ka·la·ba·tha pumpkin

calamares ⓜ pl ka·la·ma·res
calamari – popular fried or stuffed
— fritos a la romana free·tos a la
ro·ma·na squid rings fried in batter
— rellenos re·lye·nos stuffed squid

calçots ⓜ pl kal·sots spring onion-like
vegetables chargrilled and eaten with
a romesco dipping sauce

caldeirada ⓕ kal·dey·ra·da
salted cod & potatoes in a paprika
sauce • fish soup

caldereta ⓕ kal·de·re·ta stew
— asturiana as·too·rya·na fish stew
— de cordero de kor·de·ro lamb stew

caldillo ⓜ **de perro** kal·dee·lyo de pe·ro
'puppy dog soup' – stew of onions,
fresh fish & orange juice

caldo ⓜ kal·do
broth • clear soup • stock
— al estilo del Mar Menor
al es·tee·lo del mar me·nor
fish stew from the Mar Menor
— gallego ga·lye·go broth with haricot
beans, ham & sausage

callos ⓜ pl ka·lyos tripe

camarones fritos ⓜ pl ka·ma·ro·nes
free·tos deep-fried prawns

canagroc ka·na·grok mushroom

cañaillas ⓕ pl **de la Isla** ka·nyay·lyas
de la ees·la boiled sea snails

canelones ⓜ pl ka·na·lo·nes squares of
pasta for making cannelloni
— con espinaca kon es·pee·na·ka
cannelloni with spinach, anchovies &
bechamel
— con pescado kon pes·ka·do
cannelloni with cod, eggs &
mushrooms

canapés ⓜ pl **de fiambres** ka·na·pes de
fee·am·bres mini hors d'oeuvres with
ham, anchovies or cheese

cangrejo ⓜ kan·gre·kho
large-clawed crab usually eaten
steamed or boiled

cantalupo ⓜ kan·ta·loo·po
cantaloupe

canutillos ⓜ pl ka·noo·tee·lyos
cream biscuits

capones ⓜ pl **de Villalba** ka·po·nes de
vee·lyal·ba Christmas dish of chicken
marinated in brandy

caracoles ⓜ pl ka·ra·ko·les snails

caramelos ⓜ pl ka·ra·me·los
caramels • confection

cardos ⓜ pl fritos kar·dos free·tos
fried thistles

carne ⓕ kar·ne meat
— de membrillo de mem·bree·lyo
quince 'cheese'
— molida mo·lee·da minced meat

cassolada ⓕ ka·so·la·da potato &
vegetable stew with bacon & ribs

castaña ⓕ kas·ta·nya chestnut

caviar ⓜ ka·vyar caviar

caza ⓕ ka·tha game

cazón ⓜ ka·thon dogfish or shark with
a sweet scallop-like flavour

cazuelitas ⓕ pl **de langostinos**
San Rafael ka·thwe·lee·tas de
lan·gos·tee·nos san ra·fa·el
baked rice with seafood

cebolla ⓕ the·bo·lya onion

cecina ⓕ the·thee·na cured meat

cerdo ⓜ ther·do pork

cereales ⓜ pl the·re·a·les cereal

cereza ⓕ the·re·tha cherry
— silvestre seel·ves·tre
wild cherry

ciervo ⓜ thyer·vo deer

cigala ⓕ thee·ga·la crayfish

ciruela ⓕ thee·rwe·la plum
— pasa pa·sa prune

civet ⓜ **de llebre** see·vet de le·bre
hare stew

cochifrito ⓜ **de cordero**
ko·chee·free·to de kor·de·ro
lamb fried with garlic & lemon

cochinillo ⓜ ko·chee·nee·lyo
suckling pig
— **asado** a·sa·do *roast suckling pig*
— **de pelotas** de pe·lo·tas
meatball stew

coco ⓜ ko·ko *coconut*

codornices ⓕ pl **a la plancha**
ko·dor·nee·thes a la plan·cha
grilled quail

codorniz ⓕ ko·dor·neeth *quail*
— **con pimientos** kon pee·myen·tos
capsicums stuffed with quail

col ⓕ kol *cabbage*
— **lombarda** lom·bar·da *red cabbage*

coles ⓕ pl **de bruselas** ko·les de
broo·se·las *Brussels sprouts*

coliflor ⓕ ko·lee·flor *cauliflower*

conejo ⓜ ko·ne·kho *rabbit*
— **de monte** de mon·te *wild rabbit*

coquina ⓕ ko·kee·na *large clam*

corazón ⓜ ko·ra·thon *heart*

cordero ⓜ kor·de·ro *lamb*
— **al chilindrón** al chee·leen·dron
lamb in tomato & capsicum sauce
— **con almendras** kon al·men·dras
lamb in almond sauce

costillas ⓕ pl kos·tee·lyas *ribs*

crema ⓕ kre·ma *cream*
— **catalana** ka·ta·la·na *creme brulee*
— **de espinacas** de es·pee·na·kas
cream of spinach soup
— **de naranja** de na·ran·kha
orange cream dessert
— **de San José** de san kho·se
egg custard flavoured with cinnamon
— **de verduras** de ver·doo·ras
cream of vegetable soup

crocante ⓜ kro·kan·te *ice cream with
chopped nuts & chocolate*

CH

chalote ⓜ cha·lo·te *shallot*

champiñones ⓜ pl cham·pee·nyo·nes
cultivated white mushrooms

chanquetes ⓜ pl chan·ke·tes
whitebait • baby anchovies

chilindrón (al) chee·leen·dron (al)
*cooked in a tomato & red pepper
sauce*

chipirón ⓜ chee·pee·ron *baby squid –
very popular in the Basque Country*

chocolate ⓜ cho·ko·la·te *chocolate*
— **caliente** ka·lee·en·te
thick hot chocolate

chocos ⓜ pl cho·kos *squid*

chorizo ⓜ cho·ree·tho *spicy red cooked
sausage, similar to salami*
— **de Pamplona** de pam·plo·na
fine-textured, hard chorizo
— **de Salamanca** de sa·la·man·ka
chunky chorizo from Salamanca

chuletas ⓕ pl choo·le·tas
chops • cutlets
— **al sarmiento** al sar·myen·to *chops
prepared over wood from vines*
— **de buey** de bwey *ox chops*
— **de cerdo a la aragonesa**
de ther·do a la a·ra·go·ne·sa
baked pork chops with wine & onion

churros ⓜ choo·ros
*fried doughnut strips bought from
street-sellers or in cafes*

D

de soja de so·kha *with soya*

despojos ⓜ pl des·po·khos *offal*

dorada ⓕ **a la sal** do·ra·da a la sal
salted sea bream

dulce ⓜ dool·the *sweet*
— **de batata** de ba·ta·ta
sweet potato pudding from Málaga

dulces ⓜ pl dool·thes *sweets*
— **de las monjas** dool·thes de las
mon·khas *confectionery made by nuns
& sold in convents or cake shops*

E

embutidos ⓜ pl em·boo·tee·dos
generic name for cured sausages

empanada ⓕ em·pa·na·da *savoury pie*
— **de carne** de kar·ne *spicy meat pie*
— **de espinaca** de es·pee·na·ka
spinach pie

empanadilla ⓕ em·pa·na·*dee*·lya
small pie, either sweet or savoury

empanado ⓜ em·pa·*na*·do
coated in bread crumbs

emparedado ⓜ em·pa·re·*da*·do
sandwich

— **de jamón y espárragos**
de kha·*mon* ee es·*pa*·ra·gos
fried ham & asparagus rolls

empiñonado ⓜ em·pee·nyo·*na*·do *small
marzipan-filled pastry with pinenuts*

en salsa verde en *sal*·sa *ver*·de
in a parsley & garlic sauce

encurtidos ⓜ pl en·koor·*tee*·dos *pickles*

ensaimada ⓕ **mallorquina**
en·sai·*ma*·da ma·lyor·*kee*·na
spiral-shaped bun made with lard

ensalada ⓕ en·sa·*la*·da *salad*

— **de frutas** de *froo*·tas *fruit salad*

— **de patatas** de pa·*ta*·tas *potato salad*

— **del tiempo** del *tyem*·po
seasonal salad

— **mixta** *meeks*·ta *mixed salad*

escaldadillas ⓕ pl es·kal·da·*dee*·lyas
dough soaked in orange juice & fried

escalivada ⓕ es·ka·lee·*va*·da
roasted red capsicums in olive oil

escalopes ⓜ pl **de ternera rellenos**
es·ka·*lo*·pes de ter·*ne*·ra re·*lye*·nos
*deep fried veal cutlets stuffed with
egg & cheese*

espaguetis ⓜ es·pa·ge·tees
spaghetti

espárragos ⓜ pl es·*pa*·ra·gos *asparagus*

— **con dos salsas** kon dos *sal*·sas
*asparagus & tomato or paprika
mayonnaise*

— **en vinagreta** en vee·na·*gre*·ta
asparagus in vinaigrette

espinacas ⓕ pl es·pee·*na*·kas *spinach*

— **a la catalana** a la ka·ta·*la*·na
spinach with pinenuts & raisins

esqueixada ⓕ es·kee·*sha*·da *cod
dressed with olives, tomato & onion*

etxeko kopa e·*che*·ko *ko*·pa
ice cream dessert

F

fabada ⓕ **asturiana** fa·*ba*·da
as·too·*rya*·na *stew made with pork,
blood sausage & white beans*

faisán fai·*san* *pheasant*

faves ⓕ pl **a la catalana** *fa*·ves a la
ka·ta·*la*·na *broad beans with ham*

fiambres ⓜ pl fee·*am*·bres *cold meats*

— **surtidos** soor·*tee*·dos
selection of cold meats

fideos ⓜ pl fee·*de*·os *pasta noodles*

fideua ⓕ fee·*de*·wa
rice or noodles with fish & shellfish

fideus ⓜ pl **a la cassola** fee·*de*·oos a la
ka·so·la *Catalan noodle dish*

filete ⓜ fee·*le*·te
steak • any boneless slice of meat

— **a la parrilla** a la pa·*ree*·lya
grilled beef steak

— **de ternera** de ter·*ne*·ra *veal steak*

filloas ⓕ pl fee·*lyo*·as
Galician pancakes filled with cream

flan ⓜ flan *creme caramel*

flaó ⓕ fla·o *sweet cheese flan*

flor manchega ⓕ flor man·*che*·ga
deep-fried sweet wafers

frambuesa ⓕ fram·*bwe*·sa *raspberry*

frangellos ⓜ pl fran·*khe*·lyos *sweet
made from cornmeal, milk & honey*

fresa ⓕ *fre*·sa *strawberry*

fricandó ⓜ **de langostinos**
free·kan·*do* de lan·gos·*tee*·nos
shrimp in almond sauce

frite ⓜ *free*·te *lamb stew, served on
festive occasions*

fritos ⓜ pl *free*·tos *fritters*

— **con miel** kon myel
honey-roasted fritters

fritura ⓕ free·*too*·ra *mixed fried fish*

fruta ⓕ *froo*·ta *fruit*

— **variada** va·*ree*·a·da
selection of fresh fruit

frutas ⓕ pl **en almíbar** *froo*·tas en
al·*mee*·bar *fruit in syrup*

frutos ⓜ pl **secos** *froo*·tos *se*·kos
nuts & dried fruit

fuet ⓕ foo·*et* *thin pork sausage*

G

gachas ① pl **manchegas** *ga*·chas
man·che·gas *flavoured porridge*

galleta ① ga·*lye*·ta *biscuit*

gambas ① pl *gam*·bas *prawns*
— **a la plancha** a la *plan*·cha
grilled prawns
— **en gabardina** en ga·bar·*dee*·na
prawns in batter

Gamonedo ⓜ ga·mo·*ne*·do *sharp-
tasting cheese, smoked & cured*

garbanzos ⓜ pl gar·*ban*·thos *chickpeas*
— **con cebolla** kon the·*bo*·lya
chickpeas in onion sauce
— **tostados** tos·*ta*·dos
roasted chickpeas (sold as a snack)

garbure ① gar·*boo*·re *green vegetable
soup • pork & ham dish*

garúm ⓜ ga·*room olive & anchovy dip*

Gata-Hurdes ga·ta·*oor*·des *cheese*

gazpacho ⓜ gath·*pa*·cho
cold tomato soup
— **andaluz** an·da·*looth* *cold tomato
soup with chopped salad vegetables*
— **pastoril** pas·to·*reel*
rabbit stew with tomato & garlic

gazpachos ⓜ pl **manchegos**
gath·*pa*·chos man·*che*·gos
game & vegetable hotpot

Gaztazarra ⓜ gath·ta·*tha*·ra *cheese*

gitano ⓜ khee·*ta*·no
Andalusian chickpea & tripe stew

gofio ⓜ *go*·fyo
toasted cornmeal or barley

granadilla ① gra·na·*dee*·lya
passion fruit

grano ⓜ *gra*·no *grain*
— **largo** *lar*·go *long-grain (rice)*

gratinado ⓜ **de berenjenas**
gra·tee·*na*·do de be·ren·*khe*·nas
eggplant gratin

Grazalema ① gra·tha·*le*·ma
semi-cured sheep's milk cheese

guindilla ① geen·*dee*·lya
mild green chilli

guisado ⓜ gee·*sa*·do *stew*
— **de cordero** de kor·*de*·ro
lamb ragout
— **de ternera** de ter·*ne*·ra *veal ragout*

guisante ⓜ gee·*san*·te *pea*
— **seco** *se*·ko *split pea*
— **mollar** mo·*lyar snow pea*

guisantes ⓜ pl **con jamón a la
española** gee·*san*·tes kon kha·*mon* a
la es·pa·*nyo*·la *pea & ham dish*

guisat ⓜ **de marisco** gee·*sat* de
ma·*rees*·ko *stew made with seafood*

guiso ⓜ **de conejo estilo canario**
gee·*so* de ko·*ne*·kho es·*tee*·lo ka·*na*·ryo
rabbit stew

guiso ⓜ **de rabo de toro** gee·*so* de *ra*·bo
de *to*·ro *stewed bull's tail with potatoes*

H

habas ① pl a·bas *broad beans*
— **a la granadina** a la gra·na·*dee*·na
broad beans with eggs & ham
— **fritas** *free*·tas
fried broad beans (sold as a snack)

habichuela ① a·bee·*chwe*·la *white bean*

hamburguesa ① am·boor·*ge*·sa
hamburger

harina ① a·*ree*·na *flour*
— **integral** een·te·*gral wholemeal flour*

helado ⓜ e·*la*·do *ice cream*

hígado ⓜ *ee*·ga·do *liver*

higo ⓜ *ee*·go *fig*
— **seco** *se*·ko *dried fig*

hogaza ① o·*ga*·tha
dense, thick-crusted bread

hoja ① **de parra** o·kha de *pa*·ra
vine leaf

hojaldres ⓜ pl o·*khal*·dres
small flaky pastries covered in sugar

hojas ① pl **verdes** o·khas *ver*·des
green vegetables

hornazo ⓜ or·*na*·tho
bread stuffed with sausage

hortalizas ① pl or·ta·*lee*·thas
vegetables

huevo m *we·vo egg*
— **cocido** ko·*thee*·do *boiled egg*
— **de chocolate** de cho·ko·*la*·te *chocolate egg*
— **frito** *free*·to *fried egg*

huevos m pl *we*·vos *egg dishes*
— **a la flamenca** a la fla·*men*·ka *baked vegetables with egg & ham*
— **al estilo Sóller** al es·*tee*·lo so·lyer *fried eggs served with a milk & vegetable sauce*
— **en salsa agria** en *sal*·sa a·grya *boiled eggs in wine & vinegar*
— **escalfados** es·kal·*fa*·dos *poached eggs*
— **revueltos** re·*vwel*·tos *scrambled eggs*

J

jabalí m kha·ba·*lee wild boar*
— **con salsa de castaños** kon *sal*·sa de kas·*ta*·nyos *wild boar in chestnut sauce*

jamón m kha·mon *ham*
— **cocido** ko·*thee*·do *cooked ham*
— **ibérico** ee·*ber*·ik·o *ham from the Iberian pig, said to be the best in Spain*
— **serrano** se·*ra*·no *cured mountain ham*

jengibre m khen·*gee*·bre *ginger*

jerez (al) khe·*reth* (al) *in a sherry sauce*

judía f khoo·*dee*·a *fresh green bean • dried kidney bean*

judías f pl **del tío Lucas** khoo·*dee*·as del *tee*·o *loo*·kas *bean stew with garlic & bacon*

judías f pl **verdes a la castellana** khoo·*dee*·as ver·des a la kas·te·*lya*·na *fried capsicums, garlic & green beans*

judiones m pl **de la granja** kho·dee·o·nes de la *gran*·kha *pork & bean stew*

K

kiskilla kees·*kee*·lya *shrimp (also spelled quisquilla)*

L

langosta f lan·*gos*·ta *lobster*
— **a la ibicenca** a la ee·bee·*then*·ka *lobster with stuffed squid*

langostinos m pl lan·gos·*tee*·nos *king prawns*
— **a la plancha** a la *plan*·cha *grilled king prawns*

lavanco m la·van·ko *wild duck*

lechuga f le·*choo*·ga *lettuce*

legumbres f pl le·*goom*·bres *pulses • vegetables • vegetable dishes*
— **secas** se·kas *dried pulses*

leguminosas f pl le·goo·mee·*no*·sas *legumes*

lengua f *len*·gwa *tongue*
— **a la aragonesa** a la a·ra·go·*ne*·sa *tongue in tomato & capsicum sauce*

lenguado m len·*gwa*·do *sole*
— **al chacolí con hongos** al cha·ko·*lee* kon *on*·gos *sole with white wine & mushrooms*

lenguados m pl **al plato** len·*gwa*·dos al *pla*·to *sole & mushroom casserole*

lenguas f pl **con salsa de almendras** *len*·gwas kon *sal*·sa de al·*men*·dras *tongue in almond sauce*

lentejas f pl len·*te*·khas *lentils*

liebre f *lye*·bre *hare*
— **con castañas** kon kas·*ta*·nyas *hare with chestnuts*
— **estofada** es·to·*fa*·da *stewed hare*

lima f *lee*·ma *lime*

limón m lee·mon *lemon*

lomo m *lo*·mo *fillet • loin • sirloin*
— **curado** koo·*ra*·do *cured pork sausage*
— **de cerdo** de *ther*·do *loin of pork*

longaniza f lon·ga·*nee*·tha *chorizo, long & skinny sausage*

lubina f loo·*bee*·na *sea bass*
— **a la marinera** a la ma·ree·*ne*·ra *sea bass in parsley sauce*

lucio m *loo*·thyo *pike*

LL

llagostí ⓜ **a l'allioli**
lyan·gos·tee a la·lyee·o·lee
grilled prawns in garlic mayonnaise

llenguado ⓜ **a la nyoca** lyen·gwa·do a
la *nyo*·ka *sole with pine nuts & raisins*

M

macedonia ⓕ **de frutas** ma·the·*do*·nya
de froo·tas *fruit salad*

macedonia ⓕ **de verduras**
ma·the·*do*·nya de ver·*doo*·ras
mixed vegetables

magdalena ⓕ ma·da·*le*·na
small fairy cake to dunk in coffee

magras ⓕ pl *ma*·gras
fried eggs, ham, cheese & tomato

maíz ⓜ ma·*eeth* maize • *corn*
— tierno *tyer*·no *sweetcorn*

mandarina ⓕ man·da·*ree*·na
tangerine • mandarin

mango ⓜ *man*·go *mango*

manitas ⓕ pl **de cerdo** ma·*nee*·tas de
ther·do *pig's trotters*

manitas ⓕ pl **de cordero** ma·*nee*·tas de
kor·*de*·ro *leg of lamb*

manteca ⓕ man·*te*·ka *lard*

mantecado ⓜ man·te·*ka*·do
a soft lard biscuit • dairy ice cream

mantequilla ⓕ man·te·*kee*·lya *butter*
— sin sal seen sal *unsalted butter*

manzana ⓕ man·*tha*·na *apple*

manzanas ⓕ **asadas** man·*tha*·nas
a·*sa*·das *baked apples*

margarina ⓕ mar·ga·*ree*·na *margarine*

marinera (a la) ma·ree·*ne*·ra (a la)
cooked or served in a white wine sauce

mariscos ⓜ ma·*rees*·kos
shellfish • seafood

marmitako mar·mee·*ta*·ko
fresh tuna & potato casserole

marrano ⓜ ma·*ra*·no *pork*

mar y cel ⓜ mar ee sel *dish of sausages,
rabbit, shrimp & angler fish*

masa ⓕ *ma*·sa *pastry (dough)*

mayonesa ⓕ ma·yo·*ne*·sa *mayonnaise*

medallones ⓜ pl **de merluza**
me·da·*lyo*·nes de mer·*loo*·tha
hake steaks

mejillones ⓜ pl me·khee·*lyo*·nes *mussels*
— al vino blanco al vee·no *blan*·ko
mussels in white wine
— con salsa kon *sal*·sa
mussels with tomato sauce

mel ⓕ **i mató** mel ee ma·*to*
a dessert of curd cheese with honey

melocotón ⓜ me·lo·ko·*ton* *peach*

melocotones ⓜ pl **al vino** me·lo·ko·*to*·nes
al vee·no *peaches in red wine*

melón ⓜ me·*lon* *melon*

membrillo ⓜ mem·*bree*·lyo *quince*

menestra ⓕ me·*nes*·tra
mixed vegetable stew
— de pollo de *po*·lyo
chicken & vegetable stew

merengue ⓜ me·*ren*·ge *meringue*

merluza ⓕ mer·*loo*·tha *hake*

mermelada ⓕ mer·me·*la*·da *marmalade*

mero ⓜ *me*·ro
halibut • grouper • sea bass

miel ⓕ myel *honey*
— de azahar de a·*tha*·ar
orange blossom honey
— de caña de *ka*·nya *treacle*

migas ⓕ pl *mee*·gas
fried cubes of bread with capsicums
— a la aragonesa a la a·ra·go·*ne*·sa
*fried bread with bacon rashers in
tomato sauce*
— mulatas moo·*la*·tas *cubes of bread
soaked in chocolate & fried*

mojarra ⓕ mo·*kha*·ra *type of sea bream*

moje ⓜ **manchego** mo·*khe* man·*che*·go
cold broth with black olives

mojete ⓜ mo·*khe*·te
*dipping sauce for bread, made from
potatoes, garlic, tomatoes & paprika*
— murciano moor·*thya*·no
fish & capsicum dish

mojo ⓜ *mo*·kho *spicy capsicum sauce*

mollejas ⓕ pl mo·*lye*·khas *sweetbreads*

mollete ⓜ mo·lye·te *soft round bap roll*
monas ⓕ pl **de pascua** mo·nas de pas·kwa *Easter cakes • figures made of chocolate*
mongetes ⓕ pl **seques i butifarra** mon·zhe·tes se·kes ee boo·tee·fa·ra *haricot beans with roasted pork sausage*
mora ⓕ mo·ra *blackberry*
moraga ⓕ **de sardina** mo·ra·ga de sar·dee·na *fresh anchovies on a spit*
morcilla ⓕ mor·thee·lya *black pudding, often stewed with beans & vegetables*
mortadela ⓕ mor·ta·de·la *mortadella sausage*
morteruelo ⓜ mor·te·rwe·lo *pate dish containing offal, game & spices*
mostachones ⓜ pl mos·ta·cho·nes *small cakes for dipping in coffee or hot chocolate (also spelled* mostatxones*)*
mostaza ⓕ mos·ta·tha *mustard*
— en grano en gra·no *mustard seed*
múgil ⓜ moo·kheel *grey mullet*
mujol ⓜ **guisado** moo·khol gee·sa·do *red mullet*
mus ⓜ **de chocolate** moos de cho·ko·la·te *chocolate mousse*
muslo ⓜ moos·lo *(chicken) leg & thigh*

N

nabo ⓜ na·bo *root vegetable • turnip*
naranja ⓕ na·ran·kha *orange*
nata ⓕ na·ta *cream*
— agria a·grya *sour cream*
— montada mon·ta·da *whipped cream*
natillas ⓕ pl na·tee·lyas *creamy custard dessert*
— de chocolate de cho·ko·la·te *chocolate custard*
navaja ⓕ na·va·kha *razor clam*
nécora ⓕ ne·ko·ra *small crab*
nueces ⓕ pl new·thes *nuts*
nuez ⓕ nweth *nut*
— de América de a·me·ree·ka *pecan nut*
— de nogal de no·gal *walnut*

Ñ

ñora ⓕ nyo·ra *sweet red capsicum (usually dried)*

O

oca ⓕ o·ka *goose*
olla ⓕ o·lya *meat & vegetable stew • cooking pot*
oreja ⓕ **de mar** o·re·kha de mar *abalone*
ostiones ⓜ pl **a la gaditana** os·tyo·nes a la ga·dee·ta·na *Cádiz oysters with garlic, parsley & bread crumbs*
ostra ⓕ os·tra *oyster*
oveja ⓕ o·ve·kha *mutton*

P

pá ⓜ **amb oli** pa amb o·lee *toasted bread with garlic & olive oil*
pacana ⓕ pa·ka·na *pecan*
paella ⓕ pa·e·lya *rice dish which has many regional variations*
— marinera ma·ree·ne·ra *paella with fish & seafood*
— zamorana tha·mo·ra·na *paella with meat*
palitos ⓜ pl **de queso** pa·lee·tos de ke·so *cheese straws*
palmera ⓕ pal·me·ra *leaf-shaped flaky pastry, often coated in chocolate*
palomitas ⓕ pl pa·lo·mee·tas *popcorn*
pan ⓜ pan *bread*
— aceite a·they·te *flat round bread*
— árabe a·ra·be *pita bread*
— de Alá de a·la *'Allah's Bread' – dessert*
— de boda de bo·da *sculpted bread traditionally made for weddings*
— de centeno de then·te·no *rye bread*
— duro doo·ro *stale bread, used for toasting & eating with olive oil*
— integral een·te·gral *wholemeal bread*

panaché ⓜ pa·na·*che*
  mixed vegetable stew

panallets ⓜ pl pa·na·*lyets*
  marzipan sweets

panceta ① pan·*the*·ta
  salt-cured, streaky bacon

panchineta ① pan·chee·*ne*·ta
  almond tart

panecillo ⓜ pa·ne·*thee*·lyo
  small bread roll

panojas ① pl **malagueñas** pa·*no*·khas
  ma·la·ge·nyas sardine dish

papas ① pl **arrugadas**
  pa·pas a·roo·*ga*·das
  potatoes boiled in their jackets

pargo ⓜ *par*·go sea bream

parrillada ① pa·ree·*lya*·da grilled meat
  — **de mariscos** de ma·*rees*·kos
  seafood grill

pastel ⓜ pas·*tel* cake
  — **de boda** de *bo*·da wedding cake
  — **de chocolate** de cho·ko·*la*·te
  chocolate cake
  — **de cierva** de *thyer*·va meat pie
  — **de cumpleaños** de koom·ple·a·*nyos*
  birthday cake

pastelitos ⓜ pl **de miel** pas·te·*lee*·tos
  de myel honey fritters

pataco ⓜ pa·*ta*·ko
  tuna & potato stew

patatas ① pl pa·*ta*·tas potatoes
  — **a la riojana** a la ree·*o*·kha·na
  potatoes with chorizo & paprika
  — **alioli** a·lee·o·lee
  potatoes in garlic mayonnaise
  — **bravas** *bra*·vas
  potatoes in spicy tomato sauce
  — **con chorizo** kon cho·*ree*·tho
  potatoes with chorizo
  — **estofadas** es·to·*fa*·das
  boiled potatoes

pato ⓜ pa·to duck
  — **a la sevillana** a la se·vee·*lya*·na
  duck with orange sauce
  — **alcaparrada** al·ka·pa·*ra*·da
  duck with capers & almonds

pavo ⓜ *pa*·vo turkey

pececillos ⓜ pl pe·the·*thee*·lyos
  small fish

pechina ① pe·*chee*·na scallop

pecho ⓜ *pe*·cho breast of lamb

pechuga ① pe·*choo*·ga
  breast of poultry

pepinillo ⓜ pe·pee·*nee*·lyo gherkin

pepino ⓜ pe·*pee*·no cucumber

pepitoria ① pe·pee·*to*·rya
  sauce made with egg & almond

pepitos ⓜ pl pe·*pee*·tos chocolate
  eclair cakes filled with custard

pera ① *pe*·ra pear

La Peral ① la pe·*ral* soft cheese

perca ① *per*·ka perch

perdices ① pl per·*dee*·thes partridges
  — **a la manchega** a la man·*che*·ga
  partridge in red wine & capsicums
  — **con chocolate** kon cho·ko·*la*·te
  partridge with chocolate

perdiz ① per·*deeth* partridge

peregrina ① pe·re·*gree*·na scallop

pericana ① pe·ree·*ka*·na dish of olives,
  cod oil, capsicums & garlic

perrito ⓜ **caliente** pe·*ree*·to ka·lee·*en*·te
  hot dog

pescada ① *á* **galega** pes·*ka*·da a
  ga·*le*·ga hake fried in olive oil &
  served with garlic & paprika sauce

pescadilla ① pes·ka·*dee*·lya
  whiting • young hake

pescaditos ⓜ pl **rebozados**
  pes·ka·*dee*·tos re·bo·*tha*·dos
  small fish fried in batter

pescado ⓜ pes·*ka*·do fish
  — **a l'all cremat** a lal kre·*mat*
  fish in burnt garlic

pescaíto ⓜ **frito** pes·ka·*ee*·to *free*·to
  tiny fried fish

pestiños ⓜ pl pes·*tee*·nyos
  honey-coated aniseed pastries, fried
  with filling

pez ① **espada** peth es·*pa*·da swordfish
  — **frito** *free*·to
  fried swordfish steaks on a skewer

picada ① pee·ka·da *mixture of garlic, parsley, toasted almonds & nuts, often used to thicken sauces*

picadillo ⑩ pee·ka·dee·lyo *salad consisting of diced vegetables*
— **de atún** de a·toon *salad made with diced tuna & capsicums*
— **de ternera** de ter·ne·ra *minced veal*

pichón ⑩ pee·chon *pigeon*

pichones ⑩ pl asados pee·cho·nes a·sa·dos *roast pigeons*

pilotes ① pl pee·lo·tes *Catalan meatballs*

pimiento ⑩ pee·myen·to *capsicum*
— **amarillo** a·ma·ree·lyo *yellow capsicum*
— **rojo** ro·kho *red capsicum*
— **verde** ver·de *green capsicum*

pimientos ⑩ pl pee·myen·tos *capsicums (the ones from El Bierzo are especially good)*
— **a la riojana** a la ree·o·kha·na *roast red capsicum fried in oil & garlic*
— **al chilindrón** al chee·leen·dron *capsicum casserole*

piña ① pee·nya *pineapple*

pinchito ⑩ **moruno** peen·chee·to mo·roo·no *lamb & chicken kebabs*

piñón ⑩ pee·nyon *pinenut*

pinta ① pee·ta *pinto bean*

pintada ① peen·ta·da *guinea fowl*

piquillo ⑩ pee·kee·lyo *sweet & spicy capsicums*

pistacho ⑩ pees·ta·cho *pistachio nut*

pisto ⑩ **manchego** pees·to man·che·go *zucchini with capsicum & tomato, fried or stewed*

plátano ⑩ pla·ta·no *banana*

pochas ① pl po·chas *beans*
— **a la riojana** a la ree·o·kha·na *beans with chorizo in spicy paprika sauce*
— **con almejas** kon al·me·khas *beans with clams*

pollo ⑩ po·lyo *chicken*
— **asado** a·sa·do *roast chicken*
— **con samfaina** kon sam·fai·na *chicken with mixed vegetables*
— **en escabeche** en es·ka·be·che *marinated chicken*
— **en salsa de ajo** en sal·sa de a·kho *chicken in garlic sauce*
— **granadina** gra·na·dee·na *chicken with wine & ham*
— **y langosta** ee lan·gos·ta *chicken with crayfish*

pulpo ⑩ **a feira** pool·po a fey·ra *spicy boiled octopus*

polvorón ⑩ pol·vo·ron *almond shortbread, often eaten at Christmas*

pomelo ⑩ po·me·lo *grapefruit*

postre ⑩ pos·tre *dessert*
— **de naranja** de na·ran·kha *cream-filled oranges*

potaje ⑩ po·ta·khe *broth*
— **castellano** kas·te·lya·no *broth with beans & sausages*
— **de garbanzos** de gar·ban·thos *broth with chickpeas*
— **de lentejas** de len·te·khas *lentil broth*

pote ⑩ **gallego** po·te ga·lye·go *stew*

potito ⑩ po·tee·to *jar of baby food*

pringada ① preen·ga·da *bread dipped in sauce • a marinated sandwich*

productos ⑩ pl **biológicos** pro·dook·tos bee·o·lo·khee·kos *organic produce*

productos ⑩ pl **del mar** pro·dook·tos del mar *seafood products*

productos ⑩ pl **lácteos** pro·dook·tos lak·te·os *dairy products*

puchero ⑩ poo·che·ro *casserole*

pudin ⑩ poo·din *pudding*

puerco ⑩ pwer·ko *pork*

puerro ⑩ pwe·ro *leek*

pulpo ⑩ pool·po *octopus*

punta ① **de diamante** poon·ta de dya·man·te *confection from Valencia*

porrusalda ① po·roo·sal·da *cod & potato stew*

Q

queso m ke·so *cheese*
 — **azul** a·thool *blue cheese*
 — **crema** kre·ma *cream cheese*
quisquilla f kees·kee·lya
 shrimp (also spelled kiskilla)

R

rábano m ra·ba·no *radish*
rabas f **en salsa verde** ra·bas en sal·sa
 ver·de *squid in green sauce*
rabassola f ra·ba·so·la *mushroom*
rape m ra·pe *monkfish*
 — **a la gallega** a la ga·lye·ga
 monkfish with potatoes & garlic sauce
 — **a la Monistrol** a la mo·nees·trol
 monkfish with bechamel sauce
redondo m re·don·do *round (of beef)*
 — **al horno** al or·no *roast beef*
regañaos m pl re·ga·nya·os
 *pastry stuffed with sardines &
 red capsicum*
relleno m re·lye·no *stuffing*
remolacha f re·mo·la·cha *beetroot*
reo m re·o *sea trout*
repollo m re·po·lyo *cabbage*
repostería f re·pos·te·ree·a
 confectionery
requesón m re·ke·son
 cottage cheese
riñón m ree·nyon *kidney*
róbalo m ro·ba·lo *haddock • sea bass*
rodaballo m ro·da·ba·lyo *turbot • brill*
romero m ro·me·ro *rosemary*
romesco m ro·mes·ko *sweet red
 capsicum, almond & garlic sauce*
rosca f **de carne** ros·ka de kar·ne
 meatloaf wrapped in bacon
rosco m ros·ko *small sweet bun*
rossejat m ro·se·dyat
 rice with fish & shellfish
rovellons m pl **a la plancha** ro·ve·lyons
 a la plan·cha *garlic mushrooms*
ruibarbo m roo·ee·bar·bo *rhubarb*

S

salchicha f sal·chee·cha *pork sausage*
salchichón m sal·chee·chon
 cured & peppery white sausage
salmón m sal·mon *salmon*
 — **a la ribereña** a la ree·be·re·nya
 salmon in a cider sauce
 — **ahumado** a·oo·ma·do
 smoked salmon
salmonete m sal·mo·ne·te *red mullet*
salmorejo m sal·mo·re·kho
 *thick gazpacho soup made from
 tomato, bread, olive oil, vinegar,
 garlic & green capsicum*
 — **de Córdoba** de kor·do·ba
 *gazpacho soup made with more
 vinegar than usual*
salpicón m sal·pee·kon
 fish or meat salad
salsa f sal·sa *sauce*
 — **alioli** a·lee·o·lee *garlic & olive oil
 vinaigrette • garlic mayonnaise*
 — **de holandesa** de o·lan·de·sa
 hollandaise sauce
 — **de mayonesa** de ma·yo·ne·sa
 mayonnaise sauce
 — **de tomate** de to·ma·te *tomato sauce*
 — **inglesa** een·gle·sa
 Worcestershire sauce
 — **tártara** tar·ta·ra *tartar sauce*
 — **verde** ver·de *parsley & garlic sauce*
samfaina f sam·fai·na
 grilled vegetable sauce
sancocho m san·ko·cho
 fish dish served with potatoes
sandía f san·dee·a *watermelon*
sándwich m san·weech *sandwich*
 — **mixto** meeks·to
 toasted ham & cheese sandwich
sanocho m **canario** sa·no·cho ka·na·ryo
 baked monkfish with potatoes
sardinas f sar·dee·nas *sardines*
 — **a la parrilla** a la pa·ree·lya
 sardines grilled
 — **en cazuela** en ka·thwe·la
 sardines served in a clay pot

sargo ⓜ sar·go *bream*

sepia ⓕ se·pya *cuttlefish*

sesos ⓜ pl se·sos *brains*

setas ⓕ pl se·tas *wild mushrooms*
— **a la kashera** a la ka·she·ra
sauteed wild mushrooms
— **rellenas** re·lye·nas
mushrooms stuffed

sofrit pagès ⓜ so·freet pa·zhes
vegetable stew

sofrito ⓜ so·free·to *fried tomato sauce*

soja ⓕ so·kha *soya bean*

soldaditos ⓜ pl **de Pavía** sol·da·dee·tos
de pa·vee·a *cod fritters*

solomillo ⓜ so·lo·mee·lyo *fillet*

sopa ⓕ so·pa *soup*
— **del día** del dee·a *soup of the day*

sopas ⓕ pl **de leche** so·pas de le·che
*pieces of bread soaked in milk &
cinnamon*

sopas ⓕ pl **engañadas**
so·pas en·ga·nya·das
*soup made from capsicum, onion
shoots, vinegar, figs & grapes*

sorbete ⓜ sor·be·te *sorbet*

sorroputún ⓜ so·ro·poo·toon
tuna casserole

suizo ⓜ swee·tho *sugared bun*

sukaldi soo·kal·dee *beef stew*

suquet ⓜ soo·ket *clams in almond sauce*

suquet de peix ⓜ soo·ket de peysh
fish stew

suspiros ⓜ pl **de monja** soos·pee·ros de
mon·kha *'nun's sighs' – custard sweets*

T

tallarines ⓜ pl ta·lya·ree·nes
pasta noodles

tarta ⓕ tar·ta *cake • tart*
— **de almendra** de al·men·dra
almond tart
— **de manzana** de man·tha·na
apple tart

tartaleta ⓕ tar·ta·le·ta *tartlet*

tartaletas ⓕ pl **de huevos revueltos**
tar·ta·le·tas de we·vos re·vwel·tos
scrambled egg tartlets

ternera ⓕ ter·ne·ra *veal*
— **a la sevillana** a la se·vee·lya·na
veal served with wine & olives
— **en cazuela con berenjenas**
en ka·thwe·la kon be·ren·khe·nas
veal & eggplant casserole

tocino ⓜ to·thee·no
salted pork • bacon
— **del cielo** del thye·lo
*creamy dessert made with egg yolk &
sugar, with a caramel topping*

tocrudo ⓜ to·kroo·do
*'everything raw' – salad of meat,
garlic, onion & green capsicum*

tomate ⓜ to·ma·te *tomatoes*
— **(de) pera** (de) pe·ra
plum tomato
— **frito** free·to *tinned tomato sauce*

tomates ⓜ pl to·ma·tes
— **enteros y pelados** en·te·ros ee
pe·la·dos *tinned whole tomatoes*
— **rellenos de atún** re·lye·nos de
a·toon *tomatoes stuffed with tuna*

toro ⓜ to·ro *bull meat*

torrefacto ⓜ to·re·fak·to
dark-roasted coffee beans

torrija ⓕ to·ree·kha *French toast*

torta ⓕ tor·ta *pie • tart • flat bread*
— **de aceite** de a·they·te *sweet, flat
cake or biscuit made with oil*
— **pascualina** pas·kwa·lee·na
spinach & egg pie, eaten at Easter

tortilla ⓕ tor·tee·lya *omelette*
— **española** es·pa·nyo·la
potato & onion omelette
— **francesa** fran·the·sa
plain omelette

tortillas ⓕ pl **de camarones** tor·tee·lyas
de ka·ma·ro·nes *shrimp fritters*

tortita ⓕ tor·tee·ta *waffle*

tostada ⓕ tos·ta·da *toasted bread*

tocino ⓜ to·thee·no *bacon*

tripas ⓕ pl tree·pas *intestines • guts*

trucha ⓕ troo·cha *trout*
— **a la marinera** a la ma·ree·ne·ra
trout in a white wine sauce

truchas ① pl *troo*·chas *trout*
— **a la navarra** a la na·*va*·ra
trout with ham
— **con vino y romero**
kon *vee*·no ee ro·*me*·ro
trout with red wine & rosemary
trufa ① *troo*·fa *truffle*
— **tarta** *tar*·ta *chocolate truffle cake*
tumbet (de peix) ⑩
toom·*bet* (de peysh) *vegetable
souffle, sometimes containing fish*
turrón ⑩ too·*ron* *Spanish nougat*

U

uva ① *oo*·va *grape*
— **de corinto** de ko·*reen*·to *currant*
— **pasa** *pa*·sa *raisin*
— **sultana** sool·*ta*·na *sultana*

V

vacuno ⑩ va·*koo*·no *beef*
venado ⑩ ve·*na*·do *venison*

verduras ① ver·*doo*·ras *vegetables*
vieira ① vee·*ey*·ra *scallop*
villagodio ⑩ vee·lya·go·*dyo* *large steak*
vinagre ⑩ vee·*na*·gre *vinegar*
visita ① vee·*see*·ta *almond cake*

Y

yemas ① pl *ye*·mas *small round cakes*
yogur ⑩ yo·*goor* *yogurt*

Z

zanahoria ① tha·na·o·*rya* *carrot*
zarangollo ⑩ tha·ran·go·*lyo*
fried zucchini
zarzamora ① thar·tha·*mo*·ra
blackberry
zarzuela ① **de mariscos** thar·*thwe*·la
de ma·*rees*·kos *spicy shellfish stew*
zarzuela ① **de pescado** thar·*thwe*·la de
pes·*ka*·do *fish in almond sauce*
zurrukutano thoo·roo·koo·*ta*·no
cod & green capsicum soup

emergencies

emergencias

Help!	*¡Socorro!*	so·*ko*·ro
Stop!	*¡Pare!*	*pa*·re
Go away!	*¡Váyase!*	va·ya·se
Thief!	*¡Ladrón!*	lad·*ron*
Fire!	*¡Fuego!*	*fwe*·go
Watch out!	*¡Cuidado!*	kwee·*da*·do

It's an emergency.
Es una emergencia. es *oo*·na e·mer·*khen*·thya

There's been an accident.
Ha habido un accidente. a a·*bee*·do oon ak·thee·*den*·te

Do you have a first-aid kit?
¿Tiene un botiquín de tye·ne oon bo·tee·*keen* de
primeros auxilios? pree·*me*·ros owk·*see*·lyos

Call the police!
¡Llame a la policía! *lya*·me a la po·lee·*thee*·a

Call a doctor!
¡Llame a un médico! *lya*·me a oon *me*·dee·ko

Call an ambulance!
¡Llame a una *lya*·me a *oo*·na
ambulancia! am·boo·*lan*·thya

Could you help me, please?
¿Me puede ayudar, me *pwe*·de a·yoo·*dar*
por favor? por fa·*vor*

I have to use the telephone.
> *Necesito usar el teléfono.*
> ne·the·*see*·to oo·*sar* el te·*le*·fo·no

I'm lost.
> *Estoy perdido/a.* m/f
> es·*toy* per·*dee*·do/a

Where are the toilets?
> *¿Dónde están los servicios?*
> *don*·de es·*tan* los ser·*vee*·thyos

the underground

Petty crime is particularly common in Madrid and Barcelona. Try not to stand near the train doors and keep money out of sight. If someone attempts to rob you, try screaming these phrases at the top of your lungs:

Leave me alone!
> *¡Déjame en paz!*
> *de*·kha·me en path

Help, thief!
> *¡Socorro, al ladron!*
> so·*ko*·ro al lad·*ron*

police

la policía

In an emergency, call the police, who will then put you through to other emergency services (fire brigade and ambulance). For more on making a call, see **communications**, page 72.

Where's the police station?
> *¿Dónde está la comisaría?*
> *don*·de es·*ta* la ko·mee·sa·*ree*·a

I want to report an offence.
> *Quiero denunciar un delito.*
> *kye*·ro de·noon·*thyar* oon de·*lee*·to

It was him/her.
> *Fue él/ella.*
> fwe el/e·lya

He/She tried to assault me.
> *Él/Ella intentó asaltarme.*
> el/e·lya een·ten·*to* a·sal·*tar*·me

He/She tried to rob me.
Él/Ella intentó robarme.   el/e·lya een·ten·to ro·bar·me

I've been robbed.
Me han robado.   me an ro·ba·do

I've been raped.
He sido violado/a. m/f   e see·do vee·o·la·do/a

My ... was stolen.
Mi ... fue robado/a. m/f   mee ... fwe ro·ba·do/a

My ... were stolen.
Mis ... fueron robados/as. m/f   mee ... fwe·ron ro·ba·dos/as

I've lost my ...   *He perdido ...*   e per·dee·do ...
  bags   *mis maletas*   mees ma·le·tas
  money   *mi dinero*   mee dee·ne·ro
  passport   *mi pasaporte*   mee pa·sa·por·te

I apologise.
Lo siento.   lo syen·to

I didn't realise I was doing anything wrong.
No sabía que estaba   no sa·bee·a ke es·ta·ba
haciendo algo mal.   a·thyen·do al·go mal

I'm innocent.
Soy inocente.   soy ee·no·then·te

I (don't) understand.
(No) Entiendo.   (no) en·tyen·do

I want to contact my embassy/consulate.
Quiero ponerme en   kye·ro po·ner·me en
contacto con mi   kon·tak·to kon mee
embajada/consulado.   em·ba·kha·da/kon·soo·la·do

Can I call a lawyer?
¿Puedo llamar a un   pwe·do lya·mar a oon
abogado?   a·bo·ga·do

I need a lawyer who speaks English.
Necesito un abogado ne·the·*see*·to oon a·bo·*ga*·do
que hable inglés. ke a·ble een·*gles*

Can I pay an on-the-spot fine?
¿Podemos pagar una po·*de*·mos pa·*gar* oo·na
multa al contado? *mool*·ta al kon·*ta*·do

Can I have a copy, please?
¿Puede darme una copia, pwe·de *dar*·me oo·na *ko*·pya
por favor? por fa·*vor*

I have insurance.
Tengo seguro. ten·go se·*goo*·ro

This drug is for personal use.
Esta droga es para uso es·ta *dro*·ga es *pa*·ra oo·so
personal. per·so·*nal*

I have a prescription for this drug.
Tengo receta para esta ten·go re·*the*·ta *pa*·ra es·ta
droga. *dro*·ga

What am I accused of?
¿De qué me acusan? de ke me a·*ku*·san

the police may say ...

You have overstayed your visa.
El plazo de tu el *pla*·tho de too
visado se ha pasado. vee·*sa*·do se a pa·*sa*·do

You'll be charged with ...
Será acusado/a de ... m/f se·*ra* a·koo·*sa*·do/a de ...

He'll/She'll be charged with ...
Él/Ella será acusado/a el/e·lya se·*ra* a·koo·*sa*·do/a
de ... de ...

assault	asalto m	a·*sal*·to
possession	posesión f	po·se·*syon*
(of illegal	(de sustancias	(de soos·*tan*·thyas
substances)	ilegales)	ee·le·*ga*·les)
shoplifting	ratería f	ra·te·*ree*·a
speeding	exceso m de	eks·*the*·so de
	velocidad	ve·lo·thee·*da*

doctor

el médico

Where's the nearest ...?	*¿Dónde está ... más cercano/a?* m/f	*don*·de es·*ta* ... mas ther·*ka*·no/a
chemist	*la farmacia* f	la far·*ma*·thya
dentist	*el dentista* m	el den·*tees*·ta
doctor	*el médico* m	el *me*·dee·ko
hospital	*el hospital* m	el os·pee·*tal*
medical centre	*el consultorio* m	el kon·sool·*to*·ryo
optometrist	*el oculista* m	el o·koo·*lees*·ta

I've been vaccinated for ...	*Estoy vacunado/a contra ...* m/f	es·*toy* va·koo·*na*·do/a *kon*·tra ...
He's/She's been vaccinated for ...	*Está vacunado/a contra ...* m/f	es·*ta* va·koo·*na*·do/a *kon*·tra ...
tetanus	*el tétano*	el *te*·ta·no
typhoid	*la tifus*	la *tee*·foos
hepatitis A/B/C	*la hepatitis A/B/C*	la e·pa·*tee*·tees a/be/the
... fever	*la fiebre ...*	la *fye*·bre ...

I need a doctor (who speaks English).
Necesito un doctor (que hable inglés).
ne·the·*see*·to oon dok·*tor* (ke *a*·ble een·*gles*)

I'm sick.
Estoy enfermo/a. m/f
es·*toy* en·*fer*·mo/a

Could I see a female doctor?
¿Puede examinarme una doctora?
pwe·de ek·sa·mee·*nar*·me *oo*·na dok·*to*·ra

For women's medical issues, see **women's health**, page 183.

the doctor may say ...

What's the problem?
¿Qué le pasa?　　　　　ke le *pa*·sa

Where does it hurt?
¿Dónde le duele?　　　*don*·de le *dwe*·le

Do you have a temperature?
¿Tiene fiebre?　　　　*tye*·ne *fye*·bre

How long have you been like this?
¿Desde cuándo se　　　*des*·de *kwan*·do se
siente así?　　　　　　*syen*·te a·*see*

Have you had this before?
¿Ha tenido esto antes?　a te·*nee*·do *es*·to *an*·tes

Have you had unprotected sex?
¿Ha tenido relaciones　a te·*nee*·do re·la·*thyo*·nes
sexuales sin　　　　　sek·*swa*·les seen
protección?　　　　　pro·tek·*thyon*

Are you allergic?
¿Tiene Usted alergias?　*tye*·ne oos·*te* a·*ler*·khyas

Are you on medication?
¿Se encuentra　　　　se en·*kwen*·tra
bajo medicación?　　　*ba*·kho me·dee·ka·*thyon*

You need to be admitted to hospital.
Necesita ingresar　　　ne·the·*see*·ta een·gre·*sar*
en un hospital.　　　　en oon os·pee·*tal*

How long are you travelling for?
¿Por cuánto tiempo　　por *kwan*·to *tyem*·po
está viajando?　　　　es·*ta* vya·*khan*·do

**You should have it checked when
you go home.**
Debería revisarlo　　　de·be·*ree*·a re·vee·*sar*·lo
cuando vuelva a casa.　*kwan*·do *vwel*·va a *ka*·sa

Do you ...?	*¿Usted ...?*	oos·te ...
drink	*bebe*	*be*·be
smoke	*fuma*	*foo*·ma
take drugs	*toma drogas*	*to*·ma *dro*·gas

I've run out of my medication.
Se me terminaron los
medicamentos.
se me ter·mee·*na*·ron los
me·dee·ka·*men*·tos

This is my usual medicine.
Éste es mi medicamento
habitual.
es·te es mee me·dee·ka·*men*·to
a·bee·too·*al*

My prescription is ...
Mi receta es ...
mee re·*the*·ta es ...

I don't want a blood transfusion.
No quiero que me hagan
una transfusión de
sangre.
no *kye*·ro ke me *a*·gan
oo·na trans·foo·*syon* de
san·gre

Please use a new syringe.
Por favor, use una
jeringa nueva.
por fa·*vor oo*·se *oo*·na
khe·*reen*·ga *nwe*·va

I need new ...	*Necesito ...*	ne·the·*see*·to ...
	nuevas.	*nwe*·vas
contact	*lentes de*	*len*·tes de
lenses	*contacto*	kon·*tak*·to
glasses	*gafas*	*ga*·fas

For cost and receipts, see **money**, page 35.

symptoms & conditions

I have ...
Tengo ...
ten·go ...

I've recently had ...
Hace poco he tenido ...
a·the *po*·ko e te·*nee*·do ...

There's a history of ...
Hay antecedentes de ...
ai an·te·the·*den*·tes de ...

I'm on regular medication for ...
Estoy bajo
medicación para ...
es·*toy ba*·kho
me·dee·ka·*thyon pa*·ra ...

health

181

asthma	*asma* m	*as*·ma
diarrhoea	*diarrea* f	dee·a·*re*·a
fever	*fiebre* f	*fye*·bre
infection	*infección* f	in·fek·*thyon*
sprain	*torcedura* f	tor·the·*doo*·ra

It hurts here.
Me duele aquí. — me *dwe*·le a·*kee*

I've been injured.
He sido herido/a. m/f — e *see*·do e·*ree*·do/a

I've been vomiting.
He estado vomitando. — e es·*ta*·do vo·mee·*tan*·do

I'm dehydrated.
Estoy deshidratado/a. m/f — es·*toy* de·seed·ra·*ta*·do/a

I can't sleep.
No puedo dormir. — no *pwe*·do dor·*meer*

I think it's the medication I'm on.
Me parece que son los — me pa·*re*·the ke son los
medicamentos que — me·dee·ka·*men*·tos ke
estoy tomando. — es·*toy* to·*man*·do

I have a rash.
Tengo una erupción — *ten*·go *oo*·na e·roop·*thyon*
cutánea. — koo·*ta*·ne·a

I have an infection.
Tengo una infección. — *ten*·go *oo*·na in·fek·*thyon*

I feel …	*Me siento …*	me *syen*·to …
better	*mejor* m&f	me·*khor*
depressed	*deprimido/a* m/f	de·pree·*mee*·do
dizzy	*mareado/a* m/f	ma·re·a·do
shivery	*destemplado/a* m/f	des·tem·*pla*·do
strange	*raro/a* m/f	*ra*·ro
weak	*débil* m&f	*de*·beel
worse	*peor* m&f	pe·*or*

For more symptoms & conditions, see the **dictionary**.

women's health

(I think) I'm pregnant.
(Creo que) Estoy embarazada.
(kre·o ke) es·*toy* em·ba·ra·*tha*·da

I haven't had my period for ... weeks.
Hace ... semanas que no me viene la regla.
a·the ... se·*ma*·nas ke no me *vye*·ne la *reg*·la

I'm on the Pill.
Tomo la píldora.
to·mo la *peel*·do·ra

I've noticed a lump here.
He notado un bulto aquí.
e no·*ta*·do oon *bool*·to a·*kee*

I have period pain.
Tengo dolor menstrual.
ten·go do·*lor* mens·troo·*al*

contraception	*anti-conceptivos* m pl	an·tee·kon·thep·*tee*·vos
pregnancy test	*prueba* f *de embarazo*	*prwe*·ba de em·ba·ra·*tho*
the morning-after pill	*píldora* f *del día siguiente*	*peel*·do·ra del *dee*·a see·*gyen*·te

the doctor may say ...

Are you pregnant?
¿Está embarazada?
es·*ta* em·ba·ra·*tha*·da

You're pregnant.
Está embarazada.
es·*ta* em·ba·ra·*tha*·da

When did you last have your period?
¿Cuándo le vino la regla por última vez?
kwan·do le *vee*·no la *reg*·la por *ool*·tee·ma veth

Are you using contraception?
¿Usa anticonceptivos?
oo·sa an·tee·kon·thep·*tee*·vos

Do you have your period?
¿Tiene la regla?
tye·ne la *reg*·la

allergies

I'm allergic to ...	Soy alérgico/a ... m/f	soy a·ler·khee·ko/a ...
He/She is allergic to ...	Es alérgico/a ... m/f	es a·ler·khee·ko/a ...
antibiotics	a los antibióticos	a los an·tee·byo·tee·kos
anti-inflammatories	a los anti-inflamatorios	a los an·tee·een·fla·ma·to·ryos
aspirin	a la aspirina	a la as·pee·ree·na
bees	a las abejas	a las a·be·khas
codeine	a la codeína	a la ko·de·ee·na
nuts	a las nueces	a las nwe·thes
peanuts	a los cacahuetes	a los ka·ka·we·tes
penicillin	a la penicilina	a la pe·nee·thee·lee·na
pollen	al polen	al po·len

For more food-related allergies, see **vegetarian & special meals**, page 160.

I have a skin allergy.
Tengo una alergia en la piel.
ten·go oo·na a·ler·khya en la pyel

I'm on a special diet.
Estoy a régimen especial.
es·toy a re·khee·men es·pe·thyal

antihistamines	anti-histamínicos m pl	an·tee·ees·ta·mee·nee·kos
inhaler	inhalador m	een·a·la·dor
injection	inyección f	een·yek·thyon
sulphur-based drugs	drogas con base de azufre f pl	dro·gas kon ba·se de a·thoo·fre

alternative treatments

tratamientos alternativos

I don't use Western medicine.
No uso la medicina occidental.
no oo·so la me·dee·thee·na ok·thee·den·tal

I prefer ...
Prefiero ...
pre·fye·ro ...

Can I see someone who practises ...?
¿Puedo ver a alguien que practique ...?
pwe·do ver al·gyen ke prak·tee·ke ...

aromatherapy	*aromaterapia* f	a·ro·ma·te·ra·pya
chiropractor	*quiropráctico* m	kee·ro·prak·tee·ko
meditation	*meditación* f	me·dee·ta·thyon
reflexology	*reflexología* f	re·flek·so·lo·khee·a

waiting room

Here are some tips on Spanish etiquette in public places.
• Men usually wait for women to be seated before they take a seat themselves, and when they finally do it's the guys who cross their legs at the knees, not the ladies.
• Yawning and stretching when you have an audience, no matter how small, is considered inappropriate.

parts of the body

las partes del cuerpo

My ... hurts.
Me duele ...
me dwe·le ...

I can't move my ...
No puedo mover ...
no pwe·do mo·ver ...

I have a cramp in my ...
Tengo calambres en ...
ten·go ka·lam·bres en ...

My ... is swollen.
Mi ... está hinchado.
mee ... es·ta een·cha·do

health

185

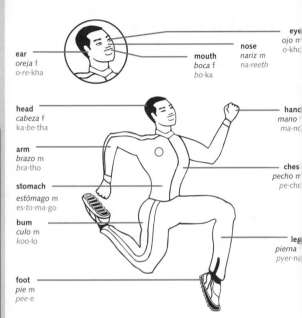

eye
ojo m
o·kho

nose
nariz m
na·reeth

mouth
boca f
bo·ka

ear
oreja f
o·re·kha

head
cabeza f
ka·be·tha

arm
brazo m
bra·tho

stomach
estómago m
es·to·ma·go

bum
culo m
koo·lo

foot
pie m
pee·e

hand
mano
ma·no

chest
pecho m
pe·cho

leg
pierna
pyer·na

For other parts of the body, see the **dictionary**.

chemist

la farmacia

Is there a (night) chemist nearby?
   *¿Hay una farmacia (de
   guardía) por aquí?*
   ai oo·na far·ma·thya (de
   gwar·dee·a) por a·kee

I need something for ...
   Necesito algo para ...
   ne·the·see·to al·go pa·ra ...

I have a prescription.
   Tengo receta médica.
   ten·go re·the·ta me·dee·ka

a to·*ma*·do es·to an·tes
¿Ha tomado esto antes? **Have you taken this before?**

de·be ter·mee·*nar* el tra·ta·*myen*·to
Debe terminar el tratamiento. **You must complete the course.**

dos *ve*·thes al *dee*·a (kon la ko·*mee*·da)
Dos veces al día (con la comida). **Twice a day (with food).**

es·ta·*ra lees*·to en (*veyn*·te mee·*noo*·tos)
Estará listo en (veinte minutos). **It'll be ready to pick up in (20 minutes).**

Do I need a prescription for ...?
¿Necesito receta para ...? ne·the·*see*·to re·*the*·ta pa·ra ...

How many times a day?
¿Cuántas veces al día? *kwan*·tas *ve*·thes al *dee*·a

For pharmaceutical items, see the **dictionary**.

dentist

el dentista

I have a broken tooth.
Se me ha roto un diente. se me a *ro*·to oon *dyen*·te

I have a toothache.
Me duele una muela. me *dwe*·le *oo*·na *mwe*·la

a·bra *Abra.* **Open wide.**
no se *mwe*·va *No se mueva.* **Don't move.**
en·*khwa*·ge *¡Enjuague!* **Rinse!**

health

I've lost a filling.
Se me ha caído un   se me a ka·*ee*·do oon
empaste.   em·*pas*·te

My orthodontic braces broke/fell off.
Se me rompió/cayó el   se me rom·*pyo*/ka·*yo* el
aparato dental.   a·pa·*ra*·to den·*tal*

My gums hurt.
Me duelen las encías.   me *dwe*·len las en·*thee*·as

I don't want it extracted.
No quiero que me lo saquen.   no *kye*·ro ke me lo *sa*·ken

I need a/an ...   *Necesito …*   ne·the·*see*·to ...
    anaesthetic   *una anestesia*   *oo*·ne a·nes·*te*·sya
    filling   *un empaste*   oon em·*pas*·te

signs

Asistencia Sanitaria	a·see·*sten*·thee·a sa·nee·*ta*·ree·a	**First Aid**
Farmacia	far·ma·*thee*·a	**Pharmacy/ Drug Store**
Horas de Visita	o·ras de vee·*see*·ta	**Visiting Hours**
Hospital	o·*spee*·tal	**Hospital**
Médico	*me*·dee·ko	**Doctor**
Planta	*plan*·ta	**Ward**
Urgencias	ur·*khen*·thee·as	**Casualty/ Emergency**

SUSTAINABLE TRAVEL

As the climate change debate heats up, the matter of sustainability becomes an important part of the travel vernacular. In practical terms, this means assessing our impact on the environment and local cultures and economies – and acting to make that impact as positive as possible. Here are some basic phrases to get you on your way …

communication & cultural differences

Would you like me to teach you some English?
¿Quieres que te enseñe   kye·res ke te en·se·nye
algo de inglés?   al·go de een·gles

Is this a local or national custom?
¿Esto es una costumbre   es·to es oo·na kos·toom·bre
local o nacional?   lo·kal o na·thyo·nal

I respect your customs.
Respeto sus costumbres.   res·pe·to soos kos·toom·bres

community benefit & involvement

What sorts of issues is this community facing?
¿A qué tipo de problemas se   a ke tee·po de pro·ble·mas se
enfrenta esta comunidad?   en·fren·ta es·ta ko·moo·nee·da

climate change	*cambio* m *climático*	kam·byo klee·ma·tee·ko
freedom of religion	*libertad* f de *religión*	lee·ber·ta de re·lee·khyon
interregional tension	*tirantez* f *interregional*	tee·ran·teth een·ter·re·khyo·nal
racism	*racismo* m	ra·thees·mo
unemployment	*desempleo* m	des·em·ple·o

I'd like to volunteer my skills.

Me gustaría ofrecer mis   me goos·ta·*ree*·a o·fre·*ther* mees
conocimientos.   ko·no·thee·*myen*·tos

Are there any volunteer programs available in the area?

¿Hay programas de   ai pro·*gra*·mas de
voluntariado en la zona?   vo·loon·ta·*rya*·do en la *tho*·na

environment

Where can I recycle this?

¿Dónde se puede   *don*·de se *pwe*·de
reciclar esto?   re·thee·*klar* es·to

transport

Can we get there by public transport?

¿Se puede ir en transporte   se *pwe*·de eer en trans·*por*·te
público?   *poo*·blee·ko

Can we get there by bike?

¿Se puede ir en bici?   se *pwe*·de eer en *bee*·thee

I'd prefer to walk there.

Prefiero ir a pie.   pre·*fye*·ro eer a pye

accommodation

I'd like to stay at a locally run hotel.

Me gustaría alojarme   me goos·ta·*ree*·a a·lo·*khar*·me
en un hotel del barrio.   en oon o·*tel* del *ba*·ryo

Are there any ecolodges here?

¿Hay algún ecolodge   ai al·*goon* e·ko·loch
por aquí?   por a·*kee*

Can I turn the air conditioning off and open the window?

¿Puedo apagar el aire   *pwe*·do a·pa·*gar* el *ai*·re
acondicionado y abrir   a·kon·dee·thyo·*na*·do ee a·*breer*
la ventana?   la ven·*ta*·na

There's no need to change my sheets.

No hace falta cambiar　　　no a·the *fal*·ta kam·byar
las sábanas.　　　las *sa*·ba·nas

shopping

Where can I buy locally produced goods/souvenirs?

¿Dónde puedo comprar　　　don·de *pwe*·do kom·*prar*
recuerdos de la zona?　　　re·*kwer*·dos de la *tho*·na

Do you sell Fair Trade products?

¿Se venden productos de　　　se *ven*·den pro·*dook*·tos de
comercio equitativo?　　　ko·*mer*·thyo e·kee·ta·*tee*·vo

food

Do you sell ...?	*¿Se venden ...?*	se *ven*·den ...
locally produced food	*comestibles de la zona*	ko·mes·*tee*·bles de la *tho*·na
organic produce	*productos agrícolas biológicos*	pro·*dook*·tos a·*gree*·ko·las bee·o·*lo*·khee·kos

Can you tell me which traditional foods I should try?

¿Que platos típicos　　　ke *pla*·tos *tee*·pee·kos
debería probar?　　　de·be·*ree*·a pro·*bar*

sightseeing

Are cultural tours available?

¿Se pueden hacer　　　se *pwe*·den a·*ther*
recorridos culturales?　　　re·ko·*ree*·dos kool·*too*·ra·les

Does the guide speak any of the regional languages?

¿El guía habla alguna　　　el *gee*·a a·bla al·*goo*·na
lengua regional?　　　*len*·gwa re·*khyo*·nal

Basque	euskera m	e·oos·ke·ra
Catalan	catalán m	ka·ta·lan
Galician	gallego m	ga·lye·go

Does your company ...?	Su empresa ...?	soo em·pre·sa ...
donate money to charity	hace donativos a organizaciones benéficas	a·the do·na·ti·vos a or·ga·nee·tha·thyo·nes be·ne·fee·kas
hire local guides	contrata a guías de la zona	kon·tra·ta a gee·as de la tho·na
visit local businesses	visita a negocios locales	vee·see·ta a ne·go·thyos lo·ka·les

A

Nouns in the dictionary have their gender indicated by ⓜ or ⓕ. If it's a plural noun, you'll also see pl. Where a word that could be either a noun or a verb has no gender indicated, it's a verb.

A

(to be) able *poder* po·*der*
aboard *a bordo* a bor·do
abortion *aborto* ⓜ a·bor·to
about *sobre* so·bre
above *arriba* a·ree·ba
abroad *en el extranjero*
   en el eks·tran·*khe*·ro
accept *aceptar* a·thep·*tar*
accident *accidente* ⓜ ak·thee·*den*·te
accommodation *alojamiento* ⓜ
   a·lo·kha·*myen*·to
across *a través* a tra·*ves*
activist *activista* ⓜ&ⓕ ak·tee·*vees*·ta
acupuncture *acupuntura* ⓕ
   a·koo·poon·*too*·ra
adaptor *adaptador* ⓜ a·dap·ta·*dor*
address *dirección* ⓕ dee·rek·*thyon*
administration *administración* ⓕ
   ad·mee·nees·tra·*thyon*
admission price *precio* ⓜ *de entrada*
   pre·thyo de en·*tra*·da
admit *admitir* ad·mee·*teer*
adult *adulto* ⓜ a·*dool*·to
advertisement *anuncio* ⓜ
   a·*noon*·thyo
advice *consejo* kon·se·kho
aerobics *aeróbic* ⓜ ai·ro·beek
Africa *África* ⓕ a·free·ka
after *después de* des·*pwes* de
aftershave *bálsamo de aftershave*
   bal·sa·mo de ahf·ter·sha·eev
again *otra vez* o·tra veth
age *edad* ⓕ e·da
aggressive *agresivo/a* ⓜ/ⓕ
   a·gre·*see*·vo/a

agree *estar de acuerdo*
   es·*tar* de a·*kwer*·do
agriculture *agricultura* ⓕ
   a·gree·kul·*too*·ra
AIDS *SIDA* ⓜ see·da
air *aire* ⓜ ai·re
air mail *por vía aérea* por vee·a a·e·re·a
air-conditioned *con aire acondicionado*
   kon ai·re a·kon·dee·thyo·na·do
air-conditioning *aire* ⓜ *acondicionado*
   ai·re a·kon·dee·thyo·na·do
airline *aerolínea* ⓕ ay·ro·lee·nya
airport *aeropuerto* ⓜ ay·ro·*pwer*·to
airport tax *tasa* ⓕ *del aeropuerto*
   ta·sa del ay·ro·*pwer*·to
alarm clock *despertador* ⓜ des·per·ta·*dor*
alcohol *alcohol* ⓜ al·*col*
all *todo* to·do
allergy *alergia* ⓕ a·*ler*·khya
allow *permitir* per·mee·*teer*
almonds *almendras* ⓕ pl al·*men*·dras
almost *casi* ka·see
alone *solo/a* ⓜ/ⓕ so·lo/a
already *ya* ya
also *también* tam·*byen*
altar *altar* ⓜ al·*tar*
altitude *altura* ⓕ al·*too*·ra
always *siempre* syem·pre
amateur *amateur* ⓜ&ⓕ a·ma·*ter*
ambassador
   embajador/embajadora ⓜ/ⓕ
   em·ba·kha·*dor*/em·ba·kha·*do*·ra
among *entre* en·tre
anarchist *anarquista* ⓜ&ⓕ
   a·nar·*kees*·ta
ancient *antiguo/a* ⓜ/ⓕ an·*tee*·gwo/a
and *y* ee
angry *enfadado/a* ⓜ/ⓕ en·fa·*da*·do/a

animal *animal* ⓜ a·nee·mal
ankle *tobillo* ⓜ to·bee·lyo
answer *respuesta* ⓕ res·pwes·ta
answering machine
    contestador ⓜ *automático*
    kon·tes·ta·dor ow·to·ma·tee·ko
ant *hormiga* ⓕ or·mee·ga
anthology *antología* ⓕ an·to·lo·khee·a
antibiotics *antibióticos* ⓜ pl
    an·tee·byo·tee·kos
antinuclear *antinuclear* an·tee·noo·kle·ar
antique *antigüedad* ⓕ an·tee·gwe·da
antiseptic *antiséptico* ⓜ
    an·tee·sep·tee·ko
any *alguno/a* ⓜ/ⓕ al·goo·no/a
appendix *apéndice* ⓜ a·pen·dee·the
apple *manzana* ⓕ man·tha·na
appointment *cita* ⓕ thee·ta
apricot *albaricoque* ⓜ al·ba·ree·ko·ke
archaeological *arqueológico/a* ⓜ/ⓕ
    ar·keo·lo·khee·ko/a
architect *arquitecto/a* ⓜ/ⓕ
    ar·kee·tek·to/a
architecture *arquitectura* ⓕ
    ar·kee·tek·too·ra
argue *discutir* dees·koo·teer
arm *brazo* ⓜ bra·tho
army *ejército* ⓜ e·kher·thee·to
arrest *detener* de·te·ner
arrivals *llegadas* ⓕ pl lye·ga·das
arrive *llegar* lye·gar
art *arte* ⓜ ar·te
art gallery *museo* ⓜ *de arte*
    moo·se·o de ar·te
artichoke *alcachofa* ⓕ al·ka·cho·fa
artist *artista* ⓜ&ⓕ ar·tees·ta
ashtray *cenicero* ⓜ the·nee·the·ro
Asia *Asia* ⓕ a·sya
ask (a question) *preguntar* pre·goon·tar
ask (for something) *pedir* pe·deer
aspirin *aspirina* ⓕ as·pee·ree·na
assault *asalto* ⓜ a·sal·to
asthma *asma* ⓕ as·ma
athletics *atletismo* ⓜ at·le·tees·mo
atmosphere *atmósfera* ⓕ at·mos·fe·ra
aubergine *berenjena* ⓕ be·ren·khe·na
aunt *tía* ⓕ tee·a

Australia *Australia* ⓕ ow·stra·lya
Australian Rules football *fútbol* ⓜ
    australiano foot·bol ow·stra·lya·no
automatic teller machine
    cajero ⓜ *automático*
    ka·khe·ro ow·to·ma·tee·ko
autumn *otoño* ⓜ o·to·nyo
avenue *avenida* ⓕ a·ve·nee·da
avocado *aguacate* ⓜ a·gwa·ka·te

B

B&W (film) *blanco y negro*
    blan·ko ee *ne*·gro
baby *bebé* ⓜ be·be
baby food *comida* ⓕ *de bebé*
    ko·mee·da de be·be
baby powder *talco* ⓜ tal·ko
babysitter *canguros* ⓜ kan·goo·ros
back (of body) *espalda* ⓕ es·pal·da
back (of chair) *respaldo* ⓜ res·pal·do
backpack *mochila* ⓕ mo·chee·la
bacon *tocino* ⓜ to·thee·no
bad *malo/a* ⓜ/ⓕ ma·lo/a
bag *bolso* ⓜ bol·so
baggage *equipaje* ⓜ e·kee·pa·khe
baggage allowance *límite de*
    equipaje lee·mee·te de e·kee·pa·khe
baggage claim
    recogida ⓕ *de equipajes*
    re·ko·khee·da de e·kee·pa·khes
bakery *panadería* ⓕ pa·na·de·ree·a
balance (account) *saldo* ⓜ sal·do
balcony *balcón* ⓜ bal·kon
ball *pelota* ⓕ pe·lo·ta
ballet *ballet* ⓜ ba·le
banana *plátano* ⓜ pla·ta·no
band *grupo* ⓜ groo·po
bandage *vendaje* ⓜ ven·da·khe
band-aids *tiritas* ⓕ pl tee·ree·tas
bank *banco* ⓜ ban·ko
bank account *cuenta* ⓕ *bancaria*
    kwen·ta ban·ka·rya
banknotes *billetes* ⓜ pl *(de banco)*
    bee·lye·tes (de ban·ko)
baptism *bautizo* ⓜ bow·tee·tho

bar *bar* ⓜ bar

bar (with music) *pub* ⓜ poob

bar work *trabajo* ⓜ *de camarero/a* ⓜ/ⓕ
tra·ba·kho de ka·ma·re·ro/a

basket *canasta* ⓕ ka·nas·ta

basketball *baloncesto* ⓜ ba·lon·thes·to

bath *bañera* ⓕ ba·nye·ra

bathing suit *bañador* ⓜ ba·nya·dor

bathroom *baño* ⓜ ba·nyo

battery (car) *batería* ⓕ ba·te·ree·a

battery (small) *pila* ⓕ pee·la

be *ser* ser • *estar* es·tar

beach *playa* ⓕ pla·ya

bean sprouts *brotes* ⓜ pl *de soja*
bro·tes de so·kha

beans *judías* khoo·dee·as

beautiful *hermoso/a* ⓜ/ⓕ er·mo·so/a

beauty salon *salón* ⓜ *de belleza*
sa·lon de be·lye·tha

because *porque* por·ke

bed *cama* ⓕ ka·ma

bedding *ropa* ⓕ *de cama* ro·pa de ka·ma

bedroom *habitación* ⓕ a·bee·ta·thyon

bee *abeja* ⓕ a·be·kha

beef *carne* ⓕ *de vaca* kar·ne de va·ka

beer *cerveza* ⓕ ther·ve·tha

beetroot *remolacha* ⓕ re·mo·la·cha

before *antes* an·tes

beggar *mendigo/a* ⓜ/ⓕ men·dee·go/a

begin *comenzar* ko·men·thar

behind *detrás de* de·tras de

Belgium *Bélgica* ⓕ bel·khee·ka

below *abajo* a·ba·kho

best *lo mejor* lo me·khor

bet *apuesta* ⓕ a·pwes·ta

better *mejor* me·khor

between *entre* en·tre

bible *biblia* ⓕ bee·blya

bicycle *bicicleta* ⓕ bee·thee·kle·ta

big *grande* gran·de

bike *bici* ⓕ bee·thee

bike chain *cadena* ⓕ *de bici*
ka·de·na de bee·thee

bike path *camino* ⓜ *de bici*
ka·mee·no de bee·thee

bill *cuenta* ⓕ kwen·ta

biodegradable *biodegradable*
bee·o·de·gra·da·ble

biography *biografía* ⓕ bee·o·gra·fee·a

bird *pájaro* ⓜ pa·kha·ro

birth certificate
partida ⓕ *de nacimiento*
par·tee·da de na·thee·myen·to

birthday *cumpleaños* ⓜ koom·ple·a·nyos

birthday cake *pastel* ⓜ *de cumpleaños*
pas·tel de koom·ple·a·nyos

biscuit *galleta* ga·lye·ta

bite (dog) *mordedura* ⓕ mor·de·doo·ra

bite (food) *bocado* ⓜ bo·ka·do

bite (insect) *picadura* ⓕ pee·ka·doo·ra

black *negro/a* ⓜ/ⓕ ne·gro/a

blanket *manta* ⓕ man·ta

bleed *sangrar* san·grar

blind *ciego/a* ⓜ/ⓕ thye·go/a

blister *ampolla* ⓕ am·po·lya

blocked *atascado/a* ⓜ/ⓕ a·tas·ka·do/a

blood *sangre* ⓕ san·gre

blood group *grupo* ⓜ *sanguíneo*
groo·po san·gee·neo

blood pressure *presión* ⓕ *arterial*
pre·syon ar·te·ryal

blood test *análisis* ⓜ *de sangre*
a·na·lee·sees de san·gre

blue *azul* a·thool

board (ship, etc) *embarcarse*
em·bar·kar·se

boarding house *pensión* ⓕ pen·syon

boarding pass *tarjeta* ⓕ *de embarque*
tar·khe·ta de em·bar·ke

bone *hueso* ⓜ we·so

book *libro* ⓜ lee·bro

book (make a reservation) *reservar*
re·ser·var

booked out *lleno/a* ⓜ/ⓕ lye·no/a

bookshop *librería* ⓕ lee·bre·ree·a

boots *botas* ⓕ pl bo·tas

border *frontera* ⓕ fron·te·ra

boring *aburrido/a* ⓜ/ⓕ a·boo·ree·do/a

borrow *tomar prestado* to·mar pres·ta·do

botanic garden *jardín* ⓜ *botánico*
khar·deen bo·ta·nee·ko

both *dos* ⓜ/ⓕ pl dos

bottle *botella* ⓕ bo·te·lya

bottle opener *abrebotellas* ⓜ
a·bre·bo·te·lyas

bowl *bol* ⓜ bol

box *caja* ⓕ *ka*·kha

boxer shorts *calzones* ⓜ pl kal·*tho*·nes

boxing *boxeo* ⓜ bo·se·o

boy *chico* ⓜ chee·ko

boyfriend *novio* ⓜ *no*·vyo

bra *sujetador* ⓜ soo·khe·ta·*dor*

brakes *frenos* ⓕ pl *fre*·nos

branch office *sucursal* ⓕ soo·koor·*sal*

brandy *coñac* ⓜ ko·*nyak*

brave *valiente* va·*lyen*·te

bread *pan* ⓜ pan

   brown bread *pan moreno* pan mo·re·no

   bread rolls *bollos* bo·lyos

   rye *pan de centeno* pan de then·te·no

   sourdough *pan de masa fermentada*
   pan de *ma*·sa fer·men·ta·da

   white bread *pan blanco* pan blan·ko

   wholemeal *integral* een·te·*gral*

break *romper* rom·*per*

break down *descomponerse*
des·kom·po·*ner*·se

breakfast *desayuno* ⓜ des·a·*yoo*·no

breasts *senos* ⓜ pl se·nos

breathe *respirar* res·pee·*rar*

brewery *fábrica* ⓕ *de cerveza*
fab·ree·ka de ther·ve·tha

bribe *soborno* ⓜ so·*bor*·no

bribe *sobornar* so·bor·*nar*

bridge *puente* ⓜ *pwen*·te

briefcase *maletín* ⓜ ma·le·*teen*

brilliant *cojonudo/a* ⓜ/ⓕ
ko·kho·*noo*·do/a

bring *traer* tra·*er*

brochure *folleto* ⓜ fo·*lye*·to

broken *roto/a* ⓜ/ⓕ ro·to/a

bronchitis *bronquitis* ⓜ bron·*kee*·tees

brother *hermano* ⓜ er·*ma*·no

brown *marrón* ma·*ron*

bruise *cardenal* ⓜ kar·de·*nal*

brussels sprouts *coles* ⓜ pl *de Bruselas*
ko·les de broo·se·las

bucket *cubo* ⓜ koo·bo

Buddhist *budista* ⓜ&ⓕ boo·*dees*·ta

buffet *buffet* ⓜ boo·*fe*

bug *bicho* ⓜ bee·cho

build *construir* kons·troo·*eer*

building *edificio* ⓜ e·dee·fee·thyo

bull *toro* ⓜ *to*·ro

bullfight *corrida* ⓕ ko·ree·da

bullring *plaza* ⓕ *de toros*
pla·tha de *to*·ros

bum (of body) *culo* ⓜ koo·lo

burn *quemadura* ⓕ ke·ma·*doo*·ra

bus *autobús* ⓜ ow·to·*boos*

bus (intercity) *autocar* ⓜ ow·to·*kar*

bus station *estación de autobuses/
autocares* ⓕ es·ta·*thyon* de
ow·to·*boo*·ses/ow·to·*ka*·res

bus stop *parada* ⓕ *de autobús*
pa·*ra*·da de ow·to·*boos*

business *negocios* ⓜ pl ne·go·thyos

business class *clase* ⓕ *preferente*
kla·se pre·fe·*ren*·te

business person *comerciante* ⓜ&ⓕ
ko·mer·*thyan*·te

busker *artista callejero/a* ⓜ/ⓕ
ar·*tees*·ta ka·lye·*khe*·ro/a

busy *ocupado/a* ⓜ/ⓕ o·koo·*pa*·do/a

but *pero* pe·ro

butcher's shop *carnicería* ⓕ
kar·nee·the·*ree*·a

butter *mantequilla* ⓕ man·te·*kee*·lya

butterfly *mariposa* ⓕ ma·ree·po·sa

buttons *botones* ⓜ pl bo·*to*·nes

buy *comprar* kom·*prar*

C

cabbage *col* kol

cable *cable* ⓜ *ka*·ble

cable car *teleférico* ⓜ te·le·fe·ree·ko

café *café* ⓜ ka·fe

cake *pastel* ⓜ pas·*tel*

cake shop *pastelería* ⓕ pas·te·le·*ree*·a

calculator *calculadora* ⓕ kal·koo·la·*do*·ra

calendar *calendario* ⓜ ka·len·*da*·ryo

calf *ternero* ⓜ ter·*ne*·ro
camera *cámara* ⓕ *(fotográfica)*
  ka·ma·ra (fo·to·*gra*·fee·ka)
camera shop *tienda* ⓕ *de fotografía*
  tyen·da de fo·to·gra·*fee*·a
camp *acampar* a·kam·*par*
camping store *tienda* ⓕ *de*
  provisiones de cámping *tyen*·da de
  pro·vee·*syo*·nes de *kam*·peen
campsite *cámping* ⓜ *kam*·peen
can *lata* ⓕ *la*·ta
can (be able) *poder* po·*der*
can opener *abrelatas* ⓜ a·bre·*la*·tas
Canada *Canadá* ⓕ ka·na·*da*
cancel *cancelar* kan·the·*lar*
cancer *cáncer* ⓜ *kan*·ther
candle *vela* ⓕ *ve*·la
cantaloupe *cantalupo* ⓜ kan·ta·*loo*·po
capsicum (red/green)
  pimiento rojo/verde
  pee·*myen*·to *ro*·kho/*ver*·de
car *coche* ⓜ *ko*·che
car hire *alquiler* ⓜ *de coche*
  al·kee·*ler* de *ko*·che
car owner's title *papeles* ⓜ pl *del*
  coche pa·*pe*·les del *ko*·che
car registration *matrícula* ⓕ
  ma·*tree*·koo·la
caravan *caravana* ⓕ ka·ra·*va*·na
cards *cartas* ⓕ pl *kar*·tas
care (about something) *preocuparse*
  por pre·o·koo·*par*·se por
care (for someone) *cuidar de* kwee·*dar* de
caring *bondadoso/a* ⓜ/ⓕ
  bon·da·*do*·so/a
carpark *aparcamiento* ⓜ a·par·ka·*myen*·to
carpenter *carpintero/a* ⓜ/ⓕ
  kar·peen·*te*·ro/a
carrot *zanahoria* ⓕ tha·na·*o*·rya
carry *llevar* lye·*var*
carton *cartón* ⓜ kar·*ton*
cash *dinero en efectivo*
  dee·*ne*·ro en e·fek·*tee*·vo
cash (a cheque) *cambiar (un cheque)*
  kam·*byar* (oon *che*·ke)

cash register *caja* ⓕ *registradora*
  ka·kha re·khees·tra·*do*·ra
cashew nut *anacardo* ⓜ a·na·*kar*·do
cashier *caja* ⓕ *ka*·kha
casino *casino* ⓜ ka·*see*·no
cassette *casete* ⓜ ka·*se*·te
castle *castillo* ⓜ kas·*tee*·lyo
casual work *trabajo* ⓜ *eventual*
  tra·*ba*·kho e·ven·*twal*
cat *gato/a* ⓜ/ⓕ *ga*·to/a
cathedral *catedral* ⓕ ka·te·*dral*
Catholic *católico/a* ⓜ/ⓕ ka·*to*·lee·ko/a
cauliflower *coliflor* ⓕ ko·lee·*flor*
caves *cuevas* ⓕ pl *kwe*·vas
CD *cómpact* ⓜ *kom*·pakt
celebrate (an event) *celebrar* the·le·*brar*
celebration *celebración* ⓕ
  the·le·bra·*thyon*
cemetery *cementerio* ⓜ the·men·*te*·ryo
cent *centavo* ⓜ then·*ta*·vo
centimetre *centímetro* ⓜ then·*tee*·me·tro
central heating *calefacción* ⓕ *central*
  ka·le·fak·*thyon* then·*tral*
centre *centro* ⓜ *then*·tro
ceramic *cerámica* ⓕ the·*ra*·mee·ka
cereal *cereales* ⓜ pl the·re·*a*·les
certificate *certificado* ⓜ
  ther·tee·fee·*ka*·do
chair *silla* ⓕ *see*·lya
champagne *champán* ⓜ cham·*pan*
chance *oportunidad* ⓕ o·por·too·nee·*da*
change (money) *cambio* ⓜ *kam*·byo
change *cambiar* kam·*byar*
changing rooms *vestuarios* ⓜ pl
  ves·*twa*·ryos
charming *encantador/encantadora* ⓜ/ⓕ
  en·kan·ta·*dor*/en·kan·ta·*do*·ra
chat up *ligar* lee·*gar*
cheap *barato/a* ⓜ/ⓕ ba·*ra*·to/a
cheat *tramposo/a* ⓜ/ⓕ tram·*po*·so/a
check *revisar* re·vee·*sar*
check (bank) *cheque* ⓜ *che*·ke
check-in *facturación* ⓕ *de equipajes*
  fak·too·ra·*thyon* de e·kee·*pa*·khes

checkpoint *control* ⓜ kon·*trol*

cheese *queso* ⓜ *ke*·so

chef *cocinero* ⓜ ko·thee·*ne*·ro

chemist (person) *farmacéutico/a* ⓜ/ⓕ far·ma·*the*·oo·ti·ko/a

chemist (shop) *farmacia* ⓕ far·*ma*·thya

chess *ajedrez* ⓜ a·khe·*dreth*

chess board *tablero* ⓜ *de ajedrez* ta·*ble*·ro de a·khe·*dreth*

chest *pecho* ⓜ *pe*·cho

chewing gum *chicle* ⓜ *chee*·kle

chicken *pollo* ⓜ *po*·lyo

chicken breast *pechuga* ⓕ pe·*choo*·ga

chickpeas *garbanzos* ⓜ pl gar·*ban*·thos

child *niño/a* ⓜ/ⓕ *nee*·nyo/a

child seat *asiento* ⓜ *de seguridad para bebés* a·*syen*·to de se·goo·ree·*da* *pa*·ra be·*bes*

childminding service *guardería* ⓕ gwar·de·*ree*·a

children *hijos* ⓜ pl ee·khos

chilli *guindilla* ⓕ geen·*dee*·lya

chilli sauce *salsa* ⓕ *de guindilla* *sal*·sa de geen·*dee*·lya

chocolate *chocolate* ⓜ cho·ko·*la*·te

choose *escoger* es·ko·*kher*

Christian *cristiano/a* ⓜ/ⓕ krees·*tya*·no/a

Christian name *nombre* ⓜ *de pila* *nom*·bre de *pee*·la

Christmas *Navidad* ⓕ na·vee·*da*

Christmas Eve *Nochebuena* ⓕ no·che·*bwe*·na

church *iglesia* ⓕ ee·*gle*·sya

cider *sidra* ⓕ *see*·dra

cigar *cigarro* ⓜ thee·*ga*·ro

cigarette *cigarillo* ⓜ thee·ga·*ree*·lyo

cigarette lighter *mechero* ⓜ me·*che*·ro

cigarette machine *máquina* ⓕ *de tabaco* *ma*·kee·na de ta·*ba*·ko

cigarette paper *papel* ⓜ *de fumar* pa·*pel* de foo·*mar*

cinema *cine* ⓜ *thee*·ne

circus *circo* ⓜ *theer*·ko

citizenship *ciudadanía* ⓕ theew·da·da·*nee*·a

city *ciudad* ⓕ theew·*da*

city centre *centro* ⓜ *de la ciudad* *then*·tro de la theew·*da*

city walls *murallas* ⓕ pl moo·*ra*·lyas

civil rights *derechos civiles* ⓜ pl de·*re*·chos thee·*vee*·les

classical *clásico/a* ⓜ/ⓕ *kla*·see·ko/a

clean *limpio/a* ⓜ/ⓕ *leem*·pyo/a

cleaning *limpieza* ⓕ leem·*pye*·tha

client *clienta/e* ⓜ/ⓕ *klee*·en·ta/e

cliff *acantilado* ⓜ a·kan·tee·*la*·do

climb *subir* soo·*beer*

cloak *capote* ⓜ ka·*po*·te

cloakroom *guardarropa* ⓜ gwar·da·*ro*·pa

clock *reloj* ⓜ re·*lokh*

close *cerrar* the·*rar*

closed *cerrado/a* ⓜ/ⓕ the·*ra*·do/a

clothes line *cuerda* ⓕ *para tender la ropa* *kwer*·da *pa*·ra ten·*der* la *ro*·pa

clothing *ropa* ⓕ *ro*·pa

clothing store *tienda* ⓕ *de ropa* *tyen*·da de *ro*·pa

cloud *nube* ⓕ *noo*·be

cloudy *nublado* noo·*bla*·do

clove (garlic) *diente* ⓜ *(de ajo)* *dyen*·te (de a·kho)

cloves *clavos* ⓜ pl *kla*·vos

clutch *embrague* ⓕ em·*bra*·ge

coach *entrenador/entrenadora* ⓜ/ⓕ en·tre·na·*dor*/en·tre·na·*do*·ra

coast *costa* ⓕ *kos*·ta

cocaine *cocaína* ⓕ ko·ka·ee·na

cockroach *cucaracha* ⓕ koo·ka·*ra*·cha

cocoa *cacao* ⓜ ka·*kow*

coconut *coco* ⓜ *ko*·ko

codeine *codeína* ⓕ ko·de·*ee*·na

coffee *café* ⓜ ka·*fe*

coins *monedas* ⓕ pl mo·*ne*·das

cold *frío/a* ⓜ/ⓕ *free*·o/a

cold (illness) *resfriado* ⓜ res·free·*a*·do

colleague *colega* ⓜ&ⓕ ko·*le*·ga

collect call
llamada ① *a cobro revertido*
lya·ma·da a *ko*·bro re·ver·*tee*·do
college *residencia* ① *de estudiantes*
re·see·*den*·thya de es·too·*dyan*·tes
colour *color* ⑨ ko·*lor*
colour (film) *película* ① *en color*
pe·lee·*koo*·la en ko·*lor*
comb *peine* ⑨ *pey*·ne
come *venir* ve·*neer*
come (arrive) *llegar* lye·*gar*
comedy *comedia* ① ko·*me*·dya
comfortable *cómodo/a* ⑨/①
ko·mo·do/a
communion *comunión* ① ko·moo·*nyon*
communist *comunista* ⑨&①
ko·moo·*nees*·ta
companion *compañero/a* ⑨/①
kom·pa·*nye*·ro/a
company *compañía* ① kom·pa·*nyee*·a
compass *brújula* ① *broo*·khoo·la
complain *quejarse* ke·*khar*·se
computer *ordenador* ⑨ or·de·na·*dor*
computer game *juegos* ⑨ pl *de*
ordenador khwe·gos de or·de·na·*dor*
concert *concierto* ⑨ kon·*thyer*·to
conditioner *acondicionador* ⑨
a·kon·dee·thyo·na·*dor*
condoms *condones* ⑨ pl kon·*do*·nes
confession *confesión* ① kon·fe·*syon*
confirm *confirmar* kon·feer·*mar*
connection *conexión* ① ko·ne·*ksyon*
conservative
conservador/conservadora ⑨/①
kon·ser·va·*dor*/kon·ser·va·*do*·ra
constipation *estreñimiento* ⑨
es·tre·nyee·*myen*·to
consulate *consulado* ⑨ kon·soo·*la*·do
contact lenses *lentes* ⑨ pl *de contacto*
len·tes de kon·*tak*·to
contraceptives *anticonceptivos* ⑨ pl
an·tee·kon·thep·*tee*·vos
contract *contrato* ⑨ kon·*tra*·to
convenience store *negocio* ⑨ *de*
artículos básicos ne·go·thyo de
ar·*tee*·koo·los *ba*·see·kos

convent *convento* ⑨ kon·*ven*·to
cook *cocinero* ⑨ ko·thee·*ne*·ro
cook *cocinar* ko·thee·*nar*
cookie *galleta* ① ga·*lye*·ta
corn *maíz* ⑨ ma·*eeth*
corn flakes *copos* ⑨ pl *de maíz*
ko·pos de ma·*eeth*
corner *esquina* ① es·*kee*·na
corrupt *corrupto/a* ⑨/① ko·*roop*·to/a
cost *costar* kos·*tar*
cottage cheese *requesón* ⑨ re·ke·*son*
cotton *algodón* ⑨ al·go·*don*
cotton balls *bolas* ① pl *de algodón*
bo·las de al·go·*don*
cough *tos* ① tos
cough medicine *jarabe* ⑨ kha·*ra*·be
count *contar* kon·*tar*
counter *mostrador* ⑨ mos·tra·*dor*
country *país* ⑨ pa·*ees*
countryside *campo* ⑨ *kam*·po
coupon *cupón* ⑨ koo·*pon*
courgette *calabacín* ⑨ ka·la·ba·*theen*
court (tennis) *pista* ① *pees*·ta
cous cous *cus cus* ⑨ koos koos
cover charge *precio* ⑨ *del cubierto*
pre·thyo del koo·*byer*·to
cow *vaca* ① *va*·ka
crab *cangrejo* ⑨ kan·*gre*·kho
crackers *galletas* ① pl *saladas*
ga·*lye*·tas sa·*la*·das
crafts *artesanía* ① ar·te·sa·*nee*·a
crash *choque* ⑨ *cho*·ke
crazy *loco/a* ⑨/① *lo*·ko/a
cream (food) *crema* ① *kre*·ma
cream (moisturising) *crema* ①
hidratante *kre*·ma ee·dra·*tan*·te
cream cheese *queso* ⑨ *crema*
ke·so *kre*·ma
creche *guardería* ① gwar·de·*ree*·a
credit card *tarjeta* ① *de crédito*
tar·*khe*·ta de *kre*·dee·to
cricket *críquet* ⑨ *kree*·ket
crop *cosecha* ① ko·se·*cha*
crowded *abarrotado/a* ⑨/①
a·ba·ro·*ta*·do/a

cucumber *pepino* ⓜ pe·*pee*·no
cuddle *abrazo* ⓜ a·*bra*·tho
cup *taza* ⓕ *ta*·tha
cupboard *armario* ⓜ ar·*ma*·ryo
currency exchange *cambio* ⓜ *(de dinero)* *kam*·byo (de dee·*ne*·ro)
current (electricity) *corriente* ⓕ ko·*ryen*·te
current affairs *informativo* ⓜ een·for·ma·*tee*·vo
curry *curry* ⓜ *koo*·ree
curry powder *curry* ⓜ *en polvo* *koo*·ree en *pol*·vo
customs *aduana* ⓕ a·*dwa*·na
cut *cortar* kor·*tar*
cutlery *cubiertos* ⓜ pl koo·*byer*·tos
CV *historial* ⓜ *profesional* ees·to·*ryal* pro·fe·syo·*nal*
cycle *andar en bicicleta* an·*dar* en bee·thee·*kle*·ta
cycling *ciclismo* ⓜ thee·*klees*·mo
cyclist *ciclista* ⓜ&ⓕ thee·*klees*·ta
cystitis *cistitis* ⓕ thees·*tee*·tees

D

dad *papá* ⓜ pa·*pa*
daily *diariamente* dya·rya·*men*·te
dance *bailar* bai·*lar*
dancing *bailar* ⓜ bai·*lar*
dangerous *peligroso/a* ⓜ/ⓕ pe·lee·*gro*·so/a
dark *oscuro/a* ⓜ/ⓕ os·*koo*·ro/a
date *citarse* thee·*tar*·se
date (a person) *salir con* sa·*leer* kon
date (time) *fecha* ⓕ *fe*·cha
date of birth *fecha* ⓕ *de nacimiento* *fe*·cha de na·thee·*myen*·to
daughter *hija* ⓕ *ee*·kha
dawn *alba* ⓕ *al*·ba
day *día* ⓜ *dee*·a
day after tomorrow *pasado mañana* pa·*sa*·do ma·*nya*·na
day before yesterday *anteayer* an·te·a·*yer*
dead *muerto/a* ⓜ/ⓕ *mwer*·to/a

deaf *sordo/a* ⓜ/ⓕ *sor*·do/a
deal (cards) *repartir* re·par·*teer*
decide *decidir* de·thee·*deer*
deep *profundo/a* ⓜ/ⓕ pro·*foon*·do/a
deforestation *deforestación* ⓕ de·fo·res·ta·*thyon*
degree *título* ⓜ *tee*·too·lo
delay *demora* ⓕ de·*mo*·ra
delirious *delirante* de·lee·*ran*·te
deliver *entregar* en·tre·*gar*
democracy *democracia* ⓕ de·mo·*kra*·thya
demonstration *manifestación* ⓕ ma·ne·fes·ta·*thyon*
Denmark *Dinamarca* ⓕ dee·na·*mar*·ka
dental floss *hilo* ⓜ *dental* *ee*·lo den·*tal*
dentist *dentista* ⓜ&ⓕ den·*tees*·ta
deny *negar* ne·*gar*
deodorant *desodorante* ⓜ de·so·do·*ran*·te
depart *salir de* sa·*leer* de
department store *grande almacen* ⓜ *gran*·de al·ma·*then*
departure *salida* ⓕ sa·*lee*·da
deposit *depósito* ⓜ de·po·*see*·to
descendant *descendiente* ⓜ des·then·*dyen*·te
desert *desierto* ⓜ de·*syer*·to
design *diseño* ⓜ dee·*se*·nyo
destination *destino* ⓜ des·*tee*·no
destroy *destruir* des·troo·*eer*
detail *detalle* ⓜ de·*ta*·lye
diabetes *diabetes* ⓕ dee·a·*be*·tes
diaper *pañal* ⓜ pa·*nyal*
diaphragm *diafragma* ⓜ dee·a·*frag*·ma
diarrhoea *diarrea* ⓕ dee·a·*re*·a
diary *agenda* ⓕ a·*khen*·da
dice (die) *dados* ⓜ pl *da*·dos
dictionary *diccionario* ⓜ deek·thyo·*na*·ryo
die *morir* mo·*reer*
diet *régimen* ⓜ *re*·khee·men
different *diferente* ⓜ/ⓕ dee·fe·*ren*·te
difficult *difícil* ⓜ/ⓕ dee·*fee*·theel

dining car *vagón* ⓜ *restaurante*
va·*gon* res·tow·*ran*·te

dinner *cena* ⓕ *the*·na

direct *directo/a* ⓜ/ⓕ dee·*rek*·to/a

direct-dial *marcar directo*
mar·kar dee·*rek*·to

director *director/directora* ⓜ/ⓕ
dee·rek·tor/dee·rek·to·ra

dirty *sucio/a* ⓜ/ⓕ *soo*·thyo/a

disabled *minusválido/a* ⓜ/ⓕ
mee·noos·va·lee·do/a

disco *discoteca* ⓕ dees·ko·te·ka

discount *descuento* ⓜ des·*kwen*·to

discover *descubrir* des·koo·*breer*

discrimination *discriminación* ⓕ
dees·kree·mee·na·*thyon*

disease *enfermedad* ⓕ en·fer·me·*da*

disk *disco* ⓜ *dees*·ko

dive *bucear* boo·the·*ar*

diving *submarinismo* ⓜ
soob·ma·ree·*nees*·mo

diving equipment
equipo ⓜ *de inmersión* ⓜ
e·*kee*·po de ee·mer·*syon*

dizzy *mareado/a* ⓜ/ⓕ ma·re·a·do/a

do *hacer* a·*ther*

doctor *doctor/doctora* ⓜ/ⓕ
dok·tor/dok·to·ra

documentary *documental* ⓜ
do·koo·men·*tal*

dog *perro/a* ⓜ/ⓕ *pe*·ro/a

dole *paro* ⓜ *pa*·ro

doll *muñeca* ⓕ moo·*nye*·ka

domestic flight *vuelo* ⓜ *doméstico*
vwe·lo do·*mes*·tee·ko

donkey *burro* ⓜ *boo*·ro

door *puerta* ⓕ *pwer*·ta

dope *droga* ⓕ *dro*·ga

double *doble* ⓜ/ⓕ *do*·ble

double bed *cama* ⓕ *de matrimonio*
ka·ma de ma·tree·mo·nyo

double room *habitación* ⓕ *doble*
a·bee·ta·*thyon* do·ble

down *abajo* a·*ba*·kho

downhill *cuesta abajo* kwes·ta a·*ba*·kho

dozen *docena* ⓕ do·*the*·na

draw *dibujar* dee·boo·*khar*

dream *soñar* so·*nyar*

dress *vestido* ⓜ ves·*tee*·do

dried fruit *fruto* ⓜ *seco* froo·to se·ko

drink *bebida* ⓕ be·*bee*·da

drink *beber* be·*ber*

drive *conducir* kon·doo·*theer*

drivers licence *carnet* ⓜ *de conducir*
kar·*ne* de kon·doo·*theer*

drug *droga* ⓕ *dro*·ga

drug addiction *drogadicción* ⓕ
dro·ga·deek·*thyon*

drug dealer *traficante* ⓜ *de drogas*
tra·fee·*kan*·te de *dro*·gas

drums *batería* ⓕ ba·te·*ree*·a

drumstick (chicken) *muslo* moos·lo

drunk *borracho/a* ⓜ/ⓕ bo·ra·cho/a

dry *secar* se·kar

duck *pato* ⓜ *pa*·to

dummy (pacifier) *chupete* ⓜ choo·*pe*·te

E

each *cada* ka·da

ear *oreja* ⓕ o·re·kha

early *temprano* tem·*pra*·no

earn *ganar* ga·*nar*

earplugs *tapones* ⓜ pl *para los oídos*
ta·*po*·nes *pa*·ra los o·*ee*·dos

earrings *pendientes* ⓜ pl pen·*dyen*·tes

Earth *Tierra* ⓕ *tye*·ra

earthquake *terremoto* ⓜ te·re·*mo*·to

east *este* *es*·te

Easter *Pascua* ⓕ *pas*·kwa

easy *fácil* fa·theel

eat *comer* ko·*mer*

economy class *clase* ⓕ *turística*
kla·se too·*rees*·tee·ka

eczema *eczema* ⓕ ek·*the*·ma

editor *editor/editora* ⓜ/ⓕ
e·dee·tor/e·dee·to·ra

education *educación* ⓕ e·doo·ka·*thyon*

eggplant *berenjenas* ⓕ pl
be·ren·*khe*·nas

egg *huevo* ⓜ we·vo
elections *elecciones* ⓕ pl
    e·lek·*thyo*·nes
electrical store *tienda* ⓕ *de productos*
    eléctricos tyen·da de pro·*dook*·tos
    e·*lek*·tree·kos
electricity *electricidad* ⓕ
    e·lek·tree·thee·*da*
elevator *ascensor* ⓜ as·then·*sor*
embarrassed *avergonzado/a* ⓜ/ⓕ
    a·ver·gon·tha·do/a
embassy *embajada* ⓕ em·ba·*kha*·da
emergency *emergencia* ⓕ
    e·mer·*khen*·thya
emotional *emocional* e·mo·thyo·*nal*
employee *empleado/a* ⓜ/ⓕ
    em·ple·a·do/a
employer *jefe/a* ⓜ/ⓕ *khe*·fe/a
empty *vacío/a* ⓜ/ⓕ va·*thee*·o/a
end *fin* ⓜ feen
end *acabar* a·ka·*bar*
endangered species *especies* ⓕ pl *en*
    peligro de extinción es·*pe*·thyes en
    pe·*lee*·gro de eks·teen·*thyon*
engagement *compromiso* ⓜ
    kom·pro·*mee*·so
engine *motor* ⓜ mo·*tor*
engineer *ingeniero/a* ⓜ/ⓕ
    een·khe·*nye*·ro/a
engineering *ingeniería* ⓕ
    een·khe·nye·*ree*·a
England *Inglaterra* ⓕ een·gla·*te*·ra
English *inglés* ⓜ een·*gles*
enjoy (oneself) *divertirse* dee·ver·*teer*·se
enough *suficiente* ⓜ/ⓕ
    soo·fee·*thyen*·te
enter *entrar* en·*trar*
entertainment guide *guía* ⓕ *del ocio*
    gee·a del o·thyo
envelope *sobre* ⓜ so·bre
environment *medio* ⓜ *ambiente*
    me·dyo am·*byen*·te
epilepsy *epilepsia* ⓕ e·pee·*lep*·sya
equal opportunity
    igualdad ⓕ *de oportunidades*
    ee·gwal·*da* de o·por·too·nee·da·des

equality *igualdad* ⓕ ee·gwal·*da*
equipment *equipo* ⓜ e·*kee*·po
escalator *escaleras* ⓕ pl *mecánicas*
    es·ka·*le*·ras me·*ka*·nee·kas
euro *euro* ⓜ e·oo·ro
Europe *Europa* ⓕ e·oo·ro·pa
euthanasia *eutanasia* ⓕ e·oo·ta·*na*·sya
evening *noche* ⓕ *no*·che
everything *todo* to·do
example *ejemplo* ⓜ e·*khem*·plo
excellent *excelente* ⓜ/ⓕ eks·the·*len*·te
exchange *cambio* ⓜ *kam*·byo
exchange (money) *cambiar* kam·*byar*
exchange rate *tipo* ⓜ *de cambio*
    tee·po de kam·byo
exchange (give gifts) *regalar* re·ga·*lar*
excluded *no incluido* no een·kloo·ee·do
exhaust *tubo* ⓜ *de escape*
    too·bo de es·*ka*·pe
exhibit *exponer* eks·po·*ner*
exhibition *exposición* ⓕ
    eks·po·see·*thyon*
exit *salida* ⓕ sa·lee·da
expensive *caro/a* ⓜ/ⓕ ka·ro/a
experience *experiencia* ⓕ
    eks·pe·*ryen*·thya
express *expreso/a* ⓜ/ⓕ eks·*pre*·so/a
express mail *correo* ⓜ *urgente*
    ko·re·o oor·*khen*·te
extension (visa) *prolongación* ⓕ
    pro·lon·ga·*thyon*
eye *ojo* ⓜ o·kho
eye drops *gotas* ⓕ pl *para los ojos*
    go·tas pa·ra los o·khos

F

fabric *tela* ⓕ te·la
face *cara* ⓕ ka·ra
face cloth *toallita* ⓕ to·a·*lyee*·ta
factory *fábrica* ⓕ fa·bree·ka
factory worker *obrero/a* ⓜ/ⓕ o·bre·ro/a
fall *caída* ⓕ ka·ee·da
family *familia* ⓕ fa·*mee*·lya
family name *apellido* ⓜ a·pe·*lyee*·do
famous *famoso/a* ⓜ/ⓕ fa·mo·so/a

fan (hand held) *abanico* ⓜ a·ba·*nee*·ko
fan (electric) *ventilador* ⓜ
  ven·tee·la·*dor*
fanbelt *correa* ⓕ *del ventilador*
  ko·*re*·a del ven·tee·la·*dor*
far *lejos* *le*·khos
farm *granja* ⓕ *gran*·kha
farmer *agricultor/agricultora* ⓜ/ⓕ
  a·gree·kool·*tor*/a·gree·kool·*to*·ra
fast *rápido/a* ⓜ/ⓕ *ra*·pee·do/a
fat *gordo/a* ⓜ/ⓕ *gor*·do/a
father *padre* ⓜ *pa*·dre
father-in-law *suegro* ⓜ *swe*·gro
fault *falta* ⓕ *fal*·ta
faulty *defectuoso/a* ⓜ/ⓕ
  de·fek·too·o·so/a
feed *dar de comer* dar de ko·*mer*
feel *sentir* sen·*teer*
feelings *sentimientos* ⓜ pl
  sen·tee·*myen*·tos
fence *cerca* ⓕ *ther*·ka
fencing *esgrima* ⓕ es·*gree*·ma
festival *festival* ⓜ fes·tee·*val*
fever *fiebre* ⓕ *fye*·bre
few *pocos* *po*·kos
fiance *prometido* ⓜ pro·me·*tee*·do
fiancee *prometida* ⓕ pro·me·*tee*·da
fiction *ficción* ⓕ feek·*thyon*
field *campo* ⓜ *kam*·po
fig *higo* ⓜ *ee*·go
fight *pelea* ⓕ pe·*le*·a
fight *luchar* loo·*char*
fill *llenar* lye·*nar*
fillet *filete* ⓜ fee·*le*·te
film *película* ⓕ pe·*lee*·koo·la
film speed *sensibilidad* ⓕ
  sen·see·bee·lee·*da*
filtered *con filtro* kon *feel*·tro
find *encontrar* en·kon·*trar*
fine *multa* ⓕ *mool*·ta
finger *dedo* ⓜ *de*·do
finish *terminar* ter·mee·*nar*
fire *fuego* ⓜ *fwe*·go
firewood *leña* ⓕ *le*·nya
first *primero/a* ⓜ/ⓕ pree·*me*·ro/a

first class *primera clase* pree·*me*·ra *kla*·se
first-aid kit *maletín* ⓜ *de primeros*
  auxilios ma·le·*teen* de pree·*me*·ros
  ow·*ksee*·lyos
fish *pez* ⓜ peth
fish (as food) *pescado* ⓜ pes·*ka*·do
fish shop *pescadería* ⓕ pes·ka·de·*ree*·a
fishing *pesca* ⓕ *pes*·ka
flag *bandera* ⓕ ban·*de*·ra
flannel *franela* ⓕ fra·*ne*·la
flashlight *linterna* ⓕ leen·*ter*·na
flat *llano/a* ⓜ/ⓕ *lya*·no/a
flea *pulga* ⓕ *pool*·ga
flooding *inundación* ⓕ ee·noon·da·*thyon*
floor *suelo* ⓜ *swe*·lo
florist *florista* ⓜ&ⓕ flo·*rees*·ta
flour *harina* ⓕ a·*ree*·na
flower *flor* ⓕ flor
flower seller
  vendedor/vendedora ⓜ/ⓕ *de flores*
  ven·de·*dor*/ven·de·*do*·ra de *flo*·res
fly *volar* vo·*lar*
foggy *brumoso/a* ⓜ/ⓕ broo·*mo*·so
follow *seguir* se·*geer*
food *comida* ⓕ ko·*mee*·da
food supplies *víveres* ⓜ pl *vee*·ve·res
foot *pie* ⓜ pye
football *fútbol* ⓜ *foot*·bol
footpath *acera* ⓕ a·*the*·ra
foreign *extranjero/a* ⓜ/ⓕ
  eks·tran·*khe*·ro/a
forest *bosque* ⓜ *bos*·ke
forever *para siempre* *pa*·ra *syem*·pre
forget *olvidar* ol·vee·*dar*
forgive *perdonar* per·do·*nar*
fork *tenedor* ⓜ te·ne·*dor*
fortnight *quincena* ⓕ keen·*the*·na
foul *sucio/a* ⓜ/ⓕ *soo*·thee·o/a
foyer *vestíbulo* ⓜ ves·*tee*·boo·lo
fragile *frágil* *fra*·kheel
France *Francia* ⓕ *fran*·thya
free (not bound) *libre* *lee*·bre
free (of charge) *gratis* *gra*·tees
freeze *helarse* e·*lar*·se
friend *amigo/a* ⓜ/ⓕ a·*mee*·go/a

frost *escarcha* ① es·kar·cha
frozen foods *productos congelados* ⑩ pl pro·*dook*·tos kon·khe·*la*·dos
fruit *fruta* ① *froo*·ta
fruit picking *recolección* ① de fruta re·ko·lek·*thyon* de *froo*·ta
fry *freír* fre·*eer*
frying pan *sartén* ① sar·*ten*
fuck *follar* fo·*lyar*
full *lleno/a* ⑩/① *lye*·no/a
full-time *a tiempo completo* a *tyem*·po kom·*ple*·to
fun *diversión* ① dee·ver·*syon*
funeral *funeral* ⑩ foo·ne·*ral*
funny *gracioso/a* ⑩/① gra·*thyo*·so/a
furniture *muebles* ⑩ pl *mwe*·bles
future *futuro* ⑩ foo·*too*·ro

G

gay *gay* gai
general *general* khe·ne·*ral*
Germany *Alemania* ① a·le·*ma*·nya
gift *regalo* ⑩ re·*ga*·lo
gig *bolo* ⑩ *bo*·lo
gin *ginebra* ① khee·*ne*·bra
ginger *jengibre* ⑩ khen·*khee*·bre
girl *chica* ① *chee*·ka
girlfriend *novia* ① *no*·vya
give *dar* dar
glandular fever *fiebre* ① *glandular* *fye*·bre glan·doo·*lar*
glass (material) *vidrio* ⑩ *vee*·dryo
glass (drinking) *vaso* ⑩ *va*·so
glasses *gafas* ① pl *ga*·fas
gloves *guantes* ⑩ pl *gwan*·tes
go *ir* eer
go out with *salir con* sa·*leer* kon
go shopping *ir de compras* eer de *kom*·pras
goal *gol* ⑩ gol
goalkeeper *portero/a* ⑩/① por·*te*·ro/a
goat *cabra* ① *ka*·bra
goat's cheese *queso* ⑩ de cabra *ke*·so de *ka*·bra
god *Dios* ⑩ dyos

goggles *gafas* ① pl de submarinismo *ga*·fas de soob·ma·ree·*nees*·mo
golf ball *pelota* ① de golf pe·*lo*·ta de golf
golf course *campo* ⑩ de golf *kam*·po de golf
good *bueno/a* ⑩/① *bwe*·no/a
government *gobierno* ⑩ go·*byer*·no
gram *gramo* ⑩ *gra*·mo
grandchild *nieto/a* ⑩/① *nye*·to/a
grandfather *abuelo* ⑩ a·*bwe*·lo
grandmother *abuela* ① a·*bwe*·la
grapefruit *pomelo* ⑩ po·*me*·lo
grapes *uvas* ① pl *oo*·vas
graphic art *arte* ⑩ *gráfico* *ar*·te *gra*·fee·ko
grass *hierba* ① *yer*·ba
grave *tumba* ① *toom*·ba
gray *gris* grees
great *fantástico/a* ⑩/① fan·*tas*·tee·ko/a
green *verde* *ver*·de
greengrocery (shop) *verdulería* ① ver·doo·le·*ree*·a
grocer (shopkeeper) *verdulero/a* ⑩/① ver·doo·*le*·ro/a
grey *gris* grees
grocery *tienda* ① de comestibles *tyen*·da de ko·mes·*tee*·bles
grow *crecer* kre·*ther*
g-string *tanga* ① *tan*·ga
guess *adivinar* a·dee·vee·*nar*
guide (audio) *guía* ① audio *gee*·a ow·dyo
guide (person) *guía* ⑩&① *gee*·a
guide dog *perro lazarillo* ⑩ *pe*·ro la·tha·ree·lyo
guidebook *guía* ① *gee*·a
guided tour *recorrido* ⑩ *guiado* re·ko·*ree*·do gee·*a*·do
guilty *culpable* kool·*pa*·ble
guitar *guitarra* ① gee·*ta*·ra
gum *chicle* ⑩ *chee*·kle
gymnastics *gimnasia* ① *rítmica* kheem·*na*·sya *reet*·mee·ka
gynaecologist *ginecólogo* ⑩ khee·ne·*ko*·lo·go

H

hair *pelo* ⓜ pe·lo
hairbrush *cepillo* ⓜ the·pee·lyo
hairdresser *peluquero/a* ⓜ/ⓕ
　pe·loo·ke·ro/a
halal *halal* a·lal
half *medio/a* ⓜ/ⓕ me·dyo/a
half a litre *medio litro* ⓜ me·dyo lee·tro
hallucinate *alucinar* a·loo·thee·nar
ham *jamón* ⓜ kha·mon
hammer *martillo* ⓜ mar·tee·lyo
hammock *hamaca* ⓕ a·ma·ka
hand *mano* ⓕ ma·no
handbag *bolso* ⓜ bol·so
handicrafts *artesanía* ⓕ ar·te·sa·nee·a
handlebar *manillar* ⓜ ma·nee·lyar
handmade *hecho a mano* e·cho a ma·no
handsome *hermoso* ⓜ er·mo·so
happy *feliz* fe·leeth
harassment *acoso* ⓜ al a·ko·so
harbour *puerto* ⓜ pwer·to
hard *duro/a* ⓜ/ⓕ doo·ro/a
hardware store *ferretería* ⓕ fe·re·te·ree·a
hash *hachís* ⓜ a·chees
hat *sombrero* ⓜ som·bre·ro
have *tener* te·ner
have a cold *estar constipado/a* ⓜ/ⓕ
　es·tar kons·tee·pa·do
have fun *divertirse* dee·ver·teer·se
hay fever *alergia* ⓕ al polen
　a·ler·khya al po·len
he *él* el
head *cabeza* ⓕ ka·be·tha
headache *dolor* ⓜ *de cabeza*
　do·lor de ka·be·tha
headlights *faros* ⓜ pl fa·ros
health *salud* ⓕ sa·loo
hear *oír* o·eer
hearing aid *audífono* ⓜ ow·dee·fo·no
heart *corazón* ⓜ ko·ra·thon
heart condition *condición* ⓕ *cardíaca*
　kon·dee·thyon kar·dee·a·ka
heat *calor* ⓜ ka·lor
heater *estufa* ⓕ es·too·fa
heavy *pesado/a* ⓜ/ⓕ pe·sa·do/a

helmet *casco* ⓜ kas·ko
help *ayudar* a·yoo·dar
hepatitis *hepatitis* ⓕ e·pa·tee·tees
her *su* soo
herbalist *herbolario/a* ⓜ/ⓕ
　er·bo·la·ree·o/a
herbs *hierbas* ⓕ pl yer·bas
here *aquí* a·kee
heroin *heroína* ⓕ e·ro·ee·na
herring *arenque* ⓜ a·ren·ke
high *alto/a* ⓜ/ⓕ al·to/a
high school *instituto* ⓜ eens·tee·too·to
hike *ir de excursión*
　eer de eks·koor·syon
hiking *excursionismo* ⓜ
　eks·koor·syo·nees·mo
hiking boots *botas* ⓕ pl *de montaña*
　bo·tas de mon·ta·nya
hiking routes *caminos* ⓜ pl *rurales*
　ka·mee·nos roo·ra·les
hill *colina* ⓕ ko·lee·na
Hindu *hindú* een·doo
hire *alquilar* al·kee·lar
his *su* soo
historical *histórico/a* ⓜ/ⓕ
　ees·to·ree·ko/a
hitchhike *hacer dedo* a·ther de·do
HIV positive *seropositivo/a* ⓜ/ⓕ
　se·ro·po·see·tee·vo/a
hockey *hockey* ⓜ kho·kee
holiday *día festivo* ⓕ dee·a fes·tee·vo
holidays *vacaciones* ⓕ pl
　va·ka·thyo·nes
Holy Week *Semana* ⓕ *Santa*
　se·ma·na san·ta
homeless *sin hogar* seen o·gar
homemaker *ama* ⓕ *de casa*
　a·ma de ka·sa
homosexual *homosexual* ⓜ&ⓕ
　o·mo·se·kswal
honey *miel* ⓕ myel
honeymoon *luna* ⓕ *de miel*
　loo·na de myel
horoscope *horóscopo* ⓜ o·ros·ko·po
horse *caballo* ⓜ ka·ba·lyo

horse riding *equitación* ① e·kee·ta·*thyon*
horseradish *rábano* ⑩ *picante*
ra·ba·no pee·kan·te
hospital *hospital* ⑩ os·pee·*tal*
hospitality *hosteleria* ① os·te·le·*ree*·a
hot *caliente* ka·*lyen*·te
hot water *agua caliente* ⑩
a·gwa ka·*lyen*·te
hotel *hotel* ⑩ o·*tel*
house *casa* ① *ka*·sa
housework *trabajo* ⑩ *de casa*
tra·*ba*·kho de *ka*·sa
how *cómo* *ko*·mo
how much *cuánto* *kwan*·to
hug *abrazo* ⑩ a·*bra*·tho
huge *enorme* e·*nor*·me
human rights *derechos* ⑩ pl *humanos*
de·*re*·chos o·*ma*·nos
humanities *humanidades* ① pl
oo·ma·nee·*da*·des
hungry *hambriento/a* ⑩/①
am·*bryen*·to/a
hungry *tener hambre* te·*ner* am·bre
hunting *caza* ① *ka*·tha
hurt *dañar* da·*nyar*
husband *marido* ⑩ ma·*ree*·do

I

I *yo* yo
ice *hielo* ⑩ *ye*·lo
ice axe *piolet* ⑩ pyo·*le*
ice cream *helado* ⑩ e·*la*·do
ice cream parlour *heladería* ①
e·la·de·*ree*·a
ice hockey *hockey* ⑩ *sobre hielo*
kho·kee so·bre *ye*·lo
identification *identificación* ①
ee·den·tee·fee·ka·*thyon*
identification card *carnet* ⑩ *de*
identidad kar·*net* de ee·den·tee·*da*
idiot *idiota* ⑩&① ee·*dyo*·ta
if *si* see
ill *enfermo/a* ⑩/① en·*fer*·mo/a
immigration *inmigración* ①
een·mee·gra·*thyon*

important *importante* eem·por·*tan*·te
in a hurry *de prisa* de *pree*·sa
in front of *enfrente de* en·*fren*·te de
included *incluido* een·kloo·ee·do
income tax *impuesto* ⑩ *sobre la renta*
eem·*pwes*·to so·bre la *ren*·ta
India *India* ① *een*·dya
indicator *indicador* ⑩ een·dee·ka·*dor*
indigestion *indigestion* ①
een·dee·khes·*tyon*
industry *industria* ① een·*doos*·trya
infection *infección* ① een·fek·*thyon*
inflammation *inflamación* ①
een·fla·ma·*thyon*
influenza *gripe* ① *gree*·pe
ingredient *ingrediente* ⑩
een·gre·*dyen*·te
inject *inyectarse* een·yek·*tar*·se
injection *inyección* ① een·yek·*thyon*
injury *herida* ① e·*ree*·da
innocent *inocente* ee·no·*then*·te
inside *adentro* a·*den*·tro
instructor *profesor/profesora* ⑩/①
pro·fe·*sor*/pro·fe·*sor*·ra
insurance *seguro* ⑩ se·*goo*·ro
interesting *interesante* een·te·re·*san*·te
intermission *descanso* ⑩ des·*kan*·so
international *internacional* ①
een·ter·na·thyo·*nal*
Internet *Internet* een·ter·*net*
Internet cafe *cibercafé* thee·ber·ka·*fe*
interpreter *intérprete* ⑩&①
een·*ter*·pre·te
intersection *cruce* ⑩ *croo*·the
interview *entrevista* ① en·tre·*vees*·ta
invite *invitar* een·vee·*tar*
Ireland *Irlanda* ① *plan*·cha
iron *plancha* ① *plan*·cha
island *isla* ① *ees*·la
IT *informática* ① een·for·*ma*·tee·ka
Italy *Italia* ① ee·*ta*·lya
itch *picazón* ① pee·ka·*thon*
itemised *detallado/a* ⑩/①
de·ta·*lya*·do/a
itinerary *itinerario* ① ee·tee·ne·*ra*·ryo
IUD *DIU* ⑩ de ee oo

J

jacket *chaqueta* ① cha·ke·ta
jail *cárcel* ① kar·thel
jam *mermelada* ① mer·me·la·da
Japan *Japón* ⓜ kha·pon
jar *jarra* ① kha·ra
jaw *mandíbula* ① man·dee·boo·la
jealous *celoso/a* ⓜ/① the·lo·so/a
jeans *vaqueros* ⓜ pl va·ke·ros
jeep *yip* ⓜ yeep
jet lag *jet lag* ⓜ dyet lag
jewellery shop *joyería* ① kho·ye·ree·a
Jewish *judío/a* ⓜ/① khoo·dee·o/a
job *trabajo* ⓜ tra·ba·kho
jockey *jockey* ⓜ dyo·kee
jogging *footing* ⓜ foo·teen
joke *broma* ① bro·ma
joke *bromear* bro·me·ar
journalist *periodista* ⓜ&①
    pe·ryo·dees·ta
judge *juez* ⓜ&① khweth
juice *jugo* ⓜ khoo·go •
    zumo ⓜ thoo·mo
jump *saltar* sal·tar
jumper (sweater) *jersey* ⓜ kher·say
jumper leads *cables* ⓜ pl *de arranque*
    ka·bles de a·ran·ke

K

ketchup *salsa* ① *de tomate*
    sal·sa de to·ma·te
key *llave* ① lya·ve
keyboard *teclado* ⓜ te·kla·do
kick *dar una patada* dar oo·na pa·ta·da
kick (a goal) *meter (un gol)*
    me·ter (oon gol)
kill *matar* ma·tar
kilogram *kilogramo* ⓜ kee·lo·gram·o
kilometre *kilómetro* ⓜ kee·lo·me·tro
kind *amable* a·ma·ble
kindergarten *escuela* ① *de párvulos*
    es·kwe·la de par·voo·los
king *rey* ⓜ rey

kiss *beso* ⓜ be·so
kiss *besar* be·sar
kitchen *cocina* ① ko·thee·na
kitten *gatito/a* ⓜ/① ga·tee·to/a
kiwifruit *kiwi* ⓜ kee·wee
knapsack *mochila* ① mo·chee·la
knee *rodilla* ① ro·dee·lya
knife *cuchillo* ⓜ koo·chee·lyo
know (someone) *conocer* ko·no·ther
know (something) *saber* sa·ber
Kosher *kosher* ko·sher

L

labourer *obrero/a* ⓜ/① o·bre·ro/a
lace *encaje* ⓜ en·ka·khe
lager *cerveza* ① *rubia*
    ther·ve·tha roo·bya
lake *lago* ⓜ la·go
lamb *cordero* ⓜ kor·de·ro
land *tierra* ① tye·ra
landlady *propietaria* ① pro·pye·ta·rya
landlord *propietario* ⓜ pro·pye·ta·ryo
languages *idiomas* ⓜ pl ee·dyo·mas
laptop *ordenador* ⓜ *portátil*
    or·de·na·dor por·ta·teel
lard *manteca* ① man·te·ka
large *grande* gran·de
late *tarde* tar·de
laugh *reírse* re·eer·se
laundrette *lavandería* ① la·van·de·ree·a
laundry *lavadero* ⓜ la·va·de·ro
law *ley* ① ley
lawyer *abogado/a* ⓜ/① a·bo·ga·do/a
leader *líder* ⓜ&① lee·der
leaf *hoja* ① o·kha
learn *aprender* a·pren·der
leather *cuero* ⓜ kwe·ro
leave *dejar* de·khar
lecturer *profesor/profesora* ⓜ/①
    pro·fe·sor/pro·fe·so·ra
ledge *saliente* ⓜ sa·lyen·te
leek *puerro* ⓜ pwe·ro
left *izquierda* ① eeth·kyer·da

left (behind/over) *quedar* ke·*dar*
left luggage *consigna* ① kon·*seeg*·na
left-wing *de izquierda* de eeth·*kyer*·da
leg *pierna* ① *pyer*·na
legal *legal* le·*gal*
legislation *legislación* ①
le·khees·la·*thyon*
lemon *limón* ⓜ lee·*mon*
lemonade *limonada* ① lee·mo·*na*·da
Lent *Cuaresma* ① kwa·*res*·ma
lentils *lentejas* ① pl len·*te*·khas
lesbian *lesbiana* ① les·be·*a*·na
less *menos* me·nos
letter *carta* ① *kar*·ta
lettuce *lechuga* ① le·*choo*·ga
liar *mentiroso/a* ⓜ/① men·tee·ro·*so*/a
library *biblioteca* ① bee·blyo·*te*·ka
lice *piojos* ⓜ pl *pyo*·khos
license plate number *matrícula* ①
ma·*tree*·koo·la
lie (not stand) *tumbarse* toom·*bar*·se
life *vida* ① *vee*·da
lifejacket *chaleco* ⓜ *salvavidas*
cha·*le*·ko sal·va·*vee*·das
lift *ascensor* ⓜ as·then·*sor*
light (weight) *leve* *le*·ve
light *luz* ① *looth*
light bulb *bombilla* ① bom·*bee*·lya
light meter *fotómetro* ⓜ fo·*to*·me·tro
lighter *encendedor* ⓜ en·then·de·*dor*
like *gustar(le)* goos·*tar*(le)
lime *lima* ① *lee*·ma
line *línea* ① *lee*·ne·a
lip balm *bálsamo* ⓜ *de labios*
bal·sa·mo de *la*·byos
lips *labios* ⓜ pl *la*·byos
lipstick *pintalabios* ⓜ peen·ta *la*·byos
liquor store *bodega* ① bo·*de*·ga
listen *escuchar* es·koo·*char*
live (life) *vivir* vee·*veer*
live (somewhere) *ocupar* o·koo·*par*
liver *hígado* ⓜ *ee*·ga·do
lizard *lagartija* ① la·gar·*tee*·kha

local *de cercanías* de ther·ka·*nee*·as
lock *cerradura* ① the·ra·*doo*·ra
lock *cerrar* the·*rar*
locked *cerrado/a* ⓜ/① *con llave*
the·ra·do/a kon *lya*·ve
lollies *caramelos* ⓜ pl ka·ra·*me*·los
long *largo/a* ⓜ/① *lar*·go/a
long-distance *a larga distancia*
a *lar*·ga dees·*tan*·thya
look *mirar* mee·*rar*
look after *cuidar* kwee·*dar*
look for *buscar* boos·*kar*
lookout *mirador* ⓜ mee·ra·*dor*
lose *perder* per·*der*
lost *perdido/a* ⓜ/① per·*dee*·do/a
lost property office *oficina* ① *de*
objetos perdidos o·fee·*thee*·na de
ob·*khe*·tos per·*dee*·dos
loud *ruidoso/a* ⓜ/① rwee·*do*·so/a
love *querer* ke·*rer*
lover *amante* ⓜ&① a·*man*·te
low *bajo/a* ⓜ/① *ba*·kho/a
lubricant *lubricante* ⓜ loo·bree·*kan*·te
luck *suerte* ① *swer*·te
lucky *afortunado/a* ⓜ/①
a·for·too·*na*·do/a
luggage *equipaje* ⓜ e·kee·*pa*·khe
luggage lockers
consigna ① *automática*
kon·*seeg*·na ow·to·*ma*·tee·ka
luggage tag *etiqueta* ① *de equipaje*
e·tee·*ke*·ta de e·kee·*pa*·khe
lump *bulto* ⓜ *bool*·to
lunch *almuerzo* ⓜ al·*mwer*·tho
lungs *pulmones* ⓜ pl pool·*mo*·nes
luxury *lujo* ⓜ *loo*·kho

M

machine *máquina* ① *ma*·kee·na
made of (cotton) *hecho a de (algodón)*
e·cho a de (al·go·*don*)
magazine *revista* ① re·*vees*·ta
magician *mago/a* ⓜ/① *ma*·go/a
mail *correo* ⓜ ko·*re*·o

mailbox *buzón* ⓜ boo·*thon*
main *principal* preen·thee·*pal*
make *hacer* a·*ther*
make fun of *burlarse de* boor·*lar*·se de
make-up *maquillaje* ⓜ ma·kee·*lya*·khe
mammogram *mamograma* ⓜ
  ma·mo·*gra*·ma
man *hombre* ⓜ *om*·bre
manager *gerente* ⓜ&ⓕ khe·*ren*·te
mandarin *mandarina* ⓕ man·da·*ree*·na
mango *mango* ⓜ *man*·go
manual worker *obrero/a* ⓜ/ⓕ o·*bre*·ro/a
many *muchas/os* ⓜ/ⓕ pl *moo*·chas/os
map *mapa* ⓜ *ma*·pa
margarine *margarina* ⓕ mar·ga·*ree*·na
marijuana *marihuana* ⓕ ma·ree·*wa*·na
marital status *estado* ⓜ *civil*
  es·*ta*·do thee·*veel*
market *mercado* ⓜ mer·*ka*·do
marmalade *mermelada* ⓕ
  mer·me·*la*·da
marriage *matrimonio* ⓜ ma·tree·mo·*nyo*
marry *casarse* ka·*sar*·se
martial arts *artes* ⓜ pl *marciales*
  ar·tes mar·*thya*·les
mass *misa* ⓕ *mee*·sa
massage *masaje* ⓜ ma·*sa*·khe
masseur/masseuse *masajista* ⓜ&ⓕ
  ma·sa·*khees*·ta
mat *esterilla* ⓕ es·te·*ree*·lya
match *partido* ⓜ par·*tee*·do
matches *cerillas* ⓕ pl the·*ree*·lyas
mattress *colchón* ⓜ kol·*chon*
maybe *quizás* kee·*thas*
mayonnaise *mayonesa* ⓕ ma·yo·*ne*·sa
mayor *alcalde* ⓜ&ⓕ al·*kal*·de
measles *sarampión* ⓜ sa·ram·*pyon*
meat *carne* ⓕ *kar*·ne
mechanic *mecánico/a* ⓜ/ⓕ
  me·*ka*·nee·ko
media *medios* ⓜ pl *de comunicación*
  me·dyos de ko·moo·nee·ka·*thyon*
medicine *medicina* ⓕ me·dee·*thee*·na
meet *encontrar* en·kon·*trar*

melon *melón* ⓜ me·*lon*
member *miembro* ⓜ *myem*·bro
menstruation *menstruación* ⓕ
  mens·trwa·*thyon*
menu *menú* ⓜ me·*noo*
message *mensaje* ⓜ men·*sa*·khe
metal *metal* ⓜ me·*tal*
metre *metro* ⓜ *me*·tro
metro station *estación* ⓕ *de metro*
  es·ta·*thyon* de *me*·tro
microwave *microondas* ⓜ
  mee·kro·*on*·das
midnight *medianoche* ⓕ me·dya·*no*·che
migraine *migraña* ⓕ mee·*gra*·nya
military service *servicio* ⓜ *militar*
  ser·*vee*·thyo mee·lee·*tar*
milk *leche* ⓕ *le*·che
millimetre *milímetro* ⓜ mee·*lee*·me·tro
million *millón* ⓜ mee·*lyon*
mince (meat) *carne* ⓜ *molida*
  kar·ne mo·*lee*·da
mind (object) *cuidar* kwee·*dar*
mineral water *agua* ⓜ *mineral*
  a·gwa mee·ne·*ral*
mints *pastillas* ⓕ pl *de menta*
  pas·*tee*·lyas de *men*·ta
minute *minuto* ⓜ mee·*noo*·to
mirror *espejo* ⓜ es·*pe*·kho
miscarriage *aborto* ⓜ *natural*
  a·*bor*·to na·too·*ral*
miss (feel sad) *echar de menos*
  e·*char* de *me*·nos
mistake *error* ⓜ e·*ror*
mix *mezclar* meth·*klar*
mobile phone *teléfono* ⓜ *móvil*
  te·*le*·fo·no *mo*·veel
modem *módem* ⓜ *mo*·dem
moisturiser *crema* ⓕ *hidratante*
  kre·ma ee·dra·*tan*·te
monastery *monasterio* ⓜ mo·nas·*te*·ryo
money *dinero* ⓜ dee·*ne*·ro
month *mes* ⓜ mes
monument *monumento* ⓜ
  mo·noo·*men*·to

(full) moon *luna* ① *(llena)*
loo·na (lye·na)

morning (6am - 1pm) *mañana* ①
ma·nya·na

morning sickness *náuseas* ① pl *del*
embarazo now·se·as del em·ba·ra·tho

mosque *mezquita* ① meth·kee·ta

mosquito *mosquito* ⓜ mos·kee·to

mosquito coil *rollo* ⓜ *repelente contra*
mosquitos ro·lyo re·pe·len·te kon·tra
mos·kee·tos

mosquito net *mosquitera* ①
mos·kee·te·ra

mother *madre* ① ma·dre

mother-in-law *suegra* ① swe·gra

motorboat *motora* ① mo·to·ra

motorcycle *motocicleta* ①
mo·to·thee·kle·ta

motorway *autovía* ① ow·to·vee·a

mountain *montaña* ① mon·ta·nya

mountain bike *bicicleta* ① *de montaña*
bee·thee·kle·ta de mon·ta·nya

mountain path *sendero* ⓜ sen·de·ro

mountain range *cordillera* ①
kor·dee·lye·ra

mountaineering *alpinismo* ⓜ
al·pee·nees·mo

mouse *ratón* ⓜ ra·ton

mouth *boca* ① bo·ka

movie *película* ① pe·lee·koo·la

mud *lodo* ⓜ lo·do

muesli *muesli* ⓜ mwes·lee

mum *mamá* ① ma·ma

muscle *músculo* ⓜ moos·koo·lo

museum *museo* ⓜ moo·se·o

mushroom *champiñón* ⓜ
cham·pee·nyon

music *música* ① moo·see·ka

musician *músico/a* ⓜ/① moo·see·ko/a

Muslim *musulmán/musulmána* ⓜ/①
moo·sool·man/moo·sool·ma·na

mussels *mejillones* ⓜ pl
me·khee·lyo·nes

mustard *mostaza* ① mos·ta·tha

mute *mudo/a* ⓜ/① moo·do/a

my *mi* mee

N

nail clippers *cortauñas* ⓜ pl
kor·ta·oo·nyas

name *nombre* ⓜ nom·bre

napkin *servilleta* ① ser·vee·lye·ta

nappy *pañal* ⓜ pa·nyal

nappy rash *irritación* ① *de pañal*
ee·ree·ta·thyon de pa·nyal

national park *parque* ⓜ *nacional*
par·ke na·thyo·nal

nationality *nacionalidad* ①
na·thyo·na·lee·da

nature *naturaleza* ① na·too·ra·le·tha

naturopathy *naturopatia* ①
na·too·ro·pa·tya

nausea *náusea* ① now·se·a

near *cerca* ther·ka

nearby *cerca* ther·ka

nearest *más cercano/a* ⓜ/①
mas ther·ka·no/a

necessary *necesario/a* ⓜ/①
ne·the·sa·ryo/a

neck *cuello* ⓜ kwe·lyo

necklace *collar* ⓜ ko·lyar

need *necesitar* ne·the·see·tar

needle (sewing) *aguja* ① a·goo·kha

needle (syringe) *jeringa* ① khe·reen·ga

neither *tampoco* tam·po·ko

net *red* ⓜ red

Netherlands *Holanda* ① o·lan·da

never *nunca* noon·ka

new *nuevo/a* ⓜ/① nwe·vo/a

New Year *Año Nuevo* ⓜ a·nyo nwe·vo

New Year's Eve *Nochevieja* ①
no·che·vye·kha

New Zealand *Nueva Zelanda* ①
nwe·va the·lan·da

news *noticias* ① pl no·tee·thyas

news stand *quiosco* ⓜ kyos·ko

newsagency *quiosco* ⓜ kyos·ko

newspaper *periódico* ⓜ pe·ryo·dee·ko

next (month) *el próximo (mes)*
el prok·see·mo (mes)

next to *al lado de* al la·do de

nice simpático/a ⓜ/ⓕ seem·pa·tee·ko/a
nickname apodo ⓜ a·po·do
night noche ⓕ no·che
no no no
noisy ruidoso/a ⓜ/ⓕ rwee·do·so/a
none nada na·da
non-smoking no fumadores
  no foo·ma·do·res
noodles fideos ⓜ pl fee·de·os
noon mediodía ⓜ me·dyo·dee·a
north norte ⓜ nor·te
nose nariz ⓕ na·reeth
notebook cuaderno ⓜ kwa·der·no
nothing nada na·da
now ahora a·o·ra
nuclear energy energía ⓕ nuclear
  e·ner·khee·a noo·kle·ar
nuclear testing pruebas ⓕ pl
  nucleares prwe·bas noo·kle·a·res
nuclear waste
  desperdicios ⓜ pl nucleares
  des·per·dee·thyos noo·kle·a·res
number número ⓜ noo·me·ro
nun monja ⓕ mon·kha
nurse enfermero/a ⓜ/ⓕ en·fer·me·ro/a
nuts nueces ⓕ pl nwe·thes
nuts (raw) nueces ⓕ pl (crudas)
  nwe·thes (kroo·das)
nuts (roasted) nueces ⓕ pl (tostadas)
  nwe·thes (tos·ta·das)

O

oats avena ⓕ a·ve·na
ocean océano ⓜ o·the·a·no
off (food) pasado/a ⓜ/ⓕ pa·sa·do/a
office oficina ⓕ o·fee·thee·na
office worker oficinista ⓜ&ⓕ
  o·fee·thee·nees·ta
offside fuera de juego fwe·ra de khwe·go
often a menudo a me·noo·do
oil aceite ⓜ a·they·te
old viejo/a ⓜ/ⓕ vye·kho/a
olive oil aceite ⓜ de oliva
  a·they·te de o·lee·va

Olympic Games juegos ⓜ pl olímpicos
  khwe·gos o·leem·pee·kos
on en en
once vez ⓕ veth
one-way ticket billete ⓜ sencillo
  bee·lye·te sen·thee·lyo
onion cebolla ⓕ the·bo·lya
only sólo so·lo
open abierto/a ⓜ/ⓕ a·byer·to/a
open abrir a·breer
opening hours horas ⓕ pl de abrir
  o·ras de a·breer
opera ópera ⓕ o·pe·ra
opera house teatro ⓜ de la ópera
  te·a·tro de la o·pe·ra
operation operación ⓕ o·pe·ra·thyon
operator operador/operadora ⓜ/ⓕ
  o·pe·ra·dor/o·pe·ra·do·ra
opinion opinión ⓕ o·pee·nyon
opposite frente a fren·te a
or o o
orange (fruit) naranja ⓕ na·ran·kha
orange (colour) naranja na·ran·kha
orange juice zumo ⓜ de naranja
  thoo·mo de na·ran·kha
orchestra orquesta ⓕ or·kes·ta
order orden ⓜ or·den
order ordenar or·de·nar
ordinary corriente ko·ryen·te
orgasm orgasmo ⓜ or·gas·mo
original original o·ree·khee·nal
other otro/a ⓜ/ⓕ o·tro/a
our nuestro/a ⓜ/ⓕ nwes·tro/a
outside exterior ⓜ eks·te·ryor
ovarian cyst quiste ⓜ ovárico
  kees·te o·va·ree·ko
oven horno ⓜ or·no
overcoat abrigo ⓜ a·bree·go
overdose sobredosis ⓕ so·bre·do·sees
owe deber de·ver
owner dueño/a ⓜ/ⓕ dwe·nyo/a
oxygen oxígeno ⓜ o·ksee·khe·no
oyster ostra ostra
ozone layer capa ⓕ de ozono
  ka·pa de o·tho·no

P

pacemaker *marcapasos* ⓜ mar·ka·*pa*·sos
pacifier *chupete* ⓜ choo·*pe*·te
package *paquete* ⓜ pa·*ke*·te
packet *paquete* ⓜ pa·*ke*·te
padlock *candado* ⓜ kan·*da*·do
page *página* ⓕ *pa*·khee·na
pain *dolor* ⓜ do·*lor*
painful *doloroso/a* ⓜ/ⓕ do·lo·*ro*·so/a
painkillers *analgésicos* ⓜ pl
a·nal·*khe*·see·kos
paint *pintar* peen·*tar*
painter *pintor/pintora* ⓜ/ⓕ
peen·*tor*/peen·*to*·ra
painting *pintura* ⓕ peen·*too*·ra
pair (couple) *pareja* ⓕ pa·*re*·kha
palace *palacio* ⓜ pa·*la*·thyo
pan *cazuela* ⓕ ka·*thwe*·la
pants *pantalones* ⓜ pl pan·ta·*lo*·nes
panty liners *salvaeslips* ⓜ pl
sal·va·e·*sleeps*
pantyhose *medias* ⓕ pl *me*·dyas
pap smear *citología* ⓕ thee·to·lo·*khee*·a
paper *papel* ⓜ pa·*pel*
paperwork *trabajo* ⓜ *administrativo*
tra·*ba*·kho ad·mee·nees·tra·*tee*·vo
paraplegic *parapléjico/a* ⓜ/ⓕ
pa·ra·*ple*·khee·ko/a
parasailing *esquí* ⓜ *acuático con*
paracaídas es·*kee* a·*kwa*·tee·ko kon
pa·ra·ka·*ee*·das
parcel *paquete* ⓜ pa·*ke*·te
parents *padres* ⓜ pl *pa*·dres
park *parque* ⓜ *par*·ke
park (car) *estacionar* es·ta·thyo·*nar*
parliament *parlamento* ⓜ
par·la·*men*·to
parsley *perejil* ⓜ pe·re·*kheel*
part *parte* ⓕ *par*·te
part-time a *tiempo parcial*
a *tyem*·po par·*thyal*
party *fiesta* ⓕ *fyes*·ta
party (political) *partido* ⓜ par·*tee*·do
pass *pase* ⓜ *pa*·se

passenger *pasajero/a* ⓜ/ⓕ
pa·sa·*khe*·ro
passport *pasaporte* ⓜ pa·sa·*por*·te
passport number *número* ⓜ *de pasaporte*
noo·me·ro de pa·sa·*por*·te
past *pasado* ⓜ pa·*sa*·do
pasta *pasta* ⓕ *pas*·ta
pate (food) *paté* ⓜ pa·*te*
path *sendero* ⓜ sen·*de*·ro
pay *pagar* pa·*gar*
payment *pago* ⓜ *pa*·go
peace *paz* ⓕ path
peach *melocotón* ⓜ me·lo·ko·*ton*
peak *cumbre* ⓕ *koom*·bre
peanuts *cacahuetes* ⓜ pl ka·ka·*we*·tes
pear *pera* ⓕ *pe*·ra
peas *guisantes* ⓜ pl gee·*san*·tes
pedal *pedal* ⓜ pe·*dal*
pedestrian *peatón* ⓜ&ⓕ pe·a·*ton*
pedestrian crossing *paso* ⓜ *de cebra*
pa·so de *the*·bra
pen *bolígrafo* ⓜ bo·*lee*·gra·fo
pencil *lápiz* ⓜ *la*·peeth
penis *pene* ⓜ *pe*·ne
penknife *navaja* ⓕ na·*va*·kha
pensioner *pensionista* ⓜ&ⓕ
pen·syo·*nees*·ta
people *gente* ⓕ *khen*·te
pepper (vegetable) *pimiento* ⓜ
pee·*myen*·to
pepper (spice) *pimienta* ⓕ
pee·*myen*·ta
per (day) *por (dia)* por (*dee*·a)
percent *por ciento* por *thyen*·to
performance *actuación* ⓕ ak·twa·*thyon*
perfume *perfume* ⓜ per·*foo*·me
period pain *dolor* ⓜ *menstrual*
do·*lor* mens·*trwal*
permission *permiso* ⓜ per·*mee*·so
permit *permiso* ⓜ per·*mee*·so
permit *permitir* per·mee·*teer*
person *persona* ⓕ per·*so*·na
perspire *sudar* soo·*dar*
petition *petición* ⓕ pe·tee·*thyon*
petrol *gasolina* ⓕ ga·so·*lee*·na

pharmacy *farmacia* ① far·ma·thya

phone book *guía* ① *telefónica*
gee·a te·le·fo·nee·ka

phone box *cabina* ① *telefónica*
ka·bee·ka te·le·fo·nee·ka

phone card *tarjeta* ① *de teléfono*
tar·khe·ta de te·le·fo·no

photo *foto* ① fo·to

photographer *fotógrafo/a* ⑩/①
fo·to·gra·fo/a

photography *fotografía* ①
fo·to·gra·fee·a

phrasebook *libro* ⑩ *de frases*
lee·bro de fra·ses

pick up *ligar* lee·gar

pickaxe *piqueta* ① pee·ke·ta

pickles *encurtidos* ⑩ pl en·koor·tee·dos

picnic *comida* ① *en el campo*
ko·mee·da en el kam·po

pie *pastel* ⑩ pas·tel

piece *pedazo* ⑩ pe·da·tho

pig *cerdo* ⑩ ther·do

pill *pastilla* ① pas·tee·lya

pillow *almohada* ① al·mwa·da

pillowcase *funda* ① *de almohada*
foon·da de al·mwa·da

pineapple *piña* ① pee·nya

pink *rosa* ro·sa

pistachio *pistacho* ⑩ pees·ta·cho

place *lugar* ⑩ loo·gar

place of birth *lugar* ⑩ *de nacimiento*
loo·gar de na·thee·myen·to

plane *avión* ⑩ a·vyon

planet *planeta* ① pla·ne·ta

plant *planta* ① plan·ta

plant *sembrar* sem·brar

plastic *plástico* ⑩ plas·tee·ko

plate *plato* ⑩ pla·to

plateau *meseta* ① me·se·ta

platform *plataforma* ① pla·ta·for·ma

play *obra* ① o·bra

play (musical instrument) *tocar* to·kar

play (sport/games) *jugar* khoo·gar

plug *tapar* ta·par

plum *ciruela* thee·rwe·la

pocket *bolsillo* ⑩ bol·see·lyo

poetry *poesía* ① po·e·see·a

point *apuntar* a·poon·tar

point (tip) *punto* ⑩ poon·to

poisonous *venenoso/a* ⑩/①
ve·ne·no·so/a

poker *póquer* ⑩ po·ker

police *policía* ① po·lee·thee·a

police station *comisaría* ①
ko·mee·sa·ree·a

policy *política* ① po·lee·tee·ka

policy (insurance) *póliza* ① po·lee·tha

politician *político* ⑩ po·lee·tee·ko

politics *política* ① po·lee·tee·ka

pollen *polen* ⑩ po·len

polls *sondeos* ⑩ pl son·de·os

pollution *contaminación* ①
kon·ta·mee·na·thyon

pool (swimming) *piscina* ①
pees·thee·na

poor *pobre* po·bre

popular *popular* po·poo·lar

pork *cerdo* ⑩ ther·do

pork sausage *chorizo* ⑩ cho·ree·tho

port *puerto* ⑩ pwer·to

port (wine) *oporto* ⑩ o·por·to

possible *posible* po·see·ble

post code *código postal* ⑩
ko·dee·go pos·tal

post office *correos* ⑩ ko·re·os

postage *franqueo* ① fran·ke·o

postcard *postal* ① pos·tal

poster *póster* ⑩ pos·ter

pot (kitchen) *cazuela* ① ka·thwe·la

pot (plant) *tiesto* ⑩ tyes·to

potato *patata* ① pa·ta·ta

pottery *alfarería* ① al·fa·re·ree·a

pound (money) *libra* ① lee·bra

poverty *pobreza* ① po·bre·tha

power *poder* ⑩ po·der

prawns *gambas* ① pl gam·bas

prayer *oración* ① o·ra·thyon

prayer book *devocionario* ⑩
de·vo·thyo·na·ryo

prefer *preferir* pre·fe·reer
pregnancy test *prueba* ① *del embarazo* prwe·ba del em·ba·ra·tho
pregnant *embarazada* ① em·ba·ra·tha·da
premenstrual tension *tensión* ① *premenstrual* ten·syon pre·mens·trwal
prepare *preparar* pre·pa·rar
president *presidente/a* ⓜ/① pre·see·den·te/a
pressure *presión* ① pre·syon
pretty *bonito/a* ⓜ/① bo·nee·to/a
prevent *prevenir* pre·ve·neer
price *precio* ⓜ pre·thyo
priest *sacerdote* ⓜ sa·ther·do·te
prime minister *primer ministro/ primera ministra* ⓜ/① pree·mer mee·nees·tro/pree·me·ra mee·nees·tra
prison *cárcel* ① kar·thel
prisoner *prisionero/a* ⓜ/① pree·syon·ne·ro/a
private *privado/a* ⓜ/① pree·va·do/a
private hospital *clínica* ① klee·nee·ka
produce *producir* pro·doo·theer
profit *beneficio* ⓜ be·ne·fee·thyo
programme *programa* ⓜ pro·gra·ma
projector *proyector* ⓜ pro·yek·tor
promise *promesa* ① pro·me·sa
protect *proteger* pro·te·kher
protected (species) *protegido/a* ⓜ/① pro·te·khee·do/a
protest *protesta* ① pro·tes·ta
protest *protestar* pro·tes·tar
provisions *provisiones* ① pl pro·bee·syo·nes
prune *ciruela* ① *pasa* thee·rwe·la pa·sa
pub *pub* ⓜ poob
public telephone *teléfono* ⓜ *público* te·le·fo·no poo·blee·ko
public toilet *servicios* ⓜ pl ser·vee·thyos
pull *tirar* tee·rar
pump *bomba* ① bom·ba

pumpkin *calabaza* ① ka·la·ba·tha
puncture *pinchar* peen·char
punish *castigar* kas·tee·gar
puppy *cachorro* ⓜ ka·cho·ro
pure *puro/a* ⓜ/① poo·ro/a
purple *lila* lee·la
push *empujar* em·poo·khar
put *poner* po·ner

Q

qualifications *cualificaciones* ① pl kwa·lee·fee·ka·thyo·nes
quality *calidad* ① ka·lee·da
quarantine *cuarentena* ① kwa·ren·te·na
quarrel *pelea* ① pe·le·a
quarter *cuarto* ⓜ kwar·to
queen *reina* ① rey·na
question *pregunta* ① pre·goon·ta
question *cuestionar* kwes·tyo·nar
queue *cola* ① ko·la
quick *rápido/a* ⓜ/① ra·pee·do/a
quiet *tranquilo/a* ⓜ/① tran·kee·lo/a
quiet *tranquilidad* ① tran·kee·lee·da
quit *dejar* de·khar

R

rabbit *conejo* ⓜ ko·ne·kho
race (people) *raza* ① ra·tha
race (sport) *carrera* ① ka·re·ra
racetrack (bicycles) *velódromo* ⓜ ve·lo·dro·mo
racetrack (cars) *circuito* ⓜ *de carreras* theer·kwee·to de ka·re·ras
racetrack (horses) *hipódromo* ⓜ ee·po·dro·mo
racetrack (runners) *pista* ① pees·ta
racing bike *bicicleta* ① *de carreras* bee·thee·kle·ta de ka·re·ras
racquet *raqueta* ① ra·ke·ta
radiator *radiador* ⓜ ra·dya·dor
radish *rábano* ⓜ ra·ba·no
railway station *estación* ① *de tren* es·ta·thyon de tren
rain *lluvia* ① lyoo·vya

raincoat *impermeable* ⓜ
 eem·per·me·a·ble
raisin *uva* ⓕ *pasa* oo·va pa·sa
rally *concentración* ⓕ
kon·then·tra·thyon
rape *violar* vyo·lar
rare *raro/a* ⓜ/ⓕ ra·ro/a
rash *irritación* ⓕ ee·ree·ta·thyon
raspberry *frambuesa* ⓕ fram·bwe·sa
rat *rata* ⓕ ra·ta
rate of pay *salario* ⓜ sa·la·ryo
raw *crudo/a* ⓜ/ⓕ kroo·do/a
razor *afeitadora* ⓕ a·fey·ta·do·ra
razor blades *cuchillas* ⓕ pl *de afeitar*
koo·chee·lyas de a·fey·tar
read *leer* le·er
ready *listo/a* ⓜ/ⓕ lees·to/a
real estate agent *agente inmobiliario* ⓜ
a·khen·te een·mo·bee·lya·ryo
realise *darse cuenta de* dar·se kwen·ta de
realistic *realista* re·a·lees·ta
reason *razón* ⓕ ra·thon
receipt *recibo* ⓜ re·thee·bo
receive *recibir* re·thee·beer
recently *recientemente* re·thyen·te·men·te
recognise *reconocer* re·ko·no·ther
recommend *recomendar* re·ko·men·dar
recording *grabación* ⓕ gra·ba·thyon
recyclable *reciclable* re·thee·kla·ble
recycle *reciclar* re·thee·klar
red *rojo/a* ⓜ/ⓕ ro·kho/a
referee *árbitro* ⓜ ar·bee·tro
reference *referencias* ⓕ pl
re·fe·ren·thyas
refrigerator *nevera* ⓕ ne·ve·ra •
frigerífico ⓜ free·ge·ree·fee·ko
refugee *refugiado/a* ⓜ/ⓕ
re·foo·khya·do/a
refund *reembolso* ⓜ re·em·bol·so
refund *reembolsar* re·em·bol·sar
refuse *negar* ne·gar
registered mail *correo* ⓜ *certificado*
ko·re·o ther·tee·fee·ka·do
regret *lamentar* la·men·tar

relationship *relación* ⓕ re·la·thyon
relax *relajarse* re·la·khar·se
relic *reliquia* ⓕ re·lee·kya
religion *religión* ⓕ re·lee·khyon
religious *religioso/a* ⓜ/ⓕ
re·lee·khyo·so/a
remember *recordar* re·kor·dar
remote *remoto/a* ⓜ/ⓕ re·mo·to/a
remote control *mando* ⓜ *a distancia*
man·do a dees·tan·thya
rent *alquiler* ⓜ al·kee·ler
rent *alquilar* al·kee·lar
repair *reparar* re·pa·rar
repeat *repetir* re·pe·teer
republic *república* ⓕ re·poo·blee·ka
reservation *reserva* ⓕ re·ser·va
reserve *reservar* re·ser·var
rest *descansar* des·kan·sar
restaurant *restaurante* ⓜ res·tow·ran·te
resumé *currículum* ⓜ
koo·ree·koo·loom
retired *jubilado/a* ⓜ/ⓕ khoo·bee·la·do/a
return *volver* vol·ver
return ticket *billete* ⓜ *de ida y vuelta*
bee·lye·te de ee·da ee vwel·ta
review *crítica* ⓕ kree·tee·ka
rhythm *ritmo* ⓜ reet·mo
rice *arroz* a·roth
rich *rico/a* ⓜ/ⓕ ree·ko/a
ride *paseo* ⓜ pa·se·o
ride *montar* mon·tar
right (correct) *correcto/a* ⓜ/ⓕ
ko·rek·to/a
right (not left) *derecha* de·re·cha
right-wing *derechista* de·re·chees·ta
ring *llamada* ⓕ lya·ma·da
ring *llamar por telefono*
lya·mar por te·le·fo·no
rip-off *estafa* ⓕ es·ta·fa
risk *riesgo* ⓜ ryes·go
river *río* ⓜ ree·o
road *carretera* ⓕ ka·re·te·ra
rob *robar* ro·bar
rock (stone) *roca* ⓕ ro·ka

rock (music) *rock* ⓜ rok
rock climbing *escalada* ⓕ es·ka·*la*·da
rock group *grupo* ⓜ *de rock*
  groo·po de rok
rollerblading *patinar* pa·tee·*nar*
romantic *romántico/a* ⓜ/ⓕ
  ro·*man*·tee·ko/a
room *habitación* ⓕ a·bee·ta·*thyon*
room number
  número ⓜ *de la habitación*
  noo·me·ro de la a·bee·ta·*thyon*
rope *cuerda* ⓕ *kwer*·da
round *redondo/a* ⓜ/ⓕ re·*don*·do/a
roundabout *glorieta* ⓕ glo·*rye*·ta
route *ruta* ⓕ *roo*·ta
rowing *remo* ⓜ *re*·mo
rubbish *basura* ⓕ ba·*soo*·ra
rug *alfombra* ⓕ al·*fom*·bra
rugby *rugby* ⓜ *roog*·bee
ruins *ruinas* ⓕ pl *rwee*·nas
rules *reglas* ⓕ pl *re*·glas
rum *ron* ron
run *correr* ko·*rer*
run out of *quedarse sin* ke·*dar*·se seen

S

sad *triste* *trees*·te
saddle *sillín* ⓜ see·*lyeen*
safe *seguro/a* ⓜ/ⓕ se·*goo*·ro/a
safe *caja* ⓕ *fuerte* ka·kha *fwer*·te
safe sex *sexo* ⓜ *seguro* *se*·kso se·*goo*·ro
saint *santo/a* ⓜ/ⓕ *san*·to/a
salad *ensalada* ⓕ en·sa·*la*·da
salami (Spanish sausage) *chorizo*
  cho·*ree*·tho
salary *salario* ⓜ sa·*la*·ryo
sales tax *IVA* ⓜ *ee*·va
salmon *salmón* ⓜ sal·*mon*
salt *sal* ⓕ sal
same *igual* ee·*gwal*
sand *arena* ⓕ a·*re*·na
sandals *sandalias* ⓕ pl san·*da*·lyas
sanitary napkins *compresas* ⓕ pl
  kom·*pre*·sas

sauna *sauna* ⓕ *sow*·na
sausage *salchicha* ⓕ sal·*chee*·cha
save *salvar* sal·*var*
save (money) *ahorrar* a·o·*rar*
say *decir* de·*theer*
scale/climb *trepar* tre·*par*
scarf *bufanda* ⓕ boo·*fan*·da
school *escuela* ⓕ es·*kwe*·la
science *ciencias* ⓕ pl *thyen*·thyas
scientist *científico/a* ⓜ/ⓕ
  thyen·*tee*·fee·ko/a
scissors *tijeras* ⓕ pl tee·*khe*·ras
score *marcar* mar·*kar*
scoreboard *marcador* ⓜ mar·ka·*dor*
Scotland *Escocia* ⓕ es·*ko*·thya
screen *pantalla* ⓕ pan·*ta*·lya
script *guión* ⓜ gee·*on*
sculpture *escultura* ⓕ es·kool·*too*·ra
sea *mar* ⓜ mar
seasick *mareado/a* ⓜ/ⓕ ma·re·a·do/a
seaside *costa* ⓕ *kos*·ta
season *estación* ⓕ es·ta·*thyon*
season (in sport) *temporada* ⓕ
  tem·po·*ra*·da
seat *asiento* ⓜ a·*syen*·to
seatbelt *cinturón* ⓜ *de seguridad*
  theen·too·*ron* de se·goo·ree·da
second *segundo/a* ⓜ/ⓕ se·*goon*·do/a
second *segundo* se·*goon*·do
second-hand *de segunda mano*
  de se·*goon*·da *ma*·no
secretary *secretario/a* ⓜ/ⓕ
  se·kre·*ta*·ryo/a
see *ver* ver
selfish *egoista* e·go·*ees*·ta
self-service *autoservicio* ⓜ
  ow·to·ser·*vee*·thyo
sell *vender* ven·*der*
send *enviar* en·vee·*ar*
sensible *prudente* proo·*den*·te
sensual *sensual* sen·*swal*
separate *separado/a* ⓜ/ⓕ se·pa·*ra*·do/a
separate *separar* se·pa·*rar*
series *serie* ⓕ *se*·rye

serious *serio/a* ⓜ/ⓕ se·ryo·a
service station *gasolinera* ⓕ ga·so·lee·ne·ra
service charge *carga* ⓕ kar·ga
several *varias/os* ⓜ/ⓕ va·ryas/os
sew *coser* ko·ser
sex *sexo* ⓜ se·kso
sexism *machismo* ⓜ ma·chees·mo
sexy *sexy* se·ksee
shadow *sombra* ⓕ som·bra
shampoo *champú* ⓜ cham·poo
shape *forma* ⓕ for·ma
share (a dorm) *compartir (un dormitorio)* kom·par·teer (oon dor·mee·to·ryo)
share (with) *compartir* kom·par·teer
shave *afeitarse* a·fey·tar·se
shaving cream *espuma* ⓕ *de afeitar* es·poo·ma de a·fey·tar
she *ella* ⓕ e·lya
sheep *oveja* ⓕ o·ve·kha
sheet (bed) *sábana* ⓕ sa·ba·na
sheet (of paper) *hoja* ⓕ o·kha
shelf *estante* ⓜ es·tan·te
ship *barco* ⓜ bar·ko
ship *enviar* en·vee·ar
shirt *camisa* ⓕ ka·mee·sa
shoe shop *zapatería* ⓕ tha·pa·te·ree·a
shoes *zapatos* ⓜ pl tha·pa·tos
shoot *disparar* dees·pa·rar
shop *tienda* ⓕ tyen·da
shoplifting *ratería* ⓕ ra·te·ree·a
shopping centre *centro comercial* then·tro ko·mer·thyal
short (height) *bajo/a* ⓜ/ⓕ ba·kho/a
short (length) *corto/a* ⓜ/ⓕ kor·to/a
shortage *escasez* ⓕ es·ka·seth
shorts *pantalones* ⓜ pl *cortos* pan·ta·lo·nes
shoulders *hombros* ⓜ pl om·bros
shout *gritar* gree·tar
show *espectáculo* ⓜ es·pek·ta·koo·lo
show *mostrar* mos·trar
show *enseñar* en·se·nyar
shower *ducha* ⓕ doo·cha

shrine *capilla* ⓕ ka·pee·lya
shut *cerrado/a* ⓜ/ⓕ the·ra·do/a
shut *cerrar* the·rar
shy *tímido/a* ⓜ/ⓕ tee·mee·do/a
sick *enfermo/a* ⓜ/ⓕ en·fer·mo/a
side *lado* ⓜ la·do
sign *señal* ⓕ se·nyal
sign *firmar* feer·mar
signature *firma* ⓕ feer·ma
silk *seda* ⓕ se·da
silver *plateado/a* ⓜ/ⓕ pla·te·a·do/a
silver *plata* ⓕ pla·ta
similar *similar* see·mee·lar
simple *sencillo/a* ⓜ/ⓕ sen·thee·lyo/a
since (mayo) *desde (mayo)* des·de (ma·yo)
sing *cantar* kan·tar
Singapore *Singapur* ⓜ seen·ga·poor
singer *cantante* ⓜ&ⓕ kan·tan·te
single *soltero/a* ⓜ/ⓕ sol·te·ro/a
single room *habitación* ⓕ *individual* a·bee·ta·thyon een·dee·vee·dwal
singlet *camiseta* ⓕ ka·mee·se·ta
sister *hermana* ⓕ er·ma·na
sit *sentarse* sen·tar·se
size (clothes) *talla* ⓕ ta·lya
skateboarding *monopatinaje* ⓜ mo·no·pa·tee·na·khe
ski *esquiar* es·kee·ar
skiing *esquí* ⓜ es·kee
skimmed milk *leche* ⓕ *desnatada* le·che des·na·ta·da
skin *piel* ⓕ pyel
skirt *falda* ⓕ fal·da
sky *cielo* ⓜ thye·lo
skydiving *paracaidismo* ⓜ pa·ra·kai·dees·mo
sleep *dormir* dor·meer
sleeping bag *saco* ⓜ *de dormir* sa·ko de dor·meer
sleeping car *coche cama* ⓜ ko·che ka·ma
sleeping pills *pastillas* ⓕ pl *para dormir* pas·tee·lyas pa·ra dor·meer
(to be) sleepy *tener sueño* te·ner swe·nyo

slide *diapositiva* ① dya·po·see·*tee*·va

slow *lento/a* ⓜ/① *len*·to/a

slowly *despacio* des·*pa*·thyo

small *pequeño/a* ⓜ/① pe·*ke*·nyo/a

smell *olor* ⓜ o·*lor*

smell *oler* o·*ler*

smile *sonreír* son·re·*eer*

smoke *fumar* foo·*mar*

snack *tentempié* ⓜ ten·tem·*pye*

snail *caracol* ⓜ ka·ra·*kol*

snake *serpiente* ① ser·*pyen*·te

snorkel *tubos* ⓜ pl *respiratorios*

snorkel *buceo* ⓜ boo·*the*·o

snow *nieve* ① *nye*·ve

snowboarding *surf* ⓜ *sobre la nieve*
soorf *so*·bre la *nye*·ve

soap *jabón* ⓜ kha·*bon*

soap opera *telenovela* ① te·le·no·ve·la

soccer *fútbol* ⓜ *foot*·bol

social welfare *estado* ⓜ *del bienestar*
es·*ta*·do del byen·es·*tar*

socialist *socialista* ⓜ&① so·thya·*lees*·ta

socks *calcetines* ⓜ pl kal·the·*tee*·nes

soft drink *refresco* ⓜ re·*fres*·ko

soldier *soldado* ⓜ sol·*da*·do

some *alguno/a* ⓜ/① al·*goon*

someone *alguien* al·*gyen*

something *algo* al·go

sometimes *de vez en cuando*
de veth en *kwan*·do

son *hijo* ⓜ *ee*·kho

song *canción* ① kan·*thyon*

soon *pronto* *pron*·to

sore *dolorido/a* ⓜ/① do·lo·*ree*·do/a

soup *sopa* ① *so*·pa

sour cream *nata* ① *agria* na·ta *a*·grya

south *sur* ⓜ soor

souvenir *recuerdo* ⓜ re·*kwer*·do

souvenir shop *tienda* ① *de recuerdos*
tyen·da de re·*kwer*·dos

soy milk *leche* ① *de soja*
le·che de so·kha

soy sauce *salsa* ① *de soja*
sal·sa de so·kha

space *espacio* ⓜ es·*pa*·thyo

Spain *España* ① es·*pa*·nya

sparkling *espumoso/a* ⓜ/①
es·poo·*mo*·so

speak *hablar* a·*blar*

special *especial* es·pe·*thyal*

specialist *especialista* ⓜ&①
es·pe·thya·*lees*·ta

speed *velocidad* ① ve·lo·thee·*da*

speeding *exceso* ⓜ *de velocidad*
eks·*the*·so de ve·lo·thee·*da*

speedometer *velocímetro* ⓜ
ve·lo·*thee*·me·tro

spider *araña* ① a·*ra*·nya

spinach *espinacas* es·pee·*na*·kas

spoon *cuchara* ① koo·*cha*·ra

sport *deportes* ⓜ pl de·*por*·tes

sports store *tienda* ① *deportivva*
tyen·da de·por·*tee*·va

sportsperson *deportista* ⓜ&①
de·por·*tees*·ta

sprain *torcedura* ① tor·the·*doo*·ra

spring (wire) *muelle* ⓜ *mwe*·lye

spring (season) *primavera* ①
pree·ma·ve·ra

square (shape) *cuadrado* ⓜ kwa·*dra*·do

(main) square *plaza* ① *(mayor)*
pla·tha ma·*yor*

stadium *estadio* ⓜ es·*ta*·dyo

stage *escenario* ⓜ es·the·*na*·ryo

stairway *escalera* ① es·ka·*le*·ra

stamp *sello* ⓜ *se*·lyo

standby ticket
billete ⓜ *de lista de espera*
bee·*lye*·te de *lees*·ta de es·*pe*·ra

stars *estrellas* ① pl es·*tre*·lyas

start *comenzar* ko·men·*thar*

station *estación* ① es·ta·*thyon*

statue *estatua* ① es·*ta*·twa

stay (remain) *quedarse* ke·*dar*·se

stay (somewhere) *alojarse* a·lo·*khar*·se

steak (beef) *bistec* ⓜ bees·*tek*

steal *robar* ro·*bar*

steep *escarpado/a* ⓜ/① es·kar·*pa*·do/a

step paso ⓜ pa·so
stereo equipo ⓜ de música
　e·kee·po de moo·see·ka
stingy tacaño/a ⓜ/ⓕ ta·ka·nyo/a
stock caldo ⓜ kal·do
stockings medias ⓕ pl me·dyas
stomach estómago ⓜ es·to·ma·go
stomachache dolor ⓜ de estómago
　do·lor de es·to·ma·go
stone piedra ⓕ pye·dra
stoned colocado/a ⓜ/ⓕ ko·lo·ka·do/a
stop parada ⓕ pa·ra·da
stop parar pa·rar
storm tormenta ⓕ tor·men·ta
story cuento ⓜ kwen·to
stove cocina ⓕ ko·thee·na
straight recto/a ⓜ/ⓕ rek·to/a
strange extraño/a ⓜ/ⓕ eks·tra·nyo/a
stranger desconocido/a ⓜ/ⓕ
　des·ko·no·thee·do/a
strawberry fresa ⓕ fre·sa
stream arroyo ⓜ a·ro·yo
street calle ⓕ ka·lye
string cuerda ⓕ kwer·da
strong fuerte fwer·te
stubborn testarudo/a ⓜ/ⓕ
　tes·ta·roo·do/a
student estudiante ⓜ&ⓕ es·too·dyan·te
studio estudio ⓜ es·too·dyo
stupid estúpido/a ⓜ/ⓕ es·too·pee·do/a
style estilo ⓜ es·tee·lo
subtitles subtítulos ⓜ pl
　soob·tee·too·los
suburb barrio ⓜ ba·ryo
subway parada ⓕ de metro
　pa·ra·da de me·tro
suffer sufrir soo·freer
sugar azúcar ⓜ a·thoo·kar
suitcase maleta ⓕ ma·le·ta
summer verano ⓜ ve·ra·no
sun sol ⓜ sol
sunblock crema ⓕ solar kre·ma so·lar
sunburn quemadura ⓕ de sol
　ke·ma·doo·ra de sol

sun-dried tomato tomate ⓜ secado al
　sol to·ma·te se·ka·do al sol
sunflower oil aceite ⓜ de girasol
　a·they·te khee·ra·sol
sunglasses gafas ⓕ pl de sol
　ga·fas de sol
(to be) sunny hace sol a·the sol
sunrise amanecer ⓜ a·ma·ne·ther
sunset puesta ⓕ del sol pwes·ta del sol
supermarket supermercado ⓜ
　soo·per·mer·ka·do
superstition superstición ⓕ
　soo·pers·tee·thyon
supporters hinchas ⓜ&ⓕ pl een·chas
surf hacer surf a·ther soorf
surface mail por vía terrestre
　por vee·a te·res·tre
surfboard tabla de surf ⓕ ta·bla de soorf
surname apellido ⓜ a·pe·lyee·do
surprise sorpresa ⓕ sor·pre·sa
survive sobrevivir so·bre·vee·veer
sweater jersey ⓜ kher·sey
Sweden Suecia ⓕ swe·thya
sweet dulce dool·the
sweets (candy) dulces ⓜ pl dool·thes
swim nadar na·dar
swimming pool piscina ⓕ pees·thee·na
swimsuit bañador ⓜ ba·nya·dor
Switzerland Suiza ⓕ swee·tha
synagogue sinagoga ⓕ see·na·go·ga
synthetic sintético/a ⓜ/ⓕ
　seen·te·tee·ko/a
syringe jeringa ⓕ khe·reen·ga

T

table mesa ⓕ me·sa
table tennis ping pong ⓜ peeng pong
tablecloth mantel ⓜ man·tel
tail rabo ⓜ ra·bo
tailor sastre ⓜ sas·tre
take (away) llevar lye·var
take (the train) tomar to·mar
take (photo) sacar sa·kar
take photographs sacar fotos
　sa·kar fo·tos

talk *hablar* a·*blar*
tall *alto/a* ⓜ/ⓕ *al*·to/a
tampons *tampones* ⓜ pl tam·*po*·nes
tanning lotion *bronceador* ⓜ
 bron·the·a·*dor*
tap *grifo* ⓜ *gree*·fo
tasty *sabroso/a* ⓜ/ⓕ sa·*bro*·so/a
tax *impuestos* ⓜ pl eem·*pwes*·tos
taxi *taxi* ⓜ *tak*·see
taxi stand *parada* ⓕ *de taxis*
 pa·*ra*·da de *tak*·sees
tea *té* ⓜ te
teacher *profesor/profesora* ⓜ/ⓕ
 pro·fe·*sor*/pro·fe·*so*·ra
team *equipo* ⓜ e·*kee*·po
teaspoon *cucharita* ⓕ koo·cha·*ree*·ta
technique *técnica* ⓕ *tek*·nee·ka
teeth *dientes* ⓜ pl *dyen*·tes
telegram *telegrama* ⓜ te·le·*gra*·ma
telephone *teléfono* ⓜ te·*le*·fo·no
telephone *llamar (por teléfono)*
 lya·*mar* (por te·*le*·fo·no)
telephone centre *central* ⓕ *telefónica*
 then·*tral* te·le·*fo*·nee·ka
telescope *telescopio* ⓜ te·les·*ko*·pyo
television *televisión* ⓕ te·le·vee·*syon*
tell *decir* de·*theer*
temperature (fever) *fiebre* ⓕ *fye*·bre
temperature (weather) *temperatura* ⓕ
 tem·pe·ra·*too*·ra
temple *templo* ⓜ *tem*·plo
tennis *tenis* ⓜ *te*·nees
tennis court *pista* ⓕ *de tenis*
 pees·ta de *te*·nees
tent *tienda* ⓕ *(de campaña)*
 tyen·da (de kam·*pa*·nya)
tent pegs *piquetas* ⓕ pl pee·*ke*·tas
terrible *terrible* te·*ree*·ble
test *prueba* ⓕ *prwe*·ba
thank *dar gracias* dar *gra*·thyas
the Pill *píldora* ⓕ *peel*·do·ra
theatre *teatro* ⓜ te·*a*·tro
their *su* soo
they *ellos/ellas* ⓜ/ⓕ e·*lyos*/e·*lyas*

thief *ladrón/ladrona* ⓜ/ⓕ
 la·*dron*/la·*dro*·na
thin *delgado/a* ⓜ/ⓕ del·*ga*·do/a
think *pensar* pen·*sar*
third *tercio* ⓜ *ter*·thyo
thirst *sed* ⓕ se
this *éste/a* ⓜ/ⓕ *es*·te/a
this month *este mes* *es*·te mes
throat *garganta* ⓕ gar·*gan*·ta
ticket *billete* ⓜ bee·*lye*·te
ticket collector *revisor/revisora* ⓜ/ⓕ
 re·vee·*sor*/re·vee·*so*·ra
ticket machine *máquina* ⓕ *de billetes*
 ma·*kee*·na de bee·*lye*·tes
ticket office *taquilla* ⓕ ta·*kee*·lya
tide *marea* ⓕ ma·*re*·a
tight *apretado/a* ⓜ/ⓕ a·pre·*ta*·do/a
time *hora* ⓕ *o*·ra • *tiempo* ⓜ *tyem*·po
time difference *diferencia* ⓕ *de horas*
 dee·fe·*ren*·thya de *o*·ras
timetable *horario* ⓜ *o*·ra·ryo
tin *hojalata* ⓕ o·kha·*la*·ta
tin opener *abrelatas* ⓜ a·bre·*la*·tas
tiny *pequeñito/a* ⓜ/ⓕ pe·ke·*nyee*·to/a
tip *propina* ⓕ pro·*pee*·na
tired *cansado/a* ⓜ/ⓕ kan·*sa*·do/a
tissues *pañuelos* ⓜ pl *de papel*
 pa·*nywe*·los de pa·*pel*
toast *tostada* ⓕ tos·*ta*·da
toaster *tostadora* ⓕ tos·ta·*do*·ra
tobacco *tabaco* ⓜ ta·*ba*·ko
tobacconist *estanquero* ⓜ es·tan·*ke*·ro
tobogganing *ir en tobogán*
 eer en to·bo·*gan*
today *hoy* oy
toe *dedo* ⓜ *del pie* *de*·do del pye
tofu *tofú* ⓜ to·*foo*
together *juntos/as* ⓜ/ⓕ *khoon*·tos/as
toilet *servicio* ⓜ ser·*vee*·thyo
toilet paper *papel* ⓜ *higiénico*
 pa·*pel* ee·*khye*·nee·ko
tomato *tomate* ⓜ to·*ma*·te
tomato sauce *salsa* ⓕ *de tomate*
 sal·sa de to·*ma*·te
tomorrow *mañana* ma·*nya*·na

tomorrow afternoon *mañana por la tarde* ma·nya·na por la *tar*·de

tomorrow evening *mañana por la noche* ma·nya·na por la *no*·che

tomorrow morning *mañana por la mañana* ma·nya·na por la ma·nya·na

tone *tono* ⓜ *to*·no

tonight *esta noche* es·ta *no*·che

too (expensive) *demasiado (caro/a)* ⓜ/ⓕ de·ma·sya·do (*ka*·ro/a)

tooth *diente* ⓜ *dyen*·te

tooth (back) *muela* ⓕ mwe·la

toothache *dolor* ⓜ *de muelas* do·*lor* de mwe·las

toothbrush *cepillo* ⓜ *de dientes* the·*pee*·lyo de *dyen*·tes

toothpaste *pasta* ⓕ *dentífrica* pas·ta den·*tee*·free·ka

toothpick *palillo* ⓜ pa·*lee*·lyo

torch *linterna* ⓕ leen·*ter*·na

touch *tocar* to·kar

tour *excursión* ⓕ eks·koor·*syon*

tourist *turista* ⓜ&ⓕ too·*rees*·ta

tourist (slang) *guiri* ⓜ gee·ree

tourist office *oficina* ⓕ *de turismo* o·fee·*thee*·na de too·*rees*·mo

towards *hacia* a·thya

towel *toalla* ⓕ to·a·lya

tower *torre* ⓕ *to*·re

toxic waste *residuos* ⓜ pl *tóxicos* re·*see*·dwos *tok*·see·kos

toyshop *juguetería* ⓕ khoo·ge·te·*ree*·a

track (car racing) *autódromo* ⓜ ow·*to*·dro·mo

track (footprints) *rastro* ⓜ *ras*·tro

trade *comercio* ⓜ ko·*mer*·thyo

traffic *tráfico* ⓜ *tra*·fee·ko

traffic lights *semáforos* ⓜ pl se·*ma*·fo·ros

trail *camino* ⓜ ka·*mee*·no

train *tren* ⓜ tren

train station *estación* ⓕ *de tren* es·ta·*thyon* de tren

tram *tranvía* ⓜ tran·*vee*·a

transit lounge *sala* ⓕ *de tránsito* sa·la de *tran*·see·to

translate *traducir* tra·doo·*theer*

transport *medios* ⓜ pl *de transporte* me·dyos de trans·*por*·te

travel *viajar* vya·*khar*

travel agency *agencia* ⓕ *de viajes* a·*khen*·thya de vya·khes

travel books *libros* ⓜ pl *de viajes* lee·bros de vya·khes

travel sickness *mareo* ⓜ ma·re·o

travellers cheque *cheques* ⓜ pl *de viajero* che·kes de vya·*khe*·ro

tree *árbol* ⓜ ar·bol

trip *viaje* ⓜ vya·khe

trousers *pantalones* ⓜ pl pan·ta·*lo*·nes

truck *camión* ⓜ ka·*myon*

trust *confianza* ⓕ kon·fee·*an*·tha

trust *confiar* kon·fee·*ar*

try *probar* pro·bar

try (to do something) *intentar (hacer algo)* een·ten·*tar* (a·*ther* al·go)

T-shirt *camiseta* ⓕ ka·mee·se·ta

tube (tyre) *cámara* ⓕ *de aire* *ka*·ma·ra de *ai*·re

tuna *atún* ⓜ a·toon

tune *melodía* ⓕ me·lo·*dee*·a

turkey *pavo* ⓜ *pa*·vo

turn *doblar* do·*blar*

TV *tele* ⓕ te·le

TV series *serie* ⓕ *se*·rye

tweezers *pinzas* ⓕ pl *peen*·thas

twice *dos veces* dos *ve*·thes

twin beds *dos camas* ⓕ pl dos *ka*·mas

twins *gemelos* ⓜ pl khe·*me*·los

type *tipo* ⓜ *tee*·po

type *escribir a máquina* es·kree·*beer* a *ma*·kee·na

typical *típico/a* ⓜ/ⓕ *tee*·pee·ko/a

tyre *neumático* ⓜ ne·oo·*ma*·tee·ko

U

ultrasound *ecografía* ⓕ e·ko·gra·*fee*·a

umbrella *paraguas* ⓜ pa·ra·gwas

umpire *árbitro* ⓜ ar·bee·tro

uncomfortable *incómodo/a* ⓜ/ⓕ een·*ko*·mo·do/a

underpants (men) *calzoncillos* ⓜ pl
kal·thon·*thee*·lyos

underpants (women) *bragas* ⓕ pl
bra·gas

understand *comprender* kom·pren·*der*

underwear *ropa interior* ⓕ
ro·pa een·te·*ryor*

unemployed *en el paro* en el *pa*·ro

unfair *injusto* een·*khoos*·to

uniform *uniforme* ⓜ oo·nee·*for*·me

universe *universo* ⓜ oo·nee·*ver*·so

university *universidad* ⓕ
oo·nee·ver·see·*da*

unleaded *sin plomo* seen *plo*·mo

unsafe *inseguro/a* ⓜ/ⓕ een·se·goo·ro/a

until (June) *hasta (junio)*
as·ta (khoo·nyo)

unusual *extraño/a* ⓜ/ⓕ eks·*tra*·nyo/a

up *arriba* a·*ree*·ba

uphill *cuesta arriba* kwes·ta a·*ree*·ba

urgent *urgente* oor·*khen*·te

USA *Los Estados* ⓜ pl *Unidos*
los es·*ta*·dos oo·*nee*·dos

useful *útil* oo·teel

V

vacant *vacante* va·*kan*·te

vacation *vacaciones* ⓕ pl
va·ka·*thyo*·nes

vaccination *vacuna* ⓕ va·*koo*·na

vagina *vagina* ⓕ va·*khee*·na

validate *validar* va·lee·*dar*

valley *valle* *va*·lye

valuable *valioso/a* ⓜ/ⓕ va·*lyo*·so/a

value *valor* ⓜ va·*lor*

van *caravana* ⓕ ka·ra·va·na

veal *ternera* ⓕ ter·ne·ra

vegetable *verdura* ⓕ ver·*doo*·ra

vegetables *verduras* ⓕ pl ver·*doo*·ras

vegetarian *vegetariano/a* ⓜ/ⓕ
ve·khe·ta·*rya*·no/a

vein *vena* ⓕ ve·na

venereal disease *enfermedad* ⓕ
venérea en·fer·me·*da* ve·ne·re·a

venue *local* ⓜ lo·*kal*

very *muy* mooy

video tape *cinta* ⓕ *de vídeo*
theen·ta de vee·de·o

view *vista* ⓕ vees·ta

village *pueblo* ⓜ pwe·blo

vine *vid* ⓕ veed

vinegar *vinagre* ⓜ vee·na·gre

vineyard *viñedo* ⓜ vee·*nye*·do

virus *virus* ⓜ vee·roos

visa *visado* ⓜ vee·sa·do

visit *visitar* vee·see·*tar*

vitamins *vitaminas* ⓕ pl
vee·ta·*mee*·nas

vodka *vodka* ⓕ vod·ka

voice *voz* ⓕ voth

volume *volumen* ⓜ vo·*loo*·men

vote *votar* vo·*tar*

wage *sueldo* ⓜ swel·do

W

wait *esperar* es·pe·*rar*

waiter *camarero/a* ⓜ/ⓕ ka·ma·re·ro/a

waiting room *sala* ⓕ *de espera*
sa·la de es·pe·ra

walk *caminar* ka·mee·*nar*

wall (inside) *pared* ⓕ pa·re

wallet *cartera* ⓕ kar·te·ra

want *querer* ke·rer

war *guerra* ⓕ ge·ra

wardrobe *vestuario* ⓜ ves·*twa*·ryo

warm *templado/a* ⓜ/ⓕ tem·*pla*·do/a

warn *advertir* ad·ver·*teer*

wash (oneself) *lavarse* la·var·se

wash (something) *lavar* la·*var*

wash cloth *toallita* ⓕ to·a·*lyee*·ta

washing machine *lavadora* ⓕ la·va·do·ra

watch *reloj* ⓜ *de pulsera*
re·*lokh* de pool·se·ra

watch *mirar* mee·*rar*

water *agua* ⓕ a·gwa
   — tap *del grifo* del gree·fo
   — bottle *cantimplora* ⓕ
   kan·teem·*plo*·ra

waterfall *cascada* ① kas·ka·da
watermelon ① *sandía* san·dee·a
waterproof *impermeable* eem·per·me·a·ble
waterskiing *esquí* ⓜ *acuático* es·kee a·kwa·tee·ko
wave *ola* ① o·la
way *camino* ⓜ ka·mee·no
we *nosotros/nosotras* ⓜ/① no·so·tros/no·so·tras
weak *débil* de·beel
wealthy *rico/a* ⓜ/① ree·ko/a
wear *llevar* lye·var
weather *tiempo* ⓜ tyem·po
wedding *boda* ① bo·da
wedding cake *tarta* ① *nupcial* tar·ta noop·thyal
wedding present *regalo* ⓜ *de bodas* re·ga·lo de bo·das
weekend *fin de semana* ⓜ feen de se·ma·na
weigh *pesar* pe·sar
weight *peso* ⓜ pe·so
weights *pesas* ① pl pe·sas
welcome *bienvenida* ① byen·ve·nee·da
welcome *dar la bienvenida* dar la byen·ve·nee·da
welfare *bienestar* ⓜ byen·es·tar
well *bien* byen
well *pozo* ⓜ po·tho
west *oeste* ⓜ o·es·te
wet *mojado/a* ⓜ/① mo·kha·do/a
what *lo que* lo ke
wheel *rueda* ① rwe·da
wheelchair *silla* ① *de ruedas* see·lya de rwe·das
when *cuando* kwan·do
where *donde* don·de
whiskey *güisqui* ⓜ gwees·kee
white *blanco/a* ⓜ/① blan·ko/a
white-water rafting *rafting* ⓜ rahf·teen
who *quien* kyen
why *por qué* por ke
wide *ancho/a* ⓜ/① an·cho/a

wife *esposa* ① es·po·sa
win *ganar* ga·nar
wind *viento* ⓜ vyen·to
window *ventana* ① ven·ta·na
window-shopping *mirar los escaparates* mee·rar los es·ka·pa·ra·tes
windscreen *parabrisas* ⓜ pa·ra·bree·sas
windsurfing *hacer windsurf* a·ther ween·soorf
wine *vino* ⓜ vee·no
wineglass *copa* ① *de vino* ko·pa de vee·no
winery *bodega* ① bo·de·ga
wings *alas* ① pl a·las
winner *ganador/ganadora* ⓜ/① ga·na·dor/ga·na·do·ra
winter *invierno* ⓜ een·vyer·no
wire *alambre* ⓜ a·lam·bre
wish *desear* de·se·ar
with *con* kon
within (an hour) *dentro de (una hora)* den·tro de (oo·na o·ra)
without *sin* seen
woman *mujer* ① moo·kher
wonderful *maravilloso/a* ⓜ/① ma·ra·vee·lyo·so/a
wood *madera* ① ma·de·ra
wool *lana* ① la·na
word *palabra* ① pa·la·bra
work *trabajo* ⓜ tra·ba·kho
work *trabajar* tra·ba·khar
work experience *experiencia* ① *laboral* eks·pe·ryen·thya la·bo·ral
work permit *permiso* ⓜ *de trabajo* per·mee·so de tra·ba·kho
workout *entreno* ⓜ en·tre·no
workshop *taller* ⓜ ta·lyer
world *mundo* ⓜ moon·do
World Cup *La Copa* ① *Mundial* la ko·pa moon·dyal
worms *lombrices* ① pl lom·bree·thes
worried *preocupado/a* ⓜ/① pre·o·koo·pa·do/a

worship *adoración* ① a·do·ra·*thyon*
wrist *muñeca* ① moo·*nye*·ka
write *escribir* es·kree·*beer*
writer *escritor/escritora* ⓜ/①
  es·kree·*tor*/es·kree·*to*·ra
wrong *equivocado/a* ⓜ/①
  e·kee·vo·*ka*·do/a

Y

yellow *amarillo/a* ⓜ/① a·ma·*ree*·lyo/a
yes *sí* see
(not) yet *todavía (no)* to·da·*vee*·a (no)
yesterday *ayer* a·*yer*

yoga *yoga* ⓜ *yo*·ga
yogurt *yogur* ⓜ yo·*goor*
you pol sg *Usted* oos·*te*
you inf sg *tú* too
young *joven* *kho*·ven
your pol sg *su* soo
your inf sg *tu* too
youth hostel *albergue* ⓜ *juvenil*
  al·*ber*·ge khoo·ve·*neel*

Z

zodiac *zodíaco* ⓜ tho·*dee*·a·ko
zoo *zoológico* ⓜ zo·o·*lo*·khee·ko

Nouns in the dictionary have their gender indicated by ⓜ or ⓕ. If it's a plural noun, you'll also see pl. Where a word that could be either a noun or a verb has no gender indicated, it's a verb.

A

abajo a·ba·kho *below*
abanico ⓜ a·ba·nee·ko *fan (hand held)*
abarrotado a·ba·ro·ta·do *crowded*
abeja ⓕ a·be·kha *bee*
abierto/a ⓜ/ⓕ a·byer·to/a *open*
abogado/a ⓜ/ⓕ a·bo·ga·do/a *lawyer*
aborto ⓜ a·bor·to *abortion*
abrazo ⓜ a·bra·tho *hug*
abrebotellas ⓜ a·bre·bo·te·lyas
  bottle opener
abrelatas ⓜ a·bre·la·tas
  can opener • tin opener
abrigo ⓜ a·bree·go *overcoat*
abrir a·breer *open*
abuela ⓕ a·bwe·la *grandmother*
abuelo ⓜ a·bwe·lo *grandfather*
aburrido/a ⓜ/ⓕ a·boo·ree·do/a
  bored • boring
acabar a·ka·bar *end*
acampar a·kam·par *camp*
acantilado ⓜ a·kan·tee·la·do *cliff*
accidente ⓜ ak·thee·den·te *accident*
aceite ⓜ a·they·te *oil*
aceptar a·thep·tar *accept*
acera ⓕ a·the·ra *footpath*
acondicionador ⓜ
  a·kon·dee·thyo·na·dor *conditioner*
acoso ⓜ a·ko·so *harassment*
activista ⓜ&ⓕ ak·tee·vees·ta *activist*
actuación ⓕ ak·twa·thyon
  performance
acupuntura ⓕ a·koo·poon·too·ra
  acupuncture
adaptador ⓜ a·dap·ta·dor *adaptor*
adentro a·den·tro *inside*
adivinar a·dee·vee·nar *guess*

administración ⓕ ad·mee·nees·tra·thyon
  administration
admitir ad·mee·teer *admit*
adoración ⓕ a·do·ra·thyon *worship*
aduana ⓕ a·dwa·na *customs*
adulto/a ⓜ/ⓕ a·dool·to/a *adult*
aeróbic ⓜ ay·ro·beek *aerobics*
aerolínea ⓕ ay·ro·lee·nya *airline*
aeropuerto ⓜ ay·ro·pwer·to *airport*
afeitadora ⓕ a·fey·ta·do·ra *razor*
afeitarse a·fey·tar·se *shave*
afortunado/a ⓜ/ⓕ a·for·too·na·do/a
  lucky
África ⓕ a·free·ka *Africa*
agencia ⓕ **de viajes** a·khen·thya de
  vya·khes *travel agency*
agenda ⓕ a·khen·da *diary*
agente ⓜ **inmobiliario** a·khen·te
  een·mo·bee·lya·ryo *real estate agent*
agresivo/a ⓜ/ⓕ a·gre·see·vo/a
  aggressive
agricultor(a) ⓜ/ⓕ a·gree·kool·tor/
  a·gree·kool·to·ra *farmer*
agricultura ⓕ a·gree·kool·too·ra
  agriculture
agua ⓕ a·gwa *water*
  — caliente ka·lyen·te *hot water*
  — mineral mee·ne·ral *mineral water*
aguacate ⓜ a·gwa·ka·te *avocado*
aguja ⓕ a·goo·kha *needle (sewing)*
ahora a·o·ra *now*
ahorrar a·o·rar *save (money)*
aire ⓜ ai·re *air*
  — acondicionado
  a·kon·dee·thyo·na·do
  air-conditioning
ajedrez ⓜ a·khe·dreth *chess*
al lado de al la·do de *next to*

alambre ⓜ a·*lam*·bre *wire*
alba ⓕ *al*·ba *dawn*
albaricoque ⓜ al·ba·ree·*ko*·ke *apricot*
albergue juvenil al·*ber*·ge khoo·ve·*neel* *youth hostel*
alcachofa ⓕ al·ka·*cho*·fa *artichoke*
alcohol ⓜ al·*col* *alcohol*
Alemania ⓕ a·le·*ma*·nya *Germany*
alérgia ⓕ a·*ler*·khya *allergy*
alérgia al polen ⓕ a·*ler*·khya al *po*·len *hay fever*
alfarería ⓕ al·fa·re·*ree*·a *pottery*
alfombra ⓕ al·*fom*·bra *rug*
algo *al*·go *something*
algodón ⓜ al·go·*don* *cotton*
alguien *al*·gyen *someone*
algún al·*goon* *some*
alguno/a ⓜ/ⓕ al·*goo*·no/a *any*
almendras ⓕ pl al·*men*·dras *almonds*
almohada ⓕ al·*mwa*·da *pillow*
almuerzo ⓜ al·*mwer*·tho *lunch*
alojamiento ⓜ a·lo·kha·*myen*·to *accommodation*
alojarse a·lo·*khar*·se *stay (somewhere)*
alpinismo ⓜ al·pee·*nees*·mo *mountaineering*
alquilar al·kee·*lar* *hire • rent*
alquiler ⓜ al·kee·*ler* *rent*
— de coche de *ko*·che *car hire*
altar ⓜ al·*tar* *altar*
alto/a ⓜ/ⓕ *al*·to/a *high • tall*
altura ⓕ al·*too*·ra *altitude*
ama de casa *a*·ma de *ka*·sa *homemaker*
amable a·*ma*·ble *kind*
amanecer ⓜ a·ma·ne·*ther* *sunrise*
amante ⓜ&ⓕ a·*man*·te *lover*
amarillo/a ⓜ/ⓕ a·ma·ree·*lyo*/a *yellow*
amigo/a ⓜ/ⓕ a·*mee*·go/a *friend*
ampolla ⓕ am·*po*·lya *blister*
anacardo ⓜ a·na·*kar*·do *cashew nut*
analgésicos ⓜ pl a·nal·*khe*·see·kos *painkillers*
análisis de sangre ⓜ a·*na*·lee·sees de *san*·gre *blood test*
anarquista ⓜ/ⓕ a·nar·*kees*·ta *anarchist*

ancho/a ⓜ/ⓕ *an*·cho/a *wide*
andar an·*dar* *walk*
animal ⓜ a·nee·*mal* *animal*
Año Nuevo a·nyo *nwe*·vo *New Year*
antes *an*·tes *before*
antibióticos ⓜ pl an·tee·byo·*tee*·kos *antibiotics*
anticonceptivos ⓜ pl an·tee·kon·thep·*tee*·vos *contraceptives*
antigüedad ⓕ an·tee·gwe·*da* *antique*
antiguo/a ⓜ/ⓕ an·tee·*gwo*/a *ancient*
antiséptico ⓜ an·tee·*sep*·tee·ko *antiseptic*
antología ⓕ an·to·lo·*khee*·a *anthology*
anuncio ⓜ a·*noon*·thyo *advertisement*
aparcamiento ⓜ a·par·ka·*myen*·to *carpark*
apellido ⓜ a·pe·*lyee*·do *surname*
apéndice ⓜ a·*pen*·dee·the *appendix*
apodo ⓜ a·*po*·do *nickname*
aprender a·pren·*der* *learn*
apretado/a ⓜ/ⓕ a·pre·*ta*·do/a *tight*
apuesta ⓕ a·*pwes*·ta *bet*
apuntar a·poon·*tar* *point*
aquí a·*kee* *here*
araña ⓕ a·*ra*·nya *spider*
árbitro ⓜ *ar*·bee·tro *referee*
árbol ⓜ *ar*·bol *tree*
arena ⓕ a·*re*·na *sand*
armario ⓜ ar·*ma*·ryo *cupboard*
arqueológico/a ⓜ/ⓕ ar·ke·o·lo·*khee*·ko/a *archaeological*
arquitecto/a ⓜ/ⓕ ar·kee·*tek*·to/a *architect*
arquitectura ⓕ ar·kee·tek·*too*·ra *architecture*
arriba a·*ree*·ba *above • up*
arroyo ⓜ a·*ro*·yo *stream*
arroz ⓜ a·*roth* *rice*
arte ⓜ *ar*·te *art*
— gráfico gra·*fee*·ko *graphic art*
artes marciales ⓜ pl *ar*·tes mar·*thya*·les *martial arts*
artesanía ⓕ ar·te·sa·*nee*·a *crafts*
artista ⓜ&ⓕ ar·*tees*·ta *artist*
ascensor ⓜ as·then·*sor* *elevator*
Asia ⓕ *a*·sya *Asia*

asiento ⓜ a·*syen*·to *seat*
  — de seguridad para bebés de
  se·goo·*ree*·da *pa*·ra be·*bes* *child seat*
asma ⓕ *as*·ma *asthma*
aspirina ⓕ as·pee·*ree*·na *aspirin*
atascado/a ⓜ/ⓕ a·tas·*ka*·do/a *blocked*
atletismo ⓜ at·le·*tees*·mo *athletics*
atmósfera ⓕ at·*mos*·fe·ra *atmosphere*
atún ⓜ a·*toon* *tuna*
audífono ⓜ ow·*dee*·fo·no *hearing aid*
Australia ⓕ ow·*stra*·lya *Australia*
autobús ⓜ ow·to·*boos* *bus*
autocar ⓜ ow·to·*kar* *bus (intercity)*
autódromo ⓜ ow·*to*·dro·mo
  track (car racing)
autoservicio ⓜ ow·to·ser·*vee*·thyo
  self-service
autovía ⓕ ow·to·*vee*·a *motorway*
avenida ⓕ a·ve·*nee*·da *avenue*
avergonzado/a ⓜ/ⓕ a·ver·gon·*tha*·do/a
  embarrassed
avión ⓜ a·*vyon* *plane*
ayer a·*yer* *yesterday*
ayudar a·yoo·*dar* *help*
azúcar ⓜ a·*thoo*·kar *sugar*
azul a·*thool* *blue*

B

bailar bai·*lar* *dance*
bajo/a ⓜ/ⓕ *ba*·kho/a
  short (height) • *low*
balcón ⓜ bal·*kon* *balcony*
ballet ⓜ ba·*le* *ballet*
baloncesto ⓜ ba·lon·*thes*·to *basketball*
bálsamo ⓜ **de aftershave** *bal*·sa·mo de
  af·ter·*sha*·eev *aftershave*
bálsamo ⓜ **de labios** *bal*·sa·mo de
  la·byos *lip balm*
bañador ⓜ ba·nya·*dor* *bathing suit*
banco ⓜ *ban*·ko *bank*
bandera ⓕ ban·*de*·ra *flag*
bañera ⓕ ba·*nye*·ra *bath*
baño ⓜ *ba*·nyo *bathroom*
bar ⓜ *bar* *bar*
barato/a ⓜ/ⓕ ba·*ra*·to/a *cheap*

barco ⓜ *bar*·ko *boat*
barrio ⓜ *ba*·ryo *suburb*
basura ⓕ ba·*soo*·ra *rubbish*
batería ⓕ ba·te·*ree*·a
  battery (car) • *drums*
bebé ⓜ be·*be* *baby*
béisbol ⓜ *beys*·bol *baseball*
beneficio ⓜ be·ne·*fee*·thyo *profit*
berenjenas ⓕ pl be·ren·*khe*·nas
  aubergine • *eggplant*
besar be·*sar* *kiss*
beso ⓜ *be*·so *kiss*
biblia ⓕ *bee*·blya *bible*
biblioteca ⓕ bee·blyo·*te*·ka *library*
bicho ⓜ *bee*·cho *bug*
bici ⓕ *bee*·thee *bike*
bicicleta ⓕ bee·thee·*kle*·ta *bicycle*
  — de carreras de ka·*re*·ras
  racing bike
  — de montaña de mon·*ta*·nya
  mountain bike
bien byen *well*
bienestar ⓜ byen·es·*tar* *welfare*
bienvenida ⓕ byen·ve·*nee*·da *welcome*
billete ⓜ bee·*lye*·te *ticket*
  — de ida y vuelta de *ee*·da ee
  vwel·ta *return ticket*
  — de lista de espera de *lees*·ta de
  es·*pe*·ra *standby ticket*
billetes ⓜ pl **de banco** bee·*lye*·tes de
  ban·ko *banknotes*
biografía ⓕ bee·o·gra·*fee*·a *biography*
bistec ⓜ bees·*tek* *steak (beef)*
blanco y negro *blan*·ko ee *ne*·gro
  B&W (film)
blanco/a ⓜ/ⓕ *blan*·ko/a *white*
boca ⓕ *bo*·ka *mouth*
bocado ⓜ bo·*ka*·do *bite (food)*
boda ⓕ *bo*·da *wedding*
bodega ⓕ bo·*de*·ga
  winery • *liquor store*
bol ⓜ bol *bowl*
bolas ⓕ pl **de algodón** *bo*·las de
  al·go·*don* *cotton balls*
bolígrafo ⓜ bo·*lee*·gra·fo *pen*
bollos ⓜ pl *bo*·lyos *rolls (bread)*

bolo ⓜ *bo*·lo *gig*
bolsillo ⓜ bol·*see*·lyo *pocket*
bolso ⓜ *bol*·so *bag • handbag*
bomba ⓕ *bom*·ba *pump • bomb*
bombilla ⓕ bom·*bee*·lya *light bulb*
bondadoso/a ⓜ/ⓕ bon·da·*do*·so/a *caring*
bonito/a ⓜ/ⓕ bo·*nee*·to/a *pretty*
bordo ⓜ *bor*·do *edge*
a bordo a *bor*·do *aboard*
borracho/a ⓜ/ⓕ bo·*ra*·cho/a *drunk*
bosque ⓜ *bos*·ke *forest*
botas ⓕ pl *bo*·tas *boots*
— **de montaña** de mon·*ta*·nya *hiking boots*
botella ⓕ bo·*te*·lya *bottle*
botones ⓜ pl bo·*to*·nes *buttons*
boxeo ⓜ bo·*kse*·o *boxing*
bragas ⓕ pl *bra*·gas *underpants (women)*
brazo ⓜ *bra*·tho *arm*
broma ⓕ *bro*·ma *joke*
bronceador ⓜ bron·the·a·*dor* *tanning lotion*
bronquitis ⓕ bron·kee·*tees* *bronchitis*
brotes ⓜ pl **de soja** *bro*·tes de so·kha *bean sprouts*
brújula ⓕ *broo*·khoo·la *compass*
brumoso broo·*mo*·so *foggy*
buceo ⓜ boo·*the*·o *snorkelling*
budista ⓜ&ⓕ boo·*dees*·ta *Buddhist*
bueno/a ⓜ/ⓕ *bwe*·no/a *good*
bufanda ⓕ boo·*fan*·da *scarf*
buffet ⓜ boo·*fe* *buffet*
bulto ⓜ *bool*·to *lump*
burlarse de boor·*lar*·se de *make fun of*
burro ⓜ *boo*·ro *donkey*
buscar boos·*kar* *look for*
buzón ⓜ boo·*thon* *mailbox*

C

caballo ⓜ ka·*ba*·lyo *horse*
cabeza ⓕ ka·*be*·tha *head*
cabina ⓕ **telefónica** ka·*bee*·na te·le·fo·*nee*·ka *phone box*
cable ⓜ *ka*·ble *cable*

cables ⓜ pl **de arranque** *ka*·bles de a·*ran*·ke *jumper leads*
cabra ⓕ *ka*·bra *goat*
cacahuetes ⓜ pl ka·ka·*we*·tes *peanuts*
cacao ⓜ ka·*kow* *cocoa*
cachorro ⓜ ka·*cho*·ro *puppy*
cada *ka*·da *each*
cadena ⓕ **de bici** ka·*de*·na de *bee*·thee *bike chain*
café ⓜ ka·*fe* *coffee • cafe*
caída ⓕ ka·*ee*·da *fall*
caja ⓕ *ka*·kha *box • cashier*
— **fuerte** *fwer*·te *safe*
— **registradora** re·khees·tra·*do*·ra *cash register*
cajero ⓜ **automático** ka·*khe*·ro ow·to·ma·*tee*·ko *automatic teller machine*
calabacín ⓜ ka·la·ba·*theen* *zucchini • courgette*
calabaza ⓕ ka·la·*ba*·tha *pumpkin*
calcetines ⓜ pl kal·the·*tee*·nes *socks*
calculadora ⓕ kal·koo·la·*do*·ra *calculator*
caldo ⓜ *kal*·do *stock*
calefacción ⓕ **central** ka·le·fak·*thyon* *then*·tral *central heating*
calendario ⓜ ka·len·*da*·ryo *calendar*
calidad ⓕ ka·lee·*da* *quality*
caliente ka·*lyen*·te *hot*
calle ⓕ *ka*·lye *street*
calor ⓜ ka·*lor* *heat*
calzoncillos ⓜ pl kal·thon·*thee*·lyos *underpants (men)*
calzones ⓜ pl kal·*tho*·nes *boxer shorts*
cama ⓕ *ka*·ma *bed*
— **de matrimonio** de ma·tree·*mo*·nyo *double bed*
cámara ⓕ **(fotográfica)** *ka*·ma·ra (fo·to·*gra*·fee·ka) *camera*
cámara ⓕ **de aire** *ka*·ma·ra de *ai*·re *tube (tyre)*
camarero/a ⓜ/ⓕ ka·ma·*re*·ro/a *waiter*
cambiar kam·*byar* *change • exchange (money)*
cambio ⓜ *kam*·byo *loose change*
— **de dinero** de dee·*ne*·ro *currency exchange*
caminar ka·mee·*nar* *walk*

camino ⓜ ka·mee·no trail • way
caminos ⓜ pl **rurales** ka·mee·nos
roo·ra·les hiking routes
camión ⓜ ka·myon truck
camisa ① ka·mee·sa shirt
camiseta ① ka·mee·se·ta
singlet • T-shirt
cámping ⓜ kam·peen campsite
campo ⓜ kam·po countryside • field
Canadá ⓜ ka·na·da Canada
canasta ① ka·nas·ta basket
cancelar kan·the·lar cancel
cáncer ⓜ kan·ther cancer
canción ① kan·thyon song
candado ⓜ kan·da·do padlock
cangrejo ⓜ kan·gre·kho crab
cansado/a ⓜ/① kan·sa·do/a tired
cantalupo ⓜ kan·ta·loo·po cantaloupe
cantante ⓜ&① kan·tan·te singer
cantar kan·tar sing
cantimplora ① kan·teem·plo·ra
water bottle
capa ① **de ozono** ka·pa de o·tho·no
ozone layer
capilla ① ka·pee·lya shrine
capote ⓜ ka·po·te cloak
cara ① ka·ra face
caracol ⓜ ka·ra·kol snail
caramelos ⓜ pl ka·ra·me·los lollies
caravana ① ka·ra·va·na
caravan • van • traffic jam
cárcel ① kar·thel prison
cardenal ⓜ kar·de·nal bruise
carne ① kar·ne meat
— **de vaca** de va·ka beef
— **molida** mo·lee·da mince meat
carnet ⓜ kar·ne licence
— **de identidad** de ee·den·tee·da
identification card
— **de conducir** de kon·doo·theer
drivers licence
carnicería ① kar·nee·the·ree·a
butcher's shop
caro/a ⓜ/① ka·ro/a expensive
carpintero ⓜ kar·peen·te·ro carpenter
carrera ① ka·re·ra race (sport)
carta ① kar·ta letter

cartas ① pl kar·tas cards
cartón ⓜ kar·ton carton • cardboard
casa ① ka·sa house
(en) casa (en) ka·sa (at) home
casarse ka·sar·se marry
cascada ① kas·ka·da waterfall
casco ⓜ kas·ko helmet
casete ⓜ ka·se·te cassette
casi ka·see almost
casino ⓜ ka·see·no casino
castigar kas·tee·gar punish
castillo ⓜ kas·tee·lyo castle
catedral ① ka·te·dral cathedral
católico/a ⓜ/① ka·to·lee·ko/a Catholic
caza ① ka·tha hunting
cazuela ① ka·thwe·la pot (kitchen)
cebolla ① the·bo·lya onion
celebración ① the·le·bra·thyon
celebration
celebrar the·le·brar celebrate (an event)
celoso/a ⓜ/① the·lo·so/a jealous
cementerio ⓜ the·men·te·ryo cemetery
cena ① the·na dinner
cenicero ⓜ the·nee·the·ro ashtray
centavo ⓜ then·ta·vo cent
centímetro ⓜ then·tee·me·tro
centimetre
central ① **telefónica** then·tral
te·le·fo·nee·ka telephone centre
centro ⓜ then·tro centre
— **comercial** ko·mer·thyal
shopping centre
— **de la ciudad** de la theew·da
city centre
cepillo ⓜ the·pee·lyo hairbrush
— **de dientes** de dyen·tes toothbrush
cerámica ① the·ra·mee·ka ceramic
cerca ① ther·ka fence
cerca ther·ka near • nearby
cerdo ⓜ ther·do pork • pig
cereales ⓜ pl the·re·a·les cereal
cerillas ① pl las the·ree·lyas matches
cerrado/a ⓜ/① the·ra·do/a closed
— **con llave** kon lya·ve locked
cerradura ① the·ra·doo·ra lock (padlock)
cerrar the·rar close • lock • shut

certificado ⓜ ther·tee·fee·ka·do *certificate*

cerveza ⓕ ther·ve·tha *beer*

— **rubia** roo·bya *lager*

cibercafé ⓜ thee·ber·ka·fe *Internet cafe*

ciclismo ⓜ thee·klees·mo *cycling*

ciclista ⓜ&ⓕ thee·klees·ta *cyclist*

ciego/a ⓜ/ⓕ thye·go/a *blind*

cielo ⓜ thye·lo *sky*

ciencias ⓕ pl thyen·thyas *science*

científico/a ⓜ/ⓕ thyen·tee·fee·ko/a *scientist*

cigarillo ⓜ thee·ga·ree·lyo *cigarette*

cigarro ⓜ thee·ga·ro *cigarette*

cine ⓜ thee·ne *cinema*

cinta ⓕ **de vídeo** theen·ta de vee·de·o *video tape*

cinturón ⓜ **de seguridad** theen·too·ron de se·goo·ree·da *seatbelt*

circuito ⓜ&ⓕ **de carreras** theer·kwee·to de ka·re·ras *racetrack (cars)*

ciruela ⓕ thee·rwe·la *plum*

— **pasa** pa·sa *prune*

cistitis ⓕ thees·tee·tees *cystitis*

cita ⓕ thee·ta *appointment*

citarse thee·tar·se *date*

citología ⓕ thee·to·lo·khee·a *pap smear*

ciudad ⓕ thew·da *city*

ciudadanía ⓕ theew·da·da·nee·a *citizenship*

clase ⓕ **preferente** kla·se pre·fe·ren·te *business class*

clase ⓕ **turística** kla·se too·rees·tee·ka *economy class*

clásico/a ⓜ/ⓕ kla·see·ko/a *classical*

clienta/e ⓜ/ⓕ klee·en·ta/e *client*

clínica ⓕ klee·nee·ka *private hospital*

cobrar (un cheque) ko·brar (oon che·ke) *cash (a cheque)*

coca ⓕ ko·ka *cocaine*

cocaína ⓕ ko·ka·ee·na *cocaine*

coche ⓜ ko·che *car*

— **cama** ka·ma *sleeping car*

cocina ⓕ ko·thee·na *kitchen • stove*

cocinar ko·thee·nar *cook*

cocinero ⓜ ko·thee·ne·ro *chef • cook*

coco ⓜ ko·ko *coconut*

codeína ⓕ ko·de·ee·na *codeine*

código ⓜ **postal** ko·dee·go pos·tal *post code*

cojonudo/a ⓜ/ⓕ ko·kho·noo·do/a *fantastic*

col ⓜ kol *cabbage*

cola ⓕ ko·la *queue*

colchón ⓜ kol·chon *mattress*

colega ⓜ&ⓕ ko·le·ga *colleague • mate*

coles ⓜ pl **de Bruselas** ko·les de broo·se·las *brussels sprouts*

coliflor ⓕ ko·lee·flor *cauliflower*

colina ⓕ ko·lee·na *hill*

collar ⓜ ko·lyar *necklace*

color ⓜ ko·lor *colour*

comedia ⓕ ko·me·dya *comedy*

comenzar ko·men·thar *begin • start*

comer ko·mer *eat*

comerciante ⓜ&ⓕ ko·mer·thyan·te *business person*

comercio ⓜ ko·mer·thyo *trade*

comezón ⓕ ko·me·thon *itch*

comida ⓕ ko·mee·da *food*

— **de bebé** de be·be *baby food*

— **en el campo** en el kam·po *picnic*

comisaría ⓕ ko·mee·sa·ree·a *police station*

cómo ko·mo *how*

cómodo/a ⓜ/ⓕ ko·mo·do/a *comfortable*

cómpact ⓜ kom·pak *CD*

compañero/a ⓜ/ⓕ kom·pa·nye·ro/a *companion*

compañía ⓕ kom·pa·nyee·a *a company*

compartir kom·par·teer *share (with)*

comprar kom·prar *buy*

comprender kom·pren·der *understand*

compresas ⓕ pl kom·pre·sas *sanitary napkins*

compromiso ⓜ kom·pro·mee·so *engagement*

comunión ⓕ ko·moo·nyon *communion*

comunista ⓜ&ⓕ ko·moo·nees·ta *communist*

con kon *with*

coñac ⓜ ko·nyak *brandy*

concentración ⓕ kon·then·tra·thyon *rally*

concierto ⓜ kon·*thyer*·to *concert*

condición ⓕ **cardíaca** kon·dee·*thyon* kar·*dee*·a·ka *heart condition*

condones ⓜ pl kon·*do*·nes *condoms*

conducir kon·doo·*theer* *drive*

conejo ⓜ ko·*ne*·kho *rabbit*

conexión ⓕ ko·nek·*syon* *connection*

confesión ⓕ kon·fe·*syon* *confession*

confianza ⓕ kon·fee·*an*·tha *trust*

confiar kon·fee·*ar* *trust*

confirmar kon·feer·*mar* *confirm*

conocer ko·no·*ther* *know (someone)*

conocido/a ⓜ/ⓕ ko·no·*thee*·do/a *famous*

consejo ⓜ kon·*se*·kho *advice*

conservador(a) ⓜ/ⓕ kon·ser·va·*dor*/ kon·ser·va·*do*·ra *conservative*

consigna ⓕ kon·*seeg*·na *left luggage*
— **automática** ow·to·ma·*tee*·ka *luggage lockers*

construir kons·*troo*·eer *build*

consulado ⓜ kon·soo·*la*·do *consulate*

contaminación ⓕ kon·ta·mee·na·*thyon* *pollution*

contar kon·*tar* *count*

contestador ⓜ **automático** kon·tes·ta·*dor* ow·to·ma·*tee*·ko *answering machine*

contrato ⓜ kon·*tra*·to *contract*

control ⓜ kon·*trol* *checkpoint*

convento ⓜ kon·*ven*·to *convent*

copa ⓕ *ko*·pa *drink*
— **de vino** de vee·no *wineglass*

copos de maíz *ko*·pos de ma·*eeth* *corn flakes*

corazón ⓜ ko·ra·*thon* *heart*

cordero ⓜ kor·*de*·ro *lamb*

cordillera ⓕ kor·dee·*lye*·ra *mountain range*

correcto/a ⓜ/ⓕ ko·*rek*·to/a *right (correct)*

correo ⓜ ko·*re*·o *mail*
— **urgente** oor·*khen*·te *express mail*

correos ko·*re*·os *post office*

correr ko·*rer* *run*

corrida ⓕ **de toros** ko·*ree*·da de *to*·ros *bullfight*

corriente ⓕ ko·*ryen*·te *current (electricity)*

corriente ko·*ryen*·te *ordinary*

corrupto/a ⓜ/ⓕ ko·*roop*·to/a *corrupt*

cortar kor·*tar* *cut*

cortaúñas ⓜ pl kor·ta·oo·*nyas* *nail clippers*

corto/a ⓜ/ⓕ *kor*·to/a *short (length)*

cosecha ⓕ ko·*se*·cha *crop*

coser ko·*ser* *sew*

costa ⓕ *kos*·ta *coast* • *seaside*

costar kos·*tar* *cost*

crecer kre·*ther* *grow*

crema ⓕ *kre*·ma *cream*
— **hidratante** ee·dra·*tan*·te *cream (moisturising)*
— **solar** so·*lar* *sunblock*

críquet ⓜ *kree*·ket *cricket*

cristiano/a ⓜ/ⓕ krees·*tya*·no/a *Christian*

crítica ⓕ *kree*·tee·ka *review*

cruce ⓜ *kroo*·the *intersection*

crudo/a ⓜ/ⓕ *kroo*·do/a *raw*

cuaderno ⓜ kwa·*der*·no *notebook* • *square*

cualificaciones ⓕ pl kwa·lee·fee·ka·*thyo*·nes *qualifications*

cuando *kwan*·do *when*

cuánto *kwan*·to *how much*

cuarentena ⓕ kwa·ren·*te*·na *quarantine*

Cuaresma ⓕ kwa·*res*·ma *Lent*

cuarto ⓜ *kwar*·to *quarter*

cubiertos ⓜ pl koo·*byer*·tos *cutlery*

cubo ⓜ *koo*·bo *bucket*

cucaracha ⓕ koo·ka·*ra*·cha *cockroach*

cuchara ⓕ koo·*cha*·ra *spoon*

cucharita ⓕ koo·cha·*ree*·ta *teaspoon*

cuchillas ⓕ pl **de afeitar** koo·*chee*·lyas de a·fey·*tar* *razor blades*

cuchillo ⓜ koo·*chee*·lyo *knife*

cuenta ⓕ *kwen*·ta *bill*
— **bancaria** ban·ka·rya *bank account*

cuento ⓜ *kwen*·to *story*

cuerda ⓕ *kwer*·da *rope* • *string*
— **para tender la ropa** pa·ra ten·*der* la *ro*·pa *clothes line*

cuero ⓜ *kwe*·ro *leather*

cuerpo ⓜ *kwer*·po *body*

cuesta abajo kwes·ta a·ba·kho *downhill*

cuesta arriba kwes·ta a·rree·ba *uphill*

cuestionar kwes·tyo·nar *question*

cuevas ① pl kwe·vas *caves*

cuidar kwee·dar
care for • mind (an object)

cuidar de kwee·dar de
care (for someone)

culo ⓜ koo·lo *bum (of body)*

culpable kool·pa·ble *guilty*

cumbre ① koom·bre *peak*

cumpleaños ⓜ koom·ple·a·nyos
birthday

currículum ⓜ koo·rree·koo·loom *resumé*

curry ⓜ koo·rree *curry*

cus cus ⓜ koos koos *cous cous*

CH

chaleco ⓜ **salvavidas** cha·le·ko
sal·va·vee·das *lifejacket*

champán ⓜ cham·pan *Champagne*

champiñón ⓜ cham·pee·nyon
mushrooms

champú ⓜ cham·poo *shampoo*

chaqueta ① cha·ke·ta *jacket*

cheque ⓜ che·ke *check (bank)*

cheques ⓜ pl **de viajero** che·kes de
vya·khe·ro *travellers cheque*

chica ① chee·ka *girl*

chicle ⓜ chee·kle *chewing gum*

chico ⓜ chee·ko *boy*

chocolate ⓜ cho·ko·la·te *chocolate*

choque ⓜ cho·ke *crash*

chorizo ⓜ cho·ree·tho
salami (Spanish sausage)

chupete ⓜ choo·pe·te *dummy • pacifier*

D

dados ⓜ pl da·dos *dice (die)*

dañar da·nyar *hurt*

dar dar *give*

— **de comer** de ko·mer *feed*

— **gracias** gra·thyas *thank*

— **la bienvenida** la byen·ve·nee·da
welcome

— **una patada** oo·na pa·ta·da *kick*

darse cuenta de dar·se kwen·ta de *realise*

de de *from*

— **(cuatro) estrellas** de (kwa·tro)
es·tre·lyas *(four-)star*

— **izquierda** de eeth·kyer·da
left-wing

— **pena** de pe·na *terrible*

— **primera clase** de pree·me·ra kla·se
first-class

— **segunda mano** de se·goon·da
ma·no *second-hand*

— **vez en cuando** de veth en
kwan·do *sometimes*

deber de·ver *owe*

débil de·beel *weak*

decidir de·thee·deer *decide*

decir de·theer *say • tell*

dedo ⓜ de·do *finger*

— **del pie** del pye *toe*

defectuoso/a ⓜ/① de·fek·too·o·so/a
faulty

deforestación ① de·fo·res·ta·thyon
deforestation

dejar de·khar *leave • quit*

delgado/a ⓜ/① del·ga·do/a *thin*

delirante de·lee·ran·te *delirious*

demasiado caro/a ⓜ/① de·ma·sya·do
ka·ro/a *too (expensive)*

democracia ① de·mo·kra·thya
democracy

demora ① de·mo·ra *delay*

dentista ⓜ&① den·tees·ta *dentist*

dentro de (una hora) den·tro de (oo·na
o·ra) *within (an hour)*

deportes ⓜ pl de·por·tes *sport*

deportista ⓜ&① de·por·tees·ta
sportsperson

depósito ⓜ de·po·see·to *deposit*

derecha ① de·re·cha *right (not left)*

derechista de·re·chees·ta *right-wing*

derechos ⓜ pl **civiles** de·re·chos
thee·vee·les *civil rights*

derechos ⓜ pl **humanos** de·re·chos oo·ma·nos *human rights*

desayuno ⓜ des·a·yoo·no *breakfast*

descansar des·kan·sar *rest*

descanso ⓜ des·kan·so *intermission*

descendiente ⓜ des·then·dyen·te *descendant*

descomponerse des·kom·po·ner·se *decompose*

descubrir des·koo·breer *discover*

descuento ⓜ des·kwen·to *discount*

desde (mayo) des·de (ma·yo) *since (may)*

desear de·se·ar *wish*

desierto ⓜ de·syer·to *desert*

desodorante ⓜ de·so·do·ran·te *deodorant*

despacio des·pa·thyo *slowly*

desperdicios ⓜ pl **nucleares** des·per·dee·thyos noo·kle·a·res *nuclear waste*

despertador ⓜ des·per·ta·dor *alarm clock*

después de des·pwes de *after*

destino ⓜ des·tee·no *destination*

destruir des·troo·eer *destroy*

detallado/a ⓜ/ⓕ de·ta·lya·do/a *itemised*

detalle ⓜ de·ta·lye *detail*

detener de·te·ner *arrest*

detrás de de·tras de *behind*

devocionario ⓜ de·vo·thyo·na·ryo *prayer book*

día ⓜ dee·a *day*
— **festivo** fes·tee·vo *holiday*

diabetes ⓕ dee·a·be·tes *diabetes*

diafragma ⓜ dee·a·frag·ma *diaphragm*

diapositiva ⓕ dya·po·see·tee·va *slide*

diariamente dya·rya·men·te *daily*

diarrea ⓕ dee·a·re·a *diarrhoea*

dieta ⓕ dee·e·ta *diet*

dibujar dee·boo·khar *draw*

diccionario ⓜ deek·thyo·na·ryo *dictionary*

diente (de ajo) dyen·te (de a·kho) *clove (garlic)*

dientes ⓜ pl dyen·tes *teeth*

diferencia ⓕ **de horas** dee·fe·ren·thya de o·ras *time difference*

diferente dee·fe·ren·te *different*

difícil dee·fee·theel *difficult*

dinero ⓜ dee·ne·ro *money*
— **en efectivo** en e·fek·tee·vo *cash*

Dios dyos *god*

dirección ⓕ dee·rek·thyon *address*

directo/a ⓜ/ⓕ dee·rek·to/a *direct*

director(a) ⓜ/ⓕ dee·rek·tor/ dee·rek·to·ra *director*

disco ⓜ dees·ko *disk*

discoteca ⓕ dees·ko·te·ka *disco*

discriminación ⓕ dees·kree·mee·na·thyon *discrimination*

discutir dees·koo·teer *argue*

diseño ⓜ dee·se·nyo *design*

disparar dees·pa·rar *shoot*

DIU ⓜ de ee oo *IUD*

diversión ⓕ dee·ver·syon *fun*

divertirse dee·ver·teer·se *enjoy (oneself)*

doblar do·blar *turn* • *bend*

doble do·ble *double*

docena ⓕ do·the·na *dozen*

doctor(a) ⓜ/ⓕ dok·tor/dok·to·ra *doctor*

dólar ⓜ do·lar *dollar*

dolor ⓜ do·lor *pain*
— **de cabeza** de ka·be·tha *headache*
— **de estómago** de es·to·ma·go *stomachache*
— **de muelas** de mwe·las *toothache*
— **menstrual** mens·trwal *period pain*

dolorido/a ⓜ/ⓕ do·lo·ree·do/a *sore*

doloroso/a ⓜ/ⓕ do·lo·ro·so/a *painful*

donde don·de *where*

dormir dor·meer *sleep*

dos ⓜ/ⓕ pl dos *two*
— **camas** ka·mas *twin beds*
— **veces** ve·thes *twice*

drama ⓜ dra·ma *drama*

droga ⓕ dro·ga *drug* • *dope*

drogadicción ⓕ dro·ga·deek·thyon *drug addiction*

drogas ⓕ pl dro·gas *drugs*

ducha ⓕ doo·cha *shower*

dueño/a ⓜ/ⓕ dwe·nyo/a *owner*

dulce dool·the *sweet*

dulces ⓜ pl dool·thes *sweets*

duro/a ⓜ/ⓕ doo·ro/a *hard*

E

eczema ① ek·*the*·ma *eczema*

edad ① e·*da* *age*

edificio ⓜ e·dee·*fee*·thyo *building*

editor(a) ⓜ/① e·dee·*tor*/e·dee·*to*·ra *editor*

educación ① e·doo·ka·*thyon* *education*

egoísta e·go·*ees*·ta *selfish*

ejemplo ⓜ e·*khem*·plo *example*

ejército ⓜ e·*kher*·thee·to *military*

él ⓜ el *he*

elecciones ① pl e·lek·*thyo*·nes *elections*

electricidad ① e·lek·tree·thee·*da* *electricity*

elegir e·le·*kheer* *pick • choose*

ella ① e·lya *she*

ellos/ellas ⓜ/① e·lyos/e·lyas *they*

embajada ① em·ba·*kha*·da *embassy*

embajador(a) ⓜ/① em·ba·kha·*dor*/em·ba·kha·*do*·ra *ambassador*

embarazada em·ba·ra·*tha*·da *pregnant*

embarcarse em·bar·*kar*·se *board (ship, etc)*

embrague ⓜ em·*bra*·ge *clutch*

emergencia ① e·mer·*khen*·thya *emergency*

emocional e·mo·thyo·*nal* *emotional*

empleado/a ⓜ/① em·ple·a·*do*/a *employee*

empujar em·poo·*khar* *push*

en en *on*
— **el extranjero** el eks·tran·*khe*·ro *abroad*
— **el paro** el *pa*·ro *unemployed*

encaje ⓜ en·*ka*·khe *lace*

encantador(a) ⓜ/① en·kan·ta·*dor*/en·kan·ta·*do*·ra *charming*

encendedor ⓜ en·then·de·*dor* *lighter*

encontrar en·kon·*trar* *find • meet*

encurtidos ⓜ pl en·koor·*tee*·dos *pickles*

energía ① nuclear e·ner·*khee*·a noo·kle·*ar* *nuclear energy*

enfadado/a ⓜ/① en·fa·*da*·do/a *angry*

enfermedad ① en·fer·me·*da* *disease*
— **venérea** ve·*ne*·re·a *venereal disease*

enfermero/a ⓜ/① en·fer·me·ro/a *nurse*

enfermo/a ⓜ/① en·*fer*·mo/a *sick*

enfrente de en·*fren*·te de *in front of*

enorme e·*nor*·me *huge*

ensalada ① en·sa·*la*·da *salad*

enseñar en·se·*nyar* *show • teach*

entrar en·*trar* *enter*

entre en·tre *among • between*

entregar en·tre·*gar* *deliver*

entrenador(a) ⓜ/① en·tre·na·*dor*/en·tre·na·*do*·ra *coach*

entreno ⓜ en·*tre*·no *workout*

entrevista ① en·tre·*vees*·ta *interview*

enviar en·vee·*ar* *send • ship off*

epilepsia ① e·pee·*lep*·sya *epilepsy*

equipaje ⓜ e·kee·*pa*·khe *luggage*

equipo ⓜ e·*kee*·po *equipment • team*
— **de inmersión** de een·mer·*syon* *diving equipment*
— **de música** ⓜ de moo·see·ka *stereo*

equitación ① e·kee·ta·*thyon* *horse riding*

equivocado/a ⓜ/① e·kee·vo·ka·do/a *wrong*

error ⓜ e·*ror* *mistake*

escalada ① es·ka·*la*·da *rock climbing*

escalera ① es·ka·*le*·ra *stairway*

escaleras ① pl mecánicas es·ka·*le*·ras me·*kan*·icas *escalator*

escarcha ① es·*kar*·cha *frost*

escarpado/a ⓜ/① es·kar·*pa*·do/a *steep*

escasez ① es·ka·*seth* *shortage*

escenario ⓜ es·the·na·ryo *stage*

Escocia ① es·*ko*·thya *Scotland*

escoger es·ko·*kher* *choose*

escribir es·kree·*beer* *write*
— **a máquina** a ma·*kee*·na *type*

escritor(a) ⓜ/① es·kree·*tor*/es·kree·*to*·ra *writer*

escuchar es·koo·*char* *listen*

escuela ① es·*kwe*·la *school*
— **de párvulos** de *par*·voo·los *kindergarten*

escultura ① es·kool·*too*·ra *sculpture*
espacio ⓜ es·*pa*·thyo *space*
espalda ① es·*pal*·da *back (body)*
España ① es·*pa*·nya *Spain*
especial es·pe·*thyal special*
especialista ⓜ&① es·pe·thya·*lees*·ta *specialist*
especies ① pl **en peligro de extinción** es·*pe*·thyes en pe·*lee*·gro de eks·*teen*·thyon *endangered species*
espectáculo ⓜ es·pek·*ta*·koo·lo *show*
espejo ⓜ es·*pe*·kho *mirror*
esperar es·pe·*rar wait*
espinaca ① es·pee·*na*·ka *spinach*
esposa ① es·*po*·sa *wife*
espuma ① **de afeitar** es·*poo*·ma de a·fey·*tar shaving cream*
espumoso/a ⓜ/①es·poo·*mo*·so/a *sparkling • foamy*
esquí ⓜ es·*kee skiing*
  — acuático a·*kwa*·tee·ko *waterskiing*
esquiar es·kee·*ar ski*
esquina ① es·*kee*·na *corner*
esta noche es·ta *no*·che *tonight*
éste/a ⓜ/① *es*·te/a *this*
estación ① es·ta·*thyon season • station*
  — de autobuses de ow·to·*boo*·ses *bus station*
  — de metro de *me*·tro *metro station*
  — de tren de tren *railway station*
estacionar es·ta·thyo·*nar park (car)*
estadio ⓜ es·*ta*·dyo *stadium*
estado ⓜ **civil** es·*ta*·do thee·*veel marital status*
estado ⓜ **del bienestar** es·*ta*·do del byen·es·*tar social welfare • well being*
estafa ① es·*ta*·fa *rip-off*
estanquero ⓜ es·tan·*ke*·ro *tobacconist*
estante ⓜ es·*tan*·te *shelf*
estar es·*tar to be*
  — constipado/a ⓜ/① kons·tee·*pa*·do/a *have a cold*
  — de acuerdo de a·*kwer*·do *agree*
estatua ① es·*ta*·twa *statue*
este *es*·te *east*
esterilla ① es·te·*ree*·lya *mat*

estilo ⓜ es·*tee*·lo *style*
estómago ⓜ es·*to*·ma·go *stomach*
estrellas ① pl es·*tre*·lyas *stars*
estreñimiento ⓜ es·tre·nyee·*myen*·to *constipation*
estudiante ⓜ&① es·too·*dyan*·te *student*
estudio ⓜ es·*too*·dyo *studio*
estufa ① es·*too*·fa *heater*
estúpido/a ⓜ/① es·*too*·pee·do/a *stupid*
etiqueta ① **de equipaje** e·tee·*ke*·ta de e·kee·*pa*·khe *luggage tag*
euro ⓜ e·*oo*·ro *euro*
Europa ① e·oo·ro·pa *Europe*
eutanasia ① e·oo·ta·*na*·sya *euthanasia*
excelente eks·the·*len*·te *excellent*
excursión ① eks·koor·*syon tour*
excursionismo ⓜ eks·koor·syo·*nees*·mo *hiking*
experiencia ① eks·pe·*ryen*·thya *experience*
  — laboral ① la·bo·*ral work experience*
exponer eks·po·*ner exhibit*
exposición ① eks·po·see·*thyon exhibition*
expreso eks·*pre*·so *express*
exterior ⓜ eks·te·*ryor outside*
extrañar eks·tra·*nyar miss (feel sad)*
extranjero/a ⓜ/① eks·tran·*khe*·ro/a *foreign*

F

fábrica ① *fa*·bree·ka *factory*
fácil *fa*·theel *easy*
facturación ① **de equipajes** fak·too·ra·*thyon* de e·kee·*pa*·khes *check-in*
falda ① *fal*·da *skirt*
falta ① *fal*·ta *fault*
familia ① fa·*mee*·lya *family*
fantástico/a ⓜ/① fan·*tas*·tee·ko/a *great*
farmacia ① far·*ma*·thya *chemist (shop) • pharmacy*
farmacéutico ⓜ far·ma·thee·*oo*·tee·ko *chemist (person)*
faros ⓜ pl *fa*·ros *headlights*

fecha ① fe·cha *date (time)*
 — **de nacimiento** de na·thee·*myen*·to
 date of birth
feliz fe·*leeth happy*
ferretería ① fe·re·te·*ree*·a *hardware store*
festival ⓜ fes·tee·*val festival*
ficción ① feek·*thyon fiction*
fideos ⓜ pl fee·*de*·os *noodles*
fiebre ① *fye*·bre *fever*
 — **glandular** glan·doo·*lar*
 glandular fever
fiesta ① *fyes*·ta *party*
filete ⓜ fee·*le*·te *fillet*
film feelm *film*
fin ⓜ feen *end*
 — **de semana** de se·*ma*·na *weekend*
final ⓜ fee·*nal end*
firma ① *feer*·ma *signature*
firmar feer·*mar sign*
flor ① flor *flower*
florista ⓜ&① flo·*rees*·ta *florist*
folleto ⓜ fo·*lye*·to *brochure*
follar fo·*lyar fuck*
footing ⓜ *foo*·teen *jogging*
forma ① *for*·ma *shape*
fotografía ① fo·to·gra·*fee*·a
 photograph
fotógrafo/a ⓜ/① fo·*to*·gra·fo/a
 photographer
fotómetro ⓜ fo·*to*·me·tro *light meter*
frágil *fra*·kheel *fragile*
frambuesa ① fram·*bwe*·sa *raspberry*
franela ① fra·*ne*·la *flannel*
franqueo ⓜ fran·*ke*·o *postage*
freír fre·*eer fry*
frenos ⓜ pl *fre*·nos *brakes*
frente a *fren*·te a *opposite*
fresa ① *fre*·sa *strawberry*
frío/a ⓜ/① *free*·o/a *cold*
frontera ① fron·*te*·ra *border*
fruta ① *froo*·ta *fruit*
fruto ⓜ *seco* froo·to *se*·ko *dried fruit*
fuego ⓜ *fwe*·go *fire*
fuera de juego *fwe*·ra de *khwe*·go
 offside
fuerte *fwer*·te *strong*

fumar foo·*mar smoke*
funda ① **de almohada** *foon*·da de
 al·*mwa*·da *pillowcase*
funeral ⓜ foo·ne·*ral funeral*
fútbol ⓜ *foot*·bol *football • soccer*
 — **australiano** ow·stra·*lya*·no
 Australian Rules football
futuro ⓜ foo·*too*·ro *future*

G

gafas ① pl *ga*·fas *glasses*
 — **de sol** de sol *sunglasses*
 — **de submarinismo** de
 soob·ma·ree·*nees*·mo *goggles*
galleta ① ga·*lye*·ta *biscuit • cookie*
galletas ① pl **saladas** ga·*lye*·tas
 sa·*la*·das *biscuits • crackers*
gambas ① pl *gam*·bas *prawns*
ganador(a) ⓜ/① ga·na·*dor*/ga·na·*do*·ra
 winner
ganar ga·*nar earn • win*
garbanzos ⓜ pl gar·*ban*·thos *chickpeas*
garganta ① gar·*gan*·ta *throat*
gasolina ① ga·so·*lee*·na *petrol*
gasolinera ① ga·so·lee·*ne*·ra
 service station
gatito/a ⓜ/① ga·*tee*·to/a *kitten*
gato/a ⓜ/① *ga*·to/a *cat*
gay gai *gay*
gemelos ⓜ pl khe·*me*·los *twins*
general khe·ne·*ral general*
gente ① *khen*·te *people*
gimnasia ① **rítmica** kheem·*na*·sya
 reet·mee·ka *gymnastics*
ginebra ① khe·*ne*·bra *gin*
ginecólogo ⓜ khe·ne·*ko*·lo·go
 gynaecologist
gobierno ⓜ go·*byer*·no *government*
gol ⓜ gol *goal*
goma ① *go*·ma *condom • rubber*
gordo/a ⓜ/① *gor*·do/a *fat*
grabación ① gra·ba·*thyon recording*
gracioso/a ⓜ/① gra·*thyo*·so/a *funny*
gramo ⓜ *gra*·mo *gram*
grande *gran*·de *big • large*

grande almacene ⓜ gran·de al·ma·*the*·ne *department store*
granja ⓕ gran·kha *farm*
gratis gra·tees *free (of charge)*
grifo ⓜ gree·fo *tap*
gripe ⓕ gree·pe *influenza*
gris grees *grey*
gritar gree·tar *shout*
grupo ⓜ groo·po *group*
— **de rock** de rok *rock band*
— **sanguíneo** san·gee·ne·o *blood group*
guantes ⓜ pl gwan·tes *gloves*
guardarropa ⓜ gwar·da·ro·pa *cloakroom*
guardería ⓕ gwar·de·ree·a *childminding service • creche*
guerra ⓕ ge·ra *war*
guía ⓜ&ⓕ gee·a *guide (person)*
guía ⓕ gee·a *guidebook*
— **audio** ow·dyo *guide (audio)*
— **del ocio** del o·thyo *entertainment guide*
— **telefónica** te·le·fo·nee·ka *phone book*
guindilla ⓕ geen·dee·lya *chilli*
guión gee·on *script*
guiri ⓜ gee·ree *tourist (slang)*
guisantes gee·san·tes *peas*
güisqui gwees·kee *whiskey*
guitarra ⓕ gee·ta·ra *guitar*
gustar(le) goos·tar(·le) *like*

H

habitación ⓕ a·bee·ta·*thyon* *bedroom • room*
— **doble** do·ble *double room*
— **individual** een·dee·vee·*dwal* *single room*
hablar a·blar *speak • talk*
hace sol a·the sol *sunny*
hacer a·ther do • make
— **dedo** de·do *hitchhike*
— **surf** soorf *surf*
— **windsurf** ween·soorf *windsurfing*

hachís ⓜ a·chees *hash*
hacia a·thya *towards*
— **abajo** a·ba·kho *down*
halal a·lal *Halal*
hamaca ⓕ a·ma·ka *hammock*
hambriento/a ⓜ/ⓕ am·bryen·to/a *hungry*
harina ⓕ a·ree·na *flour*
hasta (junio) as·ta (khoo·nyo) *until (June)*
hecho/a ⓜ/ⓕ e·cho/a *made*
— **a mano** a ma·no *handmade*
— **de (algodón)** de (al·go·*don*) *made of (cotton)*
heladería ⓕ e·la·de·ree·a *ice cream parlour*
helado ⓜ e·la·do *ice cream*
helar e·lar *freeze*
hepatitis ⓕ e·pa·tee·tees *hepatitis*
herbolario ⓜ er·bo·la·ryo *herbalist (shop)*
herida ⓕ e·ree·da *injury*
hermana ⓕ er·ma·na *sister*
hermano ⓜ er·ma·no *brother*
hermoso/a ⓜ/ⓕ er·mo·so/a *beautiful*
heroína ⓕ e·ro·ee·na *heroin*
hielo ⓜ ye·lo *ice*
hierba ⓕ yer·ba *grass*
hierbas ⓕ pl yer·bas *herbs*
hígado ⓜ ee·ga·do *liver*
higos ⓜ pl ee·gos *figs*
hija ⓕ ee·kha *daughter*
hijo ⓜ ee·kho *son*
hijos ⓜ pl ee·khos *children*
hilo ⓜ **dental** ee·lo den·tal *dental floss*
hinchas ⓜ&ⓕ pl een·chas *supporters*
hindú een·*doo Hindu*
hipódromo ⓜ ee·po·dro·mo *racetrack (horses)*
historial ⓜ **profesional** ees·to·*ryal* pro·fe·syo·*nal CV*
histórico/a ⓜ/ⓕ ees·to·ree·ko/a *historical*
hockey ⓜ kho·kee *hockey*
— **sobre hielo** so·bre ye·lo *ice hockey*
hoja ⓕ o·kha *leaf • sheet (of paper)*

hojalata ① o·kha·*la*·ta *tin*

Holanda ① o·*lan*·da *Netherlands*

hombre ⓜ *om*·bre *man*

hombros ⓜ pl om·bros *shoulders*

homosexual ⓜ&① o·mo·se·*kswal* *homosexual*

hora ① o·ra *time*

horario ⓜ o·ra·ryo *timetable*

horas ① pl **de abrir** o·ras de a·*breer* *opening hours*

hormiga ① or·*mee*·ga *ant*

horno ⓜ or·no *oven*

horóscopo ⓜ o·ros·ko·po *horoscope*

hospital ⓜ os·pee·*tal* *hospital*

hostelería ① os·te·le·*ree*·a *hospitality*

hotel ⓜ o·*tel* *hotel*

hoy oy *today*

hueso ⓜ we·so *bone*

huevo ⓜ we·vo *egg*

humanidades ① pl oo·ma·nee·*da*·des *humanities*

I

identificación ① ee·den·tee·fee·ka·*thyon* *identification*

idiomas ① pl ee·*dyo*·mas *languages*

idiota ⓜ/① ee·*dyo*·ta *idiot*

iglesia ① ee·*gle*·sya *church*

igual ee·*gwal* *same*

igualdad ① ee·gwal·*da* *equality*

impermeable ⓜ eem·per·me·a·ble *raincoat*

impermeable eem·per·me·a·ble *waterproof*

importante eem·por·*tan*·te *important*

impuesto ⓜ eem·*pwes*·to *tax*
— **sobre la renta** so·bre la *ren*·ta *income tax*

incluido een·kloo·ee·do *included*

incómodo/a ⓜ/① een·ko·mo·do/a *uncomfortable*

India ① *een*·dya *India*

indicador ⓜ een·dee·ka·*dor* *indicator*

indigestión ① een·dee·khes·*tyon* *indigestion*

industria ① een·*doos*·trya *industry*

infección ① een·fek·*thyon* *infection*

inflamación ① een·fla·ma·*thyon* *inflammation*

informática ① een·for·ma·tee·ka *IT*

ingeniería ① een·khe·nye·*ree*·a *engineering*

ingeniero/a ⓜ/① een·khe·*nye*·ro/a *engineer*

Inglaterra ① een·gla·*te*·ra *England*

inglés ⓜ een·*gles* *English*

ingrediente ⓜ een·gre·*dyen*·te *ingredient*

injusto/a ⓜ/① een·*khoos*·to/a *unfair*

inmigración ① een·mee·gra·*thyon* *immigration*

inocente ee·no·*then*·te *innocent*

inseguro/a ⓜ/① een·se·goo·ro/a *unsafe*

instituto ⓜ eens·tee·*too*·to *high school*

intentar (hacer algo) een·ten·*tar* (a·*ther* al·go) *try (to do something)*

interesante een·te·re·*san*·te *interesting*

internacional een·ter·na·thyo·*nal* *international*

Internet ⓜ een·ter·*net* *Internet*

intérprete ⓜ&① een·*ter*·pre·te *interpreter*

inundación ① ee·noon·da·*thyon* *flooding*

invierno ⓜ een·*vyer*·no *winter*

invitar een·vee·*tar* *invite*

inyección ① een·yek·*thyon* *injection*

inyectar(se) een·yek·*tar*(·se) *inject (oneself)*

ir eer *go*
— **de compras** de *kom*·pras *go shopping*
— **de excursión** de eks·koor·*syon* *hike*
— **en tobogán** en to·bo·*gan* *tobogganing*

Irlanda ① eer·*lan*·da *Ireland*

irritación ① ee·ree·ta·*thyon* *rash*
— **de pañal** de pa·*nyal* *nappy rash*

isla ① *ees*·la *island*

itinerario ⓜ ee·tee·ne·ra·ryo *itinerary*

IVA ⓜ *ee*·va *sales tax*

izquierda ① eeth·*kyer*·da *left*

J

jabón ⓜ kha·*bon* soap
jamón ⓜ kha·*mon* ham
Japón ⓜ kha·*pon* Japan
jarabe ⓜ kha·*ra*·be cough medicine
jardín ⓜ khar·*deen*
 botánico bo·*ta*·nee·ko botanic garden
jarra ⓕ *kha*·ra jar
jefe/a ⓜ/ⓕ *khe*·fe/a boss • leader
 — de sección de sek·*thyon* manager
jengibre ⓜ khen·*khee*·bre ginger
jeringa ⓕ khe·*reen*·ga syringe
jersey ⓜ kher·*sey* jumper • sweater
jet lag ⓜ dyet lag jet lag
jockey ⓜ *dyo*·kee jockey
joven *kho*·ven young
joyería ⓕ kho·ye·*ree*·a jeweller (shop)
jubilado/a ⓜ/ⓕ khoo·bee·*la*·do/a
 retired
judías ⓕ pl khoo·*dee*·as beans
judío/a ⓜ/ⓕ khoo·*dee*·o/a Jewish
juegos ⓜ pl **de ordenador** *khwe*·gos
 de or·de·na·*dor* computer games
juegos ⓜ pl **olímpicos** *khwe*·gos
 o·*leem*·pee·kos Olympic Games
juez ⓜ&ⓕ khweth judge
jugar khoo·*gar* play (sport • games)
jugo ⓜ *khoo*·go juice
juguetería ⓕ khoo·ge·te·*ree*·a toyshop
juntos/as ⓜ/ⓕ pl *khoon*·tos/as
 together

K

kilo ⓜ *kee*·lo kilogram
kilómetro ⓜ kee·*lo*·me·tro
 kilometre
kiwi ⓜ *kee*·wee kiwifruit
kosher *ko*·sher Kosher

L

La Copa ⓕ **Mundial** la *ko*·pa
 moon·*dyal* World Cup
labios ⓜ pl *la*·byos lips
lado ⓜ *la*·do side

ladrón ⓜ la·*dron* thief
lagartija ⓕ la·gar·*tee*·kha lizard
lago ⓜ *la*·go lake
lamentar la·men·*tar* regret
lana ⓕ *la*·na wool
lápiz ⓜ *la*·peeth pencil
 — de labios de *la*·byos lipstick
largo/a ⓜ/ⓕ *lar*·go/a long
lata ⓕ *la*·ta can
lavadero ⓜ la·va·*de*·ro laundry
lavadora ⓕ la·va·*do*·ra
 washing machine
lavandería ⓕ la·van·de·*ree*·a
 laundrette
lavar la·*var* wash (something)
lavarse la·*var*·se wash (oneself)
leche ⓕ *le*·che milk
 — de soja de so·kha soy milk
 — desnatada des·na·*ta*·da
 skimmed milk
lechuga ⓕ le·*choo*·ga lettuce
leer le·*er* read
legal le·*gal* legal
legislación ⓕ le·khees·la·*thyon*
 legislation
legumbre ⓕ le·*goom*·bre legume
lejos *le*·khos far
leña ⓕ *le*·nya firewood
lentejas ⓕ pl len·*te*·khas lentils
lentes ⓜ pl **de contacto** *len*·tes de
 kon·*tak*·to contact lenses
lento/a ⓜ/ⓕ *len*·to/a slow
lesbiana ⓕ les·bee·*a*·na lesbian
leve *le*·ve light
ley ⓕ ley law
libra ⓕ *lee*·bra pound (money)
libre *lee*·bre free (not bound)
librería ⓕ lee·bre·*ree*·a bookshop
libro ⓜ *lee*·bro book
 — de frases de *fra*·ses phrasebook
libros ⓜ pl **de viajes** *lee*·bros de
 vya·khes travel books
líder ⓜ *lee*·der leader
ligar lee·*gar* pick up
lila *lee*·la purple
lima *lee*·ma lime

límite ⓜ **de equipaje** *lee·mee·te de e·kee·pa·khe baggage allowance*
limón ⓜ *lee·mon lemon*
limonada ⓕ *lee·mo·na·da lemonade*
limpio/a ⓜ/ⓕ *leem·pyo/a clean*
línea ⓕ *lee·ne·a line*
linterna ⓕ *leen·ter·na flashlight • torch*
listo/a ⓜ/ⓕ *lees·to/a ready*
lo que *lo ke what*
local ⓜ *lo·kal venue*
local *lo·kal local*
loco/a ⓜ/ⓕ *lo·ko/a crazy*
lodo ⓜ *lo·do mud*
lombrices ⓕ pl *lom·bree·thes earth worms*
los dos *los dos both*
Los Estados ⓜ pl **Unidos** *los es·ta·dos oo·nee·dos USA*
lubricante ⓜ *loo·bree·kan·te lubricant*
luces ⓕ pl *loo·thes lights*
luchar contra *loo·char kon·tra fight against*
lugar ⓜ *loo·gar place*
  — **de nacimiento** *de na·thee·myen·to place of birth*
lujo ⓜ *loo·kho luxury*
luna ⓕ *loo·na moon*
  — **llena** *lye·na full moon*
  — **de miel** *de myel honeymoon*
luz ⓕ *looth light*

llamada ⓕ *lya·ma·da phone call*
  — **a cobro revertido** *a ko·bro re·ver·tee·do collect call*
llamar por telefono *lya·mar por te·le·fo·no to make a phone call*
llano/a ⓜ/ⓕ *lya·no/a flat*
llave ⓕ *lya·ve key*
llegadas ⓕ pl *lye·ga·das arrivals*
llegar *lye·gar arrive*
llenar *lye·nar fill*
lleno/a ⓜ/ⓕ *lye·no/a full*
llevar *lye·var carry • wear*
lluvia ⓕ *lyoo·vya rain*

M

machismo ⓜ *ma·chees·mo sexism*
madera ⓕ *ma·de·ra wood*
madre ⓕ *ma·dre mother*
madrugada ⓕ *ma·droo·ga·da early morning*
mago/a ⓜ/ⓕ *ma·go/a magician*
maíz ⓜ *ma·eeth corn*
maleta ⓕ *ma·le·ta suitcase*
maletín ⓜ *ma·le·teen briefcase*
  — **de primeros auxilios** ⓜ *de pree·me·ros ow·ksee·lyos first-aid kit*
malo/a ⓜ/ⓕ *ma·lo/a bad*
mamá ⓕ *ma·ma mum*
mamograma ⓜ *ma·mo·gra·ma mammogram*
mañana ⓕ *ma·nya·na tomorrow • morning (6am - 1pm)*
  — **por la mañana** *por la ma·nya·na tomorrow morning*
  — **por la noche** *por la no·che tomorrow evening*
  — **por la tarde** *por la tar·de tomorrow afternoon*
mandarina ⓕ *man·da·ree·na mandarin*
mandíbula ⓕ *man·dee·boo·la jaw*
mando ⓜ **a distancia** *man·do a dees·tan·thya remote control*
mango ⓜ *man·go mango*
manifestación ⓕ *ma·nee·fes·ta·thyon demonstration*
manillar ⓜ *ma·nee·lyar handlebar*
mano ⓕ *ma·no hand*
manta ⓕ *man·ta blanket*
manteca ⓕ *man·te·ka lard*
mantel ⓜ *man·tel tablecloth*
mantequilla ⓕ *man·te·kee·lya butter*
manzana ⓕ *man·tha·na apple*
mapa ⓜ *ma·pa map*
maquillaje ⓜ *ma·kee·lya·khe make-up*
máquina ⓕ *ma·kee·na machine*
  — **de billetes** *de bee·lye·tes ticket machine*
  — **de tabaco** *de ta·ba·ko cigarette machine*

mar ⓜ mar *sea*
marido ⓜ ma·*ree*·do *husband*
maravilloso/a ⓜ/ⓕ ma·ra·vee·*lyo*·so/a *wonderful*
marcador ⓜ mar·ka·*dor scoreboard*
marcapasos ⓜ mar·ka·*pa*·sos *pacemaker*
marcar mar·*kar score*
marea ⓕ ma·*re*·a *tide*
mareado/a ⓜ/ⓕ ma·re·a·do/a *dizzy • seasick*
mareo ⓜ ma·*re*·o *travel sickness*
margarina ⓕ mar·ga·*ree*·na *margarine*
marihuana ⓕ ma·ree·*wa*·na *marijuana*
mariposa ⓕ ma·ree·*po*·sa *butterfly*
marrón ma·*ron brown*
martillo ⓜ mar·*tee*·lyo *hammer*
más cercano/a ⓜ/ⓕ mas ther·*ka*·no/a *nearest*
masaje ⓜ ma·*sa*·khe *massage*
masajista ⓜ&ⓕ ma·sa·*khees*·ta *masseur*
matar ma·*tar kill*
matrícula ⓕ ma·*tree*·koo·la *license plate number*
matrimonio ⓜ ma·tree·*mo*·nyo *marriage*
mayonesa ⓕ ma·yo·*ne*·sa *mayonnaise*
mecánico ⓜ me·*ka*·nee·ko *mechanic*
mechero ⓜ me·*che*·ro *lighter*
medianoche ⓕ me·dya·*no*·che *midnight*
medias ⓕ pl *me*·dyas *stockings • pantyhose*
medicina ⓕ me·dee·*thee*·na *medicine*
medico/a ⓜ/ⓕ *me*·dee·co/a *doctor*
medio ambiente ⓜ *me*·dyo am·*byen*·te *environment*
medio/a ⓜ/ⓕ *me*·dyo/a *half*
mediodía ⓜ me·dyo·*dee*·a *noon*
medios de comunicación ⓜ pl *me*·dyos de ko·moo·nee·ka·*thyon media*
medios de transporte ⓜ pl *me*·dyos de trans·*por*·te *means of transport*
mejillones ⓜ pl me·khee·*lyo*·nes *mussels*
mejor me·*khor better • best*
melocotón ⓜ me·lo·ko·*ton peach*

melodía ⓕ me·lo·*dee*·a *tune*
melón ⓜ me·*lon melon*
mendigo/a ⓜ/ⓕ men·*dee*·go/a *beggar*
menos me·nos *less*
mensaje ⓜ men·*sa*·khe *message*
menstruación ⓕ mens·trwa·*thyon menstruation*
mentiroso/a ⓜ/ⓕ men·tee·ro·so/a *liar*
menú ⓜ me·*noo menu*
menudo/a ⓜ/ⓕ me·*noo*·do/a *little*
a menudo a me·*noo*·do *often*
mercado ⓜ mer·*ka*·do *market*
mermelada ⓕ mer·me·*la*·da *jam • marmalade*
mes ⓜ mes *month*
mesa ⓕ *me*·sa *table*
meseta ⓕ me·*se*·ta *plateau*
metal ⓜ me·*tal metal*
meter (un gol) me·*ter* (oon gol) *kick (a goal)*
metro ⓜ *me*·tro *metre*
mezclar meth·*klar mix*
mezquita ⓕ meth·*kee*·ta *mosque*
mi mee *my*
microondas ⓜ mee·kro·*on*·das *microwave*
miel ⓕ myel *honey*
miembro ⓜ *myem*·bro *member*
migraña ⓕ mee·*gra*·nya *migraine*
milímetro ⓜ mee·*lee*·me·tro *millimetre*
millón ⓜ mee·*lyon million*
minusválido/a ⓜ/ⓕ mee·noos·va·lee·do/a *disabled*
minuto ⓜ mee·*noo*·to *minute*
mirador ⓜ mee·ra·*dor lookout*
mirar mee·*rar look • watch*
— los escaparates los es·ka·pa·*ra*·tes *window-shopping*
misa ⓕ *mee*·sa *mass*
mochila ⓕ mo·*chee*·la *backpack*
módem ⓜ *mo*·dem *modem*
(carne) molida (*kar*·ne) mo·*lee*·da *mince (meat)*
mojado/a ⓜ/ⓕ mo·*kha*·do/a *wet*
monasterio ⓜ mo·nas·*te*·ryo *monastery*

monedas ① pl mo·ne·das *coins*

monja ① mon·kha *nun*

monopatinaje ⓜ mo·no·pa·tee·na·khe *skateboarding*

montaña ① mon·ta·nya *mountain*

montar mon·tar *ride*
— **en bicicleta** en bee·thee·kle·ta *cycle*

monumento ⓜ mo·noo·men·to *monument*

mordedura ① mor·de·doo·ra *bite (dog)*

morir mo·reer *die*

mosquitera ① mos·kee·te·ra *mosquito net*

mosquito ⓜ mos·kee·to *mosquito*

mostaza ① mos·ta·tha *mustard*

mostrador ⓜ mos·tra·dor *counter*

mostrar mos·trar *show*

motocicleta ① mo·to·thee·kle·ta *motorcycle*

motor ⓜ mo·tor *engine*

motora ① mo·to·ra *motorboat*

muchas/os ⓜ/① pl moo·chas/os *many*

mudo/a ⓜ/① moo·do/a *mute*

muebles ⓜ pl mwe·bles *furniture*

muela ① mwe·la *tooth (back)*

muelle ⓜ mwe·lye *spring*

muerto/a ⓜ/① mwer·to/a *dead*

muesli ⓜ mwes·lee *muesli*

mujer ① moo·kher *woman*

multa ① mool·ta *fine*

mundo ⓜ moon·do *world*

muñeca ① moo·nye·ka *doll • wrist*

murallas ① pl moo·ra·lyas *city walls*

músculo ⓜ moos·koo·lo *muscle*

museo ⓜ moo·se·o *museum*
— **de arte** de ar·te *art gallery*

música ① moo·see·ka *music*

músico/a ⓜ/① moo·see·ko/a *musician*
— **ambulante** am·boo·lan·te *busker*

muslo ⓜ moos·lo *drumstick (chicken)*

musulmán(a) ⓜ/① moo·sool·man/ moo·sool·ma·na *Muslim*

muy mooy *very*

N

nacionalidad ① na·thyo·na·lee·da *nationality*

nada na·da *none • nothing*

nadar na·dar *swim*

naranja ① na·ran·kha *orange*

nariz ① na·reeth *nose*

nata ① agria na·ta a·grya *sour cream*

naturaleza ① na·too·ra·le·tha *nature*

naturopatía ① na·too·ro·pa·tee·a *naturopathy*

náusea ① now·se·a *nausea*

náuseas ① pl **del embarazo** now·se·as del em·ba·ra·tho *morning sickness*

navaja ① na·va·kha *penknife*

Navidad ① na·vee·da *Christmas*

necesario/a ⓜ/① ne·the·sa·ryo/a *necessary*

necesitar ne·the·see·tar *need*

negar ne·gar *deny*

negar ne·gar *refuse*

negocio ⓜ ne·go·thyo *business*
— **de artículos básicos** de ar·tee·koo·los ba·see·kos *convenience store*

negro/a ⓜ/① ne·gro/a *black*

neumático ⓜ ne·oo·ma·tee·ko *tyre*

nevera ① ne·ve·ra *refrigerator*

nieto/a ⓜ/① nye·to/a *grandchild*

nieve ① nye·ve *snow*

niño/a ⓜ/① nee·nyo/a *child*

no no no *no*
— **fumadores** foo·ma·do·res *non-smoking*
— **incluido** een·kloo·ee·do *excluded*

noche ① no·che *evening • night*

Nochebuena ① no·che·bwe·na *Christmas Eve*

Nochevieja ① no·che·vye·kha *New Year's Eve*

nombre ⓜ nom·bre *name*
— **de pila** de pee·la *Christian name*

norte ⓜ nor·te *north*

nosotros/as ⓜ/① pl no·so·tros/ no·so·tras *we*

noticias ① pl no·tee·thyas *news*
 — **de actualidad** de ak·twal·ee·da
 current affairs
novia ① no·vya *girlfriend*
novio ⑩ no·vyo *boyfriend*
nube ① noo·be *cloud*
nublado noo·bla·do *cloudy*
nueces nwe·thes *nuts*
 — **crudas** kroo·das *raw nuts*
 — **tostadas** tos·ta·das *roasted nuts*
nuestro/a ⑩/① nwes·tro/a *our*
Nueva Zelanda ① nwe·va the·lan·da
 New Zealand
nuevo/a ⑩/① nwe·vo/a *new*
número ⑩ noo·me·ro *number*
 — **de la habitación** de la
 a·bee·ta·thyon *room number*
 — **de pasaporte** de pa·sa·por·te
 passport number
nunca noon·ka *never*

O

o o *or*
obra ① o·bra *play • building site*
obrero/a ⑩/① o·bre·ro/a
 factory worker • labourer
océano ⑩ o·the·a·no *ocean*
ocupado/a ⑩/① o·koo·pa·do/a *busy*
ocupar o·koo·par *live (somewhere)*
oeste ⑩ o·es·te *west*
oficina ① o·fee·thee·na *office*
 — **de objetos perdidos** de ob·khe·tos
 per·dee·dos *lost property office*
 — **de turismo** de too·rees·mo
 tourist office
oír o·eer *hear*
ojo ⑩ o·kho *eye*
ola ① o·la *wave*
olor ⑩ o·lor *smell*
olvidar ol·vee·dar *forget*
ópera ① o·pe·ra *opera*
operación ① o·pe·ra·thyon *operation*
opinión ① o·pee·nyon *opinion*
oporto ⑩ o·por·to *port (wine)*
oportunidad ① o·por·too·nee·da *chance*

oración ① o·ra·thyon *prayer*
orden ⑩ or·den *order (placement)*
ordenador ⑩ or·de·na·dor *computer*
 — **portátil** por·ta·teel *laptop*
ordenar or·de·nar *order*
oreja ① o·re·kha *ear*
orgasmo ⑩ or·gas·mo *orgasm*
original o·ree·khee·nal *original*
orquesta ① or·kes·ta *orchestra*
oscuro/a ⑩/① os·koo·ro/a *dark*
ostra ① os·tra *oyster*
otoño ⑩ o·to·nyo *autumn*
otra vez o·tra veth *again*
otro/a ⑩/① o·tro/a *other • another*
oveja ① o·ve·kha *sheep*
oxígeno ⑩ o·ksee·khe·no *oxygen*

P

padre ⑩ pa·dre *father*
padres ⑩ pl pa·dres *parents*
pagar pa·gar *pay*
página ① pa·khee·na *page*
pago ⑩ pa·go *payment*
país ⑩ pa·ees *country*
pájaro ⑩ pa·kha·ro *bird*
palabra ① pa·la·bra *word*
palacio ⑩ pa·la·thyo *palace*
palillo ⑩ pa·lee·lyo *toothpick*
pan ⑩ pan *bread*
 — **integral** in·te·gral
 wholemeal bread
 — **moreno** mo·re·no *brown bread*
panadería ① pa·na·de·ree·a *bakery*
pañal ⑩ pa·nyal *diaper • nappy*
pantalla ① pan·ta·lya *screen*
pantalones ⑩ pl pan·ta·lo·nes
 pants • trousers
 — **cortos** kor·tos *shorts*
pañuelos ⑩ pl **de papel** pa·nywe·los
 de pa·pel *tissues*
papá ⑩ pa·pa *dad*
papel ⑩ pa·pel *paper*
 — **de fumar** de foo·mar
 cigarette papers
 — **higiénico** ee·khye·nee·ko
 toilet paper

paquete ⓜ pa·*ke*·te
packet • package • wear

para llevar pa·ra lye·*var to take away*

parabrisas ⓜ pa·ra·*bree*·sas *windscreen*

paracaidismo ⓜ pa·ra·kai·*dees*·mo
skydiving

parada ① pa·*ra*·da *stop*
— **de autobús** de ow·to·*boos*
bus stop
— **de taxis** de *ta*·ksees *taxi stand*

paraguas ⓜ pa·*ra*·gwas *umbrella*

parapléjico/a ⓜ/① pa·ra·*ple*·khee·ko/a
paraplegic

parar pa·*rar stop*

pared ① pa·*re wall (inside)*

pareja ① pa·*re*·kha *pair (couple)*

parlamento ⓜ par·la·*men*·to *parliament*

paro ⓜ *pa*·ro *dole*

parque ⓜ *par*·ke *park*
— **nacional** na·thyo·*nal*
national park

parte ① *par*·te *part*

partida ① **de nacimiento** par·*tee*·da de
na·thee·*myen*·to *birth certificate*

partido ⓜ par·*tee*·do
match (sport) • party (political)

pasado ⓜ pa·*sa*·do *past*

pasado mañana pa·*sa*·do ma·*nya*·na
day after tomorrow

pasado/a ⓜ/① pa·*sa*·do/a *off (food)*

pasajero ⓜ pa·sa·*khe*·ro *passenger*

pasaporte ⓜ pa·sa·*por*·te *passport*

Pascua ① *pas*·kwa *Easter*

pase ⓜ *pa*·se *pass*

paseo ⓜ pa·*se*·o *street*

paso ⓜ *pa*·so *step*
— **de cebra** de *the*·bra
pedestrian crossing

pasta ① *pas*·ta *pasta*
— **dentífrica** den·*tee*·free·ka
toothpaste

pastel ⓜ pas·*tel cake • pie*
— **de cumpleaños** de
koom·ple·*a*·nyos *birthday cake*

pastelería ① pas·te·le·*ree*·a *cake shop*

pastilla ① pas·*tee*·lya *pill*

pastillas ① pl **de menta** pas·*tee*·lyas de
men·ta *mints*

pastillas ① pl **para dormir** pas·*tee*·lyas
pa·ra dor·*meer sleeping pills*

patata ① pa·*ta*·ta *potato*

paté ⓜ pa·*te pate (food)*

patinar pa·*tee*·nar
rollerblading • ice skating

pato ⓜ *pa*·to *duck*

pavo ⓜ *pa*·vo *turkey*

paz ① path *peace*

peatón ⓜ&① pe·a·*ton pedestrian*

pecho ⓜ *pe*·cho *chest*

pechuga ① pe·*choo*·ga *breast (poultry)*

pedal ⓜ pe·*dal pedal*

pedazo ⓜ pe·*da*·tho *piece*

pedir pe·*deer ask (for something)*

peine ⓜ *pey*·ne *comb*

pelea ① pe·*le*·a *fight*

película ① pe·*lee*·koo·la
movie • film (camera)
— **en color** en ko·*lor colour film*

peligroso/a ⓜ/① pe·lee·*gro*·so/a
dangerous

pelo ⓜ *pe*·lo *hair*

pelota ① pe·*lo*·ta *ball*
— **de golf** de golf *golf ball*

peluquero/a ⓜ/① pe·loo·*ke*·ro/a
hairdresser

pendientes ⓜ pl pen·*dyen*·tes *earrings*

pene ⓜ *pe*·ne *penis*

pensar pen·*sar think*

pensión ① pen·*syon boarding house*

pensionista ⓜ&① pen·syo·*nees*·ta
pensioner

pepino ⓜ pe·*pee*·no *cucumber*

pequeñito/a ⓜ/① pe·ke·*nyee*·to/a *tiny*

pequeño/a ⓜ/① pe·*ke*·nyo/a *small*

pera ① *pe*·ra *pear*

perder per·*der lose*

perdido/a ⓜ/① per·*dee*·do/a *lost*

perdonar per·do·*nar forgive*

perejil ⓜ pe·re·*kheel parsley*

perfume ⓜ per·*foo*·me *perfume*

periódico ⓜ pe·*ryo*·dee·ko *newspaper*

periodista ⓜ&① pe·ryo·*dees*·ta
journalist

permiso ⓜ per·*mee*·so
  permission • permit
  — de trabajo ⓜ de tra·*ba*·kho
  work permit
permitir per·mee·*teer* *allow • permit*
pero *pe*·ro *but*
perro/a ⓜ/ⓕ *pe*·ro/a *dog*
perro ⓜ **lazarillo** *pe*·ro la·tha·*ree*·lyo
  guide dog
persona ⓕ per·*so*·na *person*
pesado/a ⓜ/ⓕ pe·*sa*·do/a *heavy*
pesar pe·*sar* *weigh*
pesas ⓕ pl *pe*·sas *weights*
pesca ⓕ *pes*·ka *fishing*
pescadería ⓕ pes·ka·de·*ree*·a *fish shop*
pescado ⓜ pes·*ka*·do *fish (as food)*
peso ⓜ *pe*·so *weight*
petición ⓕ pe·tee·*thyon* *petition*
pez ⓜ peth *fish*
picadura ⓕ pee·ka·*doo*·ra *bite (insect)*
picazón ⓕ pee·ka·*thon* *itch*
pie ⓜ *pee*·e *foot*
piedra ⓕ *pye*·dra *stone*
piel ⓕ pyel *skin*
pierna ⓕ *pyer*·na *leg*
pila ⓕ *pee*·la *battery (small)*
píldora ⓕ *peel*·do·ra *the Pill*
pimienta ⓕ pee·*myen*·ta *pepper*
pimiento ⓜ pee·*myen*·to
  capsicum • bell pepper
  — rojo *ro*·kho *red capsicum*
  — verde *ver*·de *green capsicum*
piña ⓕ *pee*·nya *pineapple*
pinchar peen·*char* *puncture*
ping pong ⓜ peeng pong *table tennis*
pintar peen·*tar* *paint*
pintor(a) ⓜ/ⓕ peen·*tor*/peen·*to*·ra
  painter
pintura ⓕ peen·*too*·ra *painting*
pinzas ⓕ pl *peen*·thas *tweezers*
piojos ⓜ pl *pyo*·khos *lice*
piqueta ⓕ pee·*ke*·ta *pickaxe*
piquetas ⓕ pl pee·*ke*·tas *tent pegs*
piscina ⓕ pees·*thee*·na *swimming pool*
pista ⓕ *pees*·ta *court (tennis)*
  — de tenis de *te*·nees *tennis court*
pistacho ⓜ pees·*ta*·cho *pistachio*

plancha ⓕ *plan*·cha *iron*
planeta ⓜ pla·*ne*·ta *planet*
planta ⓕ *plan*·ta *plant*
plástico ⓜ *plas*·tee·ko *plastic*
plata ⓕ *pla*·ta *silver*
plataforma ⓕ pla·ta·*for*·ma *platform*
plátano ⓜ *pla*·ta·no *banana*
plateado/a ⓜ/ⓕ pla·te·*a*·do/a *silver*
plato ⓜ *pla*·to *plate*
playa ⓕ *pla*·ya *beach*
plaza ⓕ *pla*·tha *square*
  — de toros de *to*·ros *bullring*
pobre *po*·bre *poor*
pobreza ⓕ po·*bre*·tha *poverty*
pocos *po*·kos *few*
poder po·*der* *can (be able)*
poder ⓜ po·*der* *power*
poesía ⓕ po·e·*see*·a *poetry*
polen ⓜ *po*·len *pollen*
policía ⓕ po·lee·*thee*·a *police*
política ⓕ po·lee·*tee*·ka
  policy • politics
político ⓜ po·*lee*·tee·ko *politician*
póliza ⓕ *po*·lee·tha *policy (insurance)*
pollo ⓜ *po*·lyo *chicken*
pomelo ⓜ po·*me*·lo *grapefruit*
poner po·*ner* *put*
popular po·poo·*lar* *popular*
póquer ⓜ *po*·ker *poker*
por (día) por (*dee*·a) *per (day)*
por ciento por *thyen*·to *percent*
por qué por ke *why*
por vía aérea por *vee*·a a·*e*·re·a *air mail*
por vía terrestre por *vee*·a te·*res*·tre
  surface mail
porque *por*·ke *because*
portero/a ⓜ/ⓕ por·*te*·ro/a *goalkeeper*
posible po·*see*·ble *possible*
postal ⓕ pos·*tal* *postcard*
póster ⓜ *pos*·ter *poster*
potro ⓜ *po*·tro *foal*
pozo ⓜ *po*·tho *well*
precio ⓜ *pre*·thyo *price*
  — de entrada de en·*tra*·da
  admission price
  — del cubierto del koo·*byer*·to
  cover charge

preferir pre·fe·*reer* prefer

pregunta ① pre·*goon*·ta question

preguntar pre·goon·*tar* ask (a question)

preocupado/a ⓜ/① pre·o·koo·*pa*·do/a worried

preocuparse por pre·o·koo·*par*·se por care (about something)

preparar pre·pa·*rar* prepare

presidente/a ⓜ/① pre·see·*den*·te/a president

presión ① pre·*syon* pressure
— **arterial** ar·te·*ryal* blood pressure

prevenir pre·ve·*neer* prevent

primavera ① pree·ma·ve·ra spring (season)

primer ministro ⓜ pree·*mer* mee·*nees*·tro prime minister

primera ministra ① pree·*me*·ra mee·*nees*·tra prime minister

primero/a ⓜ/① pree·me·ro/a first

principal preen·thee·*pal* main

prisa ① *pree*·sa hurry

prisionero/a ⓜ/① pree·syon·*ne*·ro/a prisoner

privado/a ⓜ/① pree·va·do/a private

probar pro·*bar* try

producir pro·doo·*theer* produce

productos ⓜ pl **congelados** pro·*dook*·tos kon·khe·*la*·dos frozen foods

profesor(a) ⓜ/① pro·fe·*sor*/pro·fe·*so*·ra lecturer • instructor • teacher

profundo/a ⓜ/① pro·*foon*·do/a deep

programa ⓜ pro·*gra*·ma programme

prolongación ① pro·lon·ga·*thyon* extension (visa)

promesa ① pro·*me*·sa promise

prometida ① pro·me·*tee*·da fiancee

prometido ⓜ pro·me·*tee*·do fiance

pronto *pron*·to soon

propietaria ① pro·pye·*ta*·rya landlady

propietario ⓜ pro·pye·*ta*·ryo landlord

propina ① pro·*pee*·na tip

proteger pro·te·*kher* protect

protegido/a ⓜ/① pro·te·*khee*·do/a protected

protesta ① pro·*tes*·ta protest

provisiones ① pl pro·bee·*syo*·nes provisions

proyector ⓜ pro·yek·*tor* projector

prudente proo·*den*·te sensible

prueba ① *prwe*·ba test
— **del embarazo** del em·ba·*ra*·tho pregnancy test kit

pruebas ① pl **nucleares** *prwe*·bas noo·kle·*a*·res nuclear testing

pub ⓜ *poob* bar (with music) • pub

pueblo ⓜ *pwe*·blo village

puente ⓜ *pwen*·te bridge

puerro ⓜ *pwe*·ro leek

puerta ① *pwer*·ta door

puerto ⓜ *pwer*·to port • harbour

puesta ① **del sol** *pwes*·ta del sol sunset

pulga ① *pool*·ga flea

pulmones ⓜ pl *pool*·mo·nes lungs

punto ⓜ *poon*·to point (tip) • point (score)

puro ⓜ *poo*·ro cigar

puro/a ⓜ/① *poo*·ro/a pure

Q

(el mes) que viene (el mes) ke *vye*·ne next (month)

quedar ke·*dar* leave (behind)

quedarse ke·*dar*·se stay (remain)

quedarse sin ke·*dar*·se seen run out of

quejarse ke·*khar*·se complain

quemadura ① ke·ma·*doo*·ra burn
— **de sol** de sol sunburn

querer ke·*rer* love • want

queso ⓜ *ke*·so cheese
— **crema** *kre*·ma cream cheese
— **de cabra** de *ka*·bra goat's cheese

quien *kyen* who

quincena ① keen·*the*·na fortnight

quiosco ⓜ *kyos*·ko news stand • newsagency

quiste ⓜ **ovárico** *kees*·te o·va·*ree*·ko ovarian cyst

quizás kee·*thas* maybe

R

rábano ⓜ *ra·ba·no* radish

— picante *pee·kan·te* horseradish

rápido/a ⓜ/ⓕ *ra·pee·do/a* fast

raqueta ⓕ *ra·ke·ta* racquet

raro/a ⓜ/ⓕ *ra·ro/a* rare (item)

rastro ⓜ *ras·tro* track (footprints)

rata ⓕ *ra·ta* rat

ratón ⓜ *ra·ton* mouse

raza ⓕ *ra·tha* race (people)

razón ⓕ *ra·thon* reason

realista *re·a·lees·ta* realistic

recibir *re·thee·beer* receive

recibo ⓜ *re·thee·bo* receipt

reciclable *re·thee·kla·ble* recyclable

reciclar *re·thee·klar* recycle

recientemente *re·thyen·te·men·te* recently

recogida ⓕ **de equipajes** *re·ko·khee·da de e·kee·pa·khes* baggage claim

recolección ⓕ **de fruta** *re·ko·lek·thyon de froo·ta* fruit picking

recomendar *re·ko·men·dar* recommend

reconocer *re·ko·no·ther* recognise

recordar *re·kor·dar* remember

recorrido ⓜ **guiado** *re·ko·ree·do gee·a·do* guided tour

recto/a ⓜ/ⓕ *rek·to/a* straight

recuerdo ⓜ *re·kwer·do* souvenir

red ⓕ *red* net

redondo/a ⓜ/ⓕ *re·don·do/a* round

reembolsar *re·em·bol·sar* refund

reembolso ⓜ *re·em·bol·so* refund

referencias ⓕ pl *re·fe·ren·thyas* references

refresco ⓜ *re·fres·ko* soft drink

refugiado/a ⓜ/ⓕ *re·foo·khya·do/a* refugee

regalar *re·ga·lar* exchange (gifts)

regalo ⓜ *re·ga·lo* gift

— de bodas *de bo·das* wedding present

régimen ⓜ *re·khee·men* diet

reglas ⓕ pl *re·glas* rules

reina ⓕ *rey·na* queen

reírse *re·eer·se* laugh

relación ⓕ *re·la·thyon* relationship

relajarse *re·la·khar·se* relax

religión ⓕ *re·lee·khyon* religion

religioso/a ⓜ/ⓕ *re·lee·khyo·so/a* religious

reliquia ⓕ *re·lee·kya* relic

reloj ⓜ *re·lokh* clock

— de pulsera *de pool·se·ra* watch

remo ⓜ *re·mo* rowing

remolacha ⓕ *re·mo·la·cha* beetroot

remoto/a ⓜ/ⓕ *re·mo·to/a* remote

reparar *re·pa·rar* repair

repartir *re·par·teer* divide up (share)

repetir *re·pe·teer* repeat

república ⓕ *re·poo·blee·ka* republic

requesón ⓜ *re·ke·son* cottage cheese

reserva ⓕ *re·ser·va* reservation

reservar *re·ser·var* book (make a reservation)

resfriado ⓜ *res·free·a·do* cold

residencia ⓕ **de estudiantes** *re·see·den·thya de es·too·dyan·tes* college

residuos ⓜ pl **tóxicos** *re·see·dwos to·ksee·kos* toxic waste

respirar *res·pee·rar* breathe

respuesta ⓕ *res·pwes·ta* answer

restaurante ⓜ *res·tow·ran·te* restaurant

revisar *re·vee·sar* check

revisor(a) ⓜ/ⓕ *re·vee·sor/re·vee·so·ra* ticket collector

revista ⓕ *re·vees·ta* magazine

rey ⓜ *rey* king

rico/a ⓜ/ⓕ *ree·ko/a* rich

riesgo ⓜ *ryes·go* risk

río ⓜ *ree·o* river

ritmo ⓜ *reet·mo* rhythm

robar *ro·bar* rob • steal

roca ⓕ *ro·ka* rock

rock ⓜ *rok* rock (music)

rodilla ⓕ *ro·dee·lya* knee

rojo/a ⓜ/ⓕ *ro·kho/a* red

rollo ⓜ **repelente contra mosquitos** *ro·lyo re·pe·len·te kon·tra mos·kee·tos* mosquito coil

romántico/a ⓜ/ⓕ ro·*man*·tee·ko/a *romantic*
romper rom·*per* *break*
ron ⓜ ron *rum*
ropa ⓕ *ro*·pa *clothing*
— **de cama** de *ka*·ma *bedding*
— **interior** een·te·*ryor* *underwear*
rosa *ro*·sa *pink*
roto/a ⓜ/ⓕ *ro*·to/a *broken*
rueda ⓕ *rwe*·da *wheel*
rugby ⓜ *roog*·bee *rugby*
ruidoso/a ⓜ/ⓕ rwee·*do*·so/a *loud*
ruinas ⓕ pl *rwee*·nas *ruins*
ruta ⓕ *roo*·ta *route*

S

sábado ⓜ *sa*·ba·do *Saturday*
sábana ⓕ *sa*·ba·na *sheet (bed)*
saber sa·*ber* *know (something)*
sabroso/a ⓜ/ⓕ sa·*bro*·so/a *tasty*
sacar sa·*kar* *take out • take (photo)*
sacerdote ⓜ sa·ther·*do*·te *priest*
saco ⓜ **de dormir** *sa*·ko de dor·*meer* *sleeping bag*
sal ⓕ sal *salt*
sala ⓕ **de espera** *sa*·la de es·*pe*·ra *waiting room*
sala ⓕ **de tránsito** *sa*·la de *tran*·see·to *transit lounge*
salario ⓜ sa·*la*·ryo *rate of pay • salary*
salchicha ⓕ sal·*chee*·cha *sausage*
saldo ⓜ *sal*·do *balance (account)*
salida ⓕ sa·*lee*·da *departure • exit*
saliente ⓕ sa·*lyen*·te *ledge*
salir con sa·*leer* kon *go out with*
salir de sa·*leer* de *depart*
salmón ⓜ sal·*mon* *salmon*
salón de belleza ⓜ sa·*lon* de be·*lye*·tha *beauty salon*
salsa ⓕ *sal*·sa *sauce*
— **de guindilla** de geen·*dee*·lya *chilli sauce*
— **de soja** de *so*·kha *soy sauce*
— **de tomate** de to·*ma*·te *tomato sauce • ketchup*
saltar sal·*tar* *jump*

salud ⓕ sa·*loo* *health*
salvaeslips ⓜ pl sal·va·e·*sleeps* *panty liners*
salvar sal·*var* *save*
sandalias ⓕ pl san·*da*·lyas *sandals*
sandía ⓕ san·*dee*·a *watermelon*
sangrar san·*grar* *bleed*
sangre ⓕ *san*·gre *blood*
santo/a ⓜ/ⓕ *san*·to/a *saint*
sarampión ⓜ sa·ram·*pyon* *measles*
sartén ⓕ sar·*ten* *frying pan*
sastre ⓜ *sas*·tre *tailor*
sauna ⓕ *sow*·na *sauna*
secar se·*kar* *dry*
secretario/a ⓜ/ⓕ se·kre·*ta*·ryo/a *secretary*
sed ⓕ se *thirst*
seda ⓕ *se*·da *silk*
seguir se·*geer* *follow*
segundo/a ⓜ/ⓕ se·*goon*·do/a *second*
seguro ⓜ se·*goo*·ro *insurance*
seguro/a ⓜ/ⓕ se·*goo*·ro/a *safe*
sello ⓜ *se*·lyo *stamp*
semáforos ⓜ pl se·*ma*·fo·ros *traffic lights*
Semana ⓕ **Santa** se·*ma*·na *san*·ta *Holy Week*
sembrar sem·*brar* *plant*
semidirecto/a ⓜ/ⓕ se·mee·dee·*rek*·to/a *non-direct*
señal ⓕ se·*nyal* *sign*
sencillo/a ⓜ/ⓕ sen·*thee*·lyo/a *simple*
(un billete) sencillo (oon bee·*lye*·te) sen·*thee*·lyo *one-way (ticket)*
sendero ⓜ sen·*de*·ro *mountain path • path*
senos ⓜ pl *se*·nos *breasts*
sensibilidad ⓕ sen·see·bee·lee·*da* *sensitivity • film speed*
sensual sen·*swal* *sensual*
sentarse sen·*tar*·se *sit*
sentimientos ⓜ pl sen·tee·*myen*·tos *feelings*
sentir sen·*teer* *feel*
separado/a ⓜ/ⓕ se·pa·*ra*·do/a *separate*
separar se·pa·*rar* *separate*
ser ser *be*

serie ① se·rye *series*
serio/a ⑩/① se·ryo/a *serious*
seropositivo/a ⑩/①
se·ro·po·see·tee·vo/a *HIV positive*
serpiente ① ser·pyen·te *snake*
servicio ⑩ ser·vee·thyo *service charge*
— **militar** mee·lee·tar *military service*
— **telefónico automático**
te·le·fo·nee·ko ow·to·ma·tee·ko
direct-dial
servicios ⑩ pl ser·vee·thyos *toilets*
servilleta ① ser·vee·lye·ta *napkin*
sexo ⑩ se·kso *sex*
— **seguro** se·goo·ro *safe sex*
sexy se·ksee *sexy*
si see *if • yes*
SIDA ⑩ see·da *AIDS*
sidra ① see·dra *cider*
siempre syem·pre *always*
silla ① see·lya *chair*
— **de ruedas** de rwe·das *wheelchair*
sillín ⑩ see·lyeen *saddle*
similar see·mee·lar *similar*
simpático/a ⑩/① seem·pa·tee·ko/a *nice*
sin seen *without*
— **hogar** o·gar *homeless*
— **plomo** plo·mo *unleaded*
sinagoga ① see·na·go·ga *synagogue*
Singapur ⑩ seen·ga·poor *Singapore*
sintético/a ⑩/① seen·te·tee·ko/a
synthetic
soborno ⑩ so·bor·no *bribe*
sobre so·bre *about • on top of*
sobre ⑩ so·bre *envelope*
sobredosis ① so·bre·do·sees *overdose*
sobrevivir so·bre·vee·veer *survive*
socialista ⑩&① so·thya·lees·ta *socialist*
sol ⑩ sol *sun*
soldado ⑩ sol·da·do *soldier*
sólo so·lo *only*
solo/a ⑩/① so·lo/a *alone*
soltero/a ⑩/① sol·te·ro/a *single*
sombra ① som·bra *shadow*
sombrero ⑩ som·bre·ro *hat*
soñar so·nyar *dream*
sondeos ⑩ pl son·de·os *polls*

sonreír son·re·eer *smile*
sopa ① so·pa *soup*
sordo/a ⑩/① sor·do/a *deaf*
sorpresa ① sor·pre·sa *surprise*
su soo *her • his • their*
subir soo·beer *climb*
submarinismo ⑩ soob·ma·ree·nees·mo
diving
subtítulos ⑩ pl soob·tee·too·los *subtitles*
sucio/a ⑩/① soo·thyo/a *dirty*
sucursal ① soo·koor·sal *branch office*
sudar soo·dar *perspire*
suegra ① swe·gra *mother-in-law*
suegro ⑩ swe·gro *father-in-law*
sueldo ⑩ swel·do *wage*
suelo ⑩ swe·lo *floor*
suerte ① swer·te *luck*
suficiente soo·fee·thyen·te *enough*
sufrir soo·freer *suffer*
sujetador ⑩ soo·khe·ta·dor *bra*
supermercado ⑩ soo·per·mer·ka·do
supermarket
superstición ① soo·pers·tee·thyon
superstition
sur ⑩ soor *south*
surf ⑩ **sobre la nieve** soorf so·bre la
nye·ve *snowboarding*

T

tabaco ⑩ ta·ba·ko *tobacco*
tabla ① **de surf** ta·bla de soorf *surfboard*
tablero ⑩ **de ajedrez** ta·ble·ro de
a·khe·dreth *chess board*
tacaño/a ⑩/① ta·ka·nyo/a *stingy*
talco ⑩ tal·ko *baby powder*
talla ① ta·lya *size (clothes)*
taller ⑩ ta·lyer *workshop*
también tam·byen *also*
tampoco tam·po·ko *neither*
tampones ⑩ pl tam·po·nes *tampons*
tanga ① tan·ga *g-string*
tapones ⑩ pl **para los oídos** ta·po·nes
pa·ra los o·ee·dos *earplugs*
taquilla ① ta·kee·lya *ticket office*
tarde tar·de *late*

tarjeta tar·khe·ta *card*
— **de crédito** de kre·dee·to
credit card
— **de embarque** de em·bar·ke
boarding pass
— **de teléfono** de te·le·fo·no
phone card
tarta ① *nupcial* tar·ta noop·thyal
wedding cake
tasa ① **del aeropuerto** ta·sa del
ay·ro·pwer·to *airport tax*
taxi ⓜ ta·ksee *taxi*
taza ① ta·tha *cup*
té ⓜ te *tea*
teatro ⓜ te·a·tro *theatre*
teclado ⓜ te·kla·do *keyboard*
técnica ① tek·nee·ka *technique*
tela ① te·la *fabric*
tele ① te·le *TV*
teleférico ⓜ te·le·fe·ree·ko *cable car*
teléfono ⓜ te·le·fo·no *telephone*
— **móvil** mo·veel *mobile phone*
— **público** poo·blee·ko
public telephone
telegrama te·le·gra·ma *telegram*
telenovela ① te·le·no·ve·la *soap opera*
telescopio ⓜ te·les·ko·pyo *telescope*
televisión ① te·le·vee·syon *television*
temperatura ① tem·pe·ra·too·ra
temperature (weather)
templado/a ⓜ/① tem·pla·do/a *warm*
templo ⓜ tem·plo *temple*
temporada ① tem·po·ra·da
season (in sport)
temprano tem·pra·no *early*
tenedor ⓜ te·ne·dor *fork*
tener te·ner *have*
— **hambre** am·bre *to be hungry*
— **prisa** pree·sa *to be in a hurry*
— **sed** seth *to be thirsty*
— **sueño** swe·nyo *to be sleepy*
tenis ⓜ te·nees *tennis*
tensión ① *premenstrual* ten·syon
pre·mens·trwal *premenstrual tension*
tentempié ⓜ ten·tem·pye *snack*
tercio ⓜ ter·thyo *third*
terminar ter·mee·nar *finish*

ternera ① ter·ne·ra *veal*
ternero ⓜ ter·ne·ro *calf*
terremoto ⓜ te·re·mo·to *earthquake*
testarudo/a ⓜ/① tes·ta·roo·do/a
stubborn
tía ① tee·a *aunt*
tiempo ⓜ tyem·po *time* • *weather*
a — a tyem·po *on time*
a — completo/parcial
a tyem·po kom·ple·to/par·thyal
full-time/part-time
tienda ① **(de campaña)** tyen·da (de
kam·pa·nya) *tent*
tienda ① tyen·da *shop*
— **de comestibles** de ko·mes·tee·bles
grocery
— **de fotografía** de fo·to·gra·fee·a
camera shop
— **de eléctrodomésticos**
de e·lek·tro·do·mes·tee·kos
electrical store
— **de provisiones de cámping**
de pro·vee·syo·nes de kam·peen
camping store
— **de recuerdos** de re·kwer·dos
souvenir shop
— **de ropa** de ro·pa *clothing store*
— **deportiva** de·por·tee·va
sports store
Tierra ① tye·ra *Earth*
tierra ① tye·ra *land*
tiesto ⓜ tyes·to *pot (plant)*
tijeras ① pl tee·khe·ras *scissors*
tímido/a ⓜ/① tee·mee·do/a *shy*
típico/a ⓜ/① tee·pee·ko/a *typical*
tipo ⓜ tee·po *type*
— **de cambio** de kam·byo
exchange rate
tirar tee·rar *pull*
tiritas ① pl tee·ree·tas *band-aids*
título ⓜ tee·too·lo *degree*
toalla ① to·a·lya *towel*
toallita ① to·a·lyee·ta *face cloth*
tobillo ⓜ to·bee·lyo *ankle*
tocar to·kar *touch*
— **la guitarra** la gee·ta·ra
play (guitar)

tocino ⓜ to·*thee*·no *bacon*

todavía (no) to·da·*vee*·a (no) *(not) yet*

todo *to*·do *all* • *everything*

tofú ⓜ to·*foo* *tofu*

tomar to·*mar* *take* • *drink (something)*

tomate ⓜ to·*ma*·te *tomato*
— **secado al sol** se·*ka*·do al sol *sun-dried tomato*

tono ⓜ *to*·no *tone*

torcedura ① tor·the·*doo*·ra *sprain*

tormenta ① tor·*men*·ta *storm*

toro ⓜ *to*·ro *bull*

torre ① *to*·re *tower*

tos ① tos *cough*

tostada ① tos·*ta*·da *toast*

tostadora ① tos·ta·*do*·ra *toaster*

trabajar tra·ba·*khar* *work*

trabajo ⓜ tra·*ba*·kho *job* • *work*
— **administrativo** ad·mee·nees·tra·*tee*·vo *paperwork*
— **de camarero/a** ⓜ/① de ka·ma·*re*·ro/a *bar work*
— **de casa** de *ka*·sa *housework*
— **de limpieza** de leem·*pye*·tha *cleaning*
— **eventual** e·ven·*twal* *casual work*

traducir tra·doo·*theer* *translate*

traer tra·*er* *bring*

traficante ⓜ&① de drogas tra·fee·*kan*·te de *dro*·gas *drug dealer*

tráfico ⓜ *tra*·fee·ko *traffic*

tramposo/a ⓜ/① tram·*po*·so/a *cheat*

tranquilo/a ⓜ/① tran·*kee*·lo/a *quiet*

tranvía ⓜ tran·*vee*·a *tram*

a través a tra·*ves* *across*

tren ⓜ tren *train*
— **de cercanías** de ther·ka·*nee*·as *local train*

trepar tre·*par* *scale* • *climb*

tres en raya tres en *ra*·ya *noughts & crosses*

triste *trees*·te *sad*

tú too *you (informal)*

tu too *your*

tubo ⓜ **de escape** *too*·bo de es·*ka*·pe *exhaust*

tumba ① *toom*·ba *grave*

tumbarse toom·*bar*·se *lie (not stand)*

turista ⓜ&① too·*rees*·ta *tourist*
— **operador(a)** ⓜ/① o·pe·ra·*dor*/o·pe·ra·*do*·ra *tourist operator*

U

uniforme ⓜ oo·nee·*for*·me *uniform*

universidad ① oo·nee·ver·see·*da* *university*

universo ⓜ oo·nee·*ver*·so *universe*

urgente oor·*khen*·te *urgent*

usted oos·*te* *you (pol)*

útil *oo*·teel *useful*

uvas ① pl *oo*·vas *grapes*
— **pasas** *pa*·sas *raisins*

V

vaca ① *va*·ka *cow*

vacaciones ① pl va·ka·*thyo*·nes *holidays* • *vacation*

vacante va·*kan*·te *vacant*

vacío/a ⓜ/① va·*thee*·o/a *empty*

vacuna ① va·*koo*·na *vaccination*

vagina ① va·*khee*·na *vagina*

vagón ⓜ **restaurante** va·*gon* res·tow·*ran*·te *dining car*

validar va·lee·*dar* *validate*

valiente va·*lyen*·te *brave*

valioso/a ⓜ/① va·*lyo*·so/a *valuable*

valle ⓜ *va*·lye *valley*

valor ⓜ va·*lor* *value*

vaqueros ⓜ pl va·*ke*·ros *jeans*

varios/as ⓜ/① pl *va*·ryos/as *several*

vaso ⓜ *va*·so *(drinking) glass*

vegetariano/a ⓜ/① ve·khe·ta·*rya*·no/a *vegetarian*

vela ① *ve*·la *candle*

velocidad ① ve·lo·thee·*da* *speed*

velocímetro ⓜ ve·lo·*thee*·me·tro *speedometer*

velódromo ⓜ ve·*lo*·dro·mo *racetrack (bicycles)*

vena ① *ve*·na *vein*

vendaje ⓜ ven·*da*·khe *bandage*
vendedor(a) ⓜ/ⓕ **de flores**
 ven·de·*dor*/ven·de·*do*·ra de *flo*·res
 florist
vender ven·*der* *sell*
venenoso/a ⓜ/ⓕ ve·ne·*no*·so/a
 poisonous
venir ve·*neer* *come*
ventana ⓕ ven·*ta*·na *window*
ventilador ⓜ vee·ntee·la·*dor* *fan (machine)*
ver ver *see*
verano ⓜ ve·*ra*·no *summer*
verde *ver*·de *green*
verdulería ⓕ ver·doo·le·*ree*·a
 greengrocery (shop)
verdulero/a ⓜ/ⓕ ver·doo·*le*·ro/a
 grocer (shopkeeper)
verduras ⓕ pl ver·*doo*·ras *vegetables*
vestíbulo ⓜ ves·*tee*·boo·lo *foyer*
vestido ⓜ ves·*tee*·do *dress*
vestuario ⓜ ves·*twa*·ryo *wardrobe*
vestuarios ⓜ pl ves·*twa*·ryos
 changing room
vez ⓕ veth *once*
viajar vya·*khar* *travel*
viaje ⓜ *vya*·khe *trip*
vid ⓕ veed *vine*
vida ⓕ *vee*·da *life*
vidrio ⓜ *vee*·dryo *glass*
viejo/a ⓜ/ⓕ *vye*·kho/a *old*
viento ⓜ *vyen*·to *wind*
vinagre ⓜ vee·*na*·gre *vinegar*
viñedo ⓜ vee·*nye*·do *vineyard*
vino ⓜ *vee*·no *wine*
violar vyo·*lar* *rape*

virus ⓜ *vee*·roos *virus*
visado ⓜ vee·*sa*·do *visa*
visitar vee·see·*tar* *visit*
vista ⓕ *vees*·ta *view*
vitaminas ⓕ pl vee·ta·*mee*·nas
 vitamins
víveres ⓜ pl *vee*·ve·res *food supplies*
vivir vee·*veer* *live (life)*
vodka ⓕ *vod*·ka *vodka*
volar vo·*lar* *fly*
volumen ⓜ vo·*loo*·men *volume*
volver vol·*ver* *return*
votar vo·*tar* *vote*
voz ⓕ voth *voice*
vuelo ⓜ **doméstico** *vwe*·lo
 do·*mes*·tee·ko *domestic flight*

y ee *and*
ya ya *already*
yip ⓜ yeep *jeep*
yo yo *I*
yoga ⓜ *yo*·ga *yoga*
yogur ⓜ yo·*goor* *yogurt*

zanahoria ⓕ tha·na·o·*rya* *carrot*
zapatería ⓕ tha·pa·te·*ree*·a *shoe shop*
zapatos ⓜ pl tha·*pa*·tos *shoes*
zodíaco ⓜ tho·*dee*·a·ko *zodiac*
zoológico ⓜ zo·o·*lo*·khee·ko *zoo*
zumo ⓜ *thoo*·mo *juice*
 — de naranja de na·*ran*·kha
 orange juice

FINDER

The topics covered in this book are listed below in Spanish. If you're having trouble understanding Spanish, show this page to the person you're talking to so they can look up the relevant section.

FINDER

259

What kind of traveller are you?

A You're eating chicken for dinner *again* because it's the only word you know.

B When no one understands what you say, you step closer and shout louder.

C When the barman doesn't understand your order, you point frantically at the beer.

D You're surrounded by locals, swapping jokes, email addresses and experiences; other travellers want to borrow your phrasebook or audio guide.

If you answered A, B or C, you NEED Lonely Planet's language products...

- **Lonely Planet Phrasebooks** – every phrase you need in every language you want

- **Lonely Planet Language & Culture** – laugh and learn as you explore the richness of English idiom as it's spoken around the world

- **Lonely Planet Fast Talk** – enjoy hassle-free sightseeing, shopping and dining using our essential phrases for short trips and weekends away

- **Lonely Planet Small Talk** – pack light with our quick-hit language guide featuring 10 languages per book

- **Lonely Planet Phrasebook & Audio CD** – read, listen and talk like a local with our complete phrasebook plus a bonus CD of 400 key phrases

- **Lonely Planet Phrasebooks for iPhone and iPod touch** – download more than 600 phrases with corresponding audio, available on the App Store

...and this is why

- **Talk to everyone everywhere**
  Over 120 languages, more than any other publisher

- **The right words at the right time**
  Quick-reference colour sections, two-way dictionary, easy pronunciation, every possible subject – and audio to support it

Lonely Planet Offices

Australia
90 Maribyrnong St, Footscray,
Victoria 3011
☎ 03 8379 8000
fax 03 8379 8111
✉ talk2us@lonelyplanet.com

USA
150 Linden St, Oakland,
CA 94607
☎ 510 250 6400
Toll free 800 275 8555
fax 510 893 8572

UK
2nd fl, 186 City Rd,
London EC1V 2NT
☎ 020 7106 2100
fax 020 7106 2101

lonelyplanet.com